Enraged, Rattled, and Wronged

Enraged, Rattled, and Wronged

Entitlement's Response to Social Progress

KRISTIN J. ANDERSON

Mike—
Well you're a winner
in more ways than one!
Thank you for your
friendship.
Warmly,
Kris

OXFORD
UNIVERSITY PRESS

OXFORD
UNIVERSITY PRESS

Oxford University Press is a department of the University of Oxford. It furthers
the University's objective of excellence in research, scholarship, and education
by publishing worldwide. Oxford is a registered trade mark of Oxford University
Press in the UK and certain other countries.

Published in the United States of America by Oxford University Press
198 Madison Avenue, New York, NY 10016, United States of America.

Library of Congress Cataloging-in-Publication Data
Names: Anderson, Kristin J., 1968- author.
Title: Enraged, rattled, and wronged : entitlement's response to social
progress / Kristin J. Anderson.
Description: New York, NY : Oxford University Press, 2021. |
Includes bibliographical references and index.
Identifiers: LCCN 2021001741 (print) | LCCN 2021001742 (ebook) |
ISBN 9780197578438 (paperback) | ISBN 9780197578452 (epub) |
ISBN 9780197578469
Subjects: LCSH: Entitlement attitudes—Social aspects—United States. |
Social ethics—United States. | Attitude (Psychology) —United States. | Equality.
Classification: LCC HN90.M6 A57 2021 (print) | LCC HN90.M6 (ebook) |
DDC 303.3/720973—dc23
LC record available at https://lccn.loc.gov/2021001741
LC ebook record available at https://lccn.loc.gov/2021001742

DOI: 10.1093/oso/9780197578438.001.0001

1 3 5 7 9 8 6 4 2

Printed by LSC communications, United States of America

For the activists, organizers, dissenters, and disrupters who have put their bodies on the line in the fight for justice.

Contents

Acknowledgments

There are many people whose support was critical for this project. Several colleagues read and commented on parts of this manuscript. I am grateful for the care and commentary from Travis Crone, Nisreen Elsayegh, Bonnie Field, Campbell Leaper, Sean O'Hare, Tammis Thomas, and Raeanna Toussaint. These folks have their own work obligations that they put aside to help me make this project better. I especially want to thank Judith E. Coker and Ebony Sam, who read through multiple versions of the manuscript— Judith for keeping me coherent and grounded, and Ebony for keeping me humble.

My students at the University of Houston-Downtown inspired this work and they know well what it feels like to be on the dirty side of entitlement— they witness dominant-group power, privilege, and entitlement in their daily lives. In particular, I thank the following students for helping me think through the vast literature on entitlement: Morgan Brokaw, Shelly Burr, Haleigh Folger, Sunday Martinez, Danielle Motley, Jesly Otero, Reyes Peregrino, Luis Saldivar, and Francisca Torres. I appreciate my colleagues at University of Houston-Downtown's Center for Critical Race Studies for holding space with me during these challenging times. Thank you to the 2017–2018 Faculty Development Leave Committee at the University of Houston-Downtown for granting me a semester leave to work on this project. Thank you also to Mike Emery for encouraging me to put my analysis out to the media, and Carmen Hernández and Kevin Farren for marketing strategies. Brent Haight helped with cover design. I appreciate Katharine Pratt and Abby Gross at Oxford for moving this book through the publication process and for swiftly responding to my many queries.

Finally, I am so lucky to have these people as my friends. Their emotional sustenance and humor through the book-writing process, a global pandemic, and the crumbling of democracy kept me sane. They are: Dale Anderson, Judith Coker, Travis Crone, Roger Dunn, Bonnie Field, Bob Glazier, Chuck Jackson, Alex Rossman, Laurie Tiano, Fran Watson, Kim Watson, and Mitch Youts. Alana Anderson and Alyssa Anderson continue to inspire me. Brent

Haight, who is always in my corner, provided me space to work and, most important, light. Finally, I am indebted to Christina Hsu Accomando and her 30-year project to make me a better thinker and activist. She is expert at turning knee-jerks into analysis, and many arguments in this book that move the reader are most likely from her setting me straight.

Introduction

In order to understand how the improbable candidacy of Donald Trump became the winning candidacy in 2016, and nearly again in 2020, the news media sought out the constituency that seemed to push him to victory— White, working-class men who felt betrayed by the government during the Obama years. Trump offered these voters something Hillary Clinton did not. He convinced enough of them he was going to right the wrongs of Obama. But what wrongs needed righting? And did those voters think a wealthy New Yorker was going to help an out-of-work factory worker in Ohio, or an unemployed coalminer in Kentucky?

Pundits' and reporters' assumption that working-class White men voted for Trump because he would put them back to work turned out to be false.[1] That "economic-anxiety" argument ended up being a decoy for something else—something less palatable than the romantic notion of the hardworking bootstrapper trying to make an honest living. Or the man who used his own two hands and grit to succeed, if only the government would get out of his way. In actuality, Trump voters were no worse off financially than Clinton voters. In fact, they were *less* likely to be recently unemployed,[2] and their median income was slightly *higher* than the median income of Clinton voters.[3] Furthermore, the Republican Party has a checkered history of meeting the needs of the working class. Over the last 40 years, the Republican Party has turbo-boosted the engine of economic inequality. Under Republican administrations—and a few Democratic ones—the super wealthy have gotten wealthier, and everyone else has gotten poorer.[4]

Trump voters came from all economic backgrounds—not just the working class.[5] It is easy to understand why the super wealthy voted for Trump. They accurately believed that he would sign Republican-sponsored legislation that would make them even wealthier. And he did. But why would blue-collar individuals vote for Trump? They didn't. Unless they were White. Black and Brown blue-collar voters did not vote for Trump. One possible reason is Trump's history of bigotry. An additional reason could be an accurate assessment that Trump would not help nonwealthy voters economically. White,

Enraged, Rattled, and Wronged. Kristin J. Anderson, Oxford University Press. © Oxford University Press 2021.
DOI: 10.1093/oso/9780197578438.003.0001

working-class Trump voters also did not share wealth and income with Trump, but they did share one crucial status: race. Most Trump voters were White. Even though he did well with White women, his strongest support came from White men. Trump's racism, misogyny, xenophobia, and ableism was demonstrated over and over well before he was elected. And White voters voted for him. One charitable interpretation of the Trump voters' motivation comes from Ta-Nehisi Coates who wrote, "Certainly not every Trump voter is a white supremacist, just as not every white person in the Jim Crow South was a white supremacist. But every Trump voter felt it acceptable to hand the fate of the country over to one."[6] Trump voters knew they were voting for a bigot.

Trump's 2016 victory represents a backlash against social progress. It represents the perception of loss on the part of a constituency who has come to believe they deserve to be treated well, deserve good jobs, and deserve to be at the front of the line. They feel entitled to not be held back by "political correctness," by affirmative action, by the women of #MeToo, and by people who don't belong in their bathrooms. This constituency also believes those who have historically been on the margins of society—women, people of color, and queer individuals—are now unjustly elevated above them. Marginalized communities are "takers" not "makers" according to former Speaker of the House of Representatives, Paul Ryan.[7] They want "free stuff" from the government, in the words of Senator Mitt Romney,[8] and they are "cheaters," according to former President Trump.[9]

At the outset, let's be clear that White people—women and men—of all economic stripes, put a bigot in the White House. It is also true that working-class and poor people of all races have had their percentage of wealth diminish significantly in the last 40 years.[10] On its face, it seems as though White, working-class Trump supporters had voted against their own financial interests. What would be the motivation for that? Voters faced a choice: Challenge the elites who have kept their wages low and moved their jobs to lower-wage countries while becoming billionaires, or vote to maintain their identity and sense of belonging to their tribe—no matter the financial cost. Trump supporters chose the latter. Blame the minorities for all that is wrong. Build a wall. Batten down the hatches because "we" are losing, and "they" are winning.

This book is not about Donald Trump. It is about the political and psychological circumstances that culminated in a Trump presidency. The phenomena presented here predate Trump and have, sadly, outlasted him. I am a social psychologist, not a political scientist. My academic specialty is stereotyping, prejudice, and discrimination. I study the ways in which inequality is maintained and perpetuated.

This book explores the role of psychological entitlement in preserving inequality in the United States. Scholars and activists in recent decades have correctly incorporated the topic of privilege into discussions of prejudice and discrimination. White privilege, male privilege, heterosexual privilege, and class privilege reflect the unearned advantages given to socially-preferred groups—advantages not enjoyed by marginalized groups. As a result, activists and scholars of inequality analyze discrimination against target groups as well as the unearned privileges that come to those viewed as the societal norm—the perpetrators, supporters, and beneficiaries of inequality.

Enraged, Rattled, and Wronged examines psychological entitlement as an overlooked but essential feature of persistent inequality. *Entitlement* refers to one's sense of deservingness. This book explores the predictable and unpredictable ways entitled people resist social progress, thereby preserving and perpetuating inequality. In understanding this resistance we must understand: (1) how members of preferred groups come to understand their belief in their own worthiness relative to those in marginalized groups; (2) what happens to entitled people when they feel pushed aside and decentered, and (3) what they are willing to wreck as they scramble to keep their grip on their relative status and power.

Feelings of entitlement set the stage for rage and resentment when that sense of entitlement is questioned or threatened. This rage is not unique to our era—it happens again and again throughout history as part of a backlash by the advantaged group to progress made by those on the margins. There was the rage of the entitled when newly-freed African Americans in the South during Reconstruction made economic and political gains; there was the rage of the entitled when women attempted to control their reproduction; there was the rage of the entitled when queer people demanded marriage rights; and there was the rage of the entitled when transgender people insisted on having public lives with public accommodations.

This book explores how members of socially-preferred groups internalize the message of superiority offered by our culture and then act in ways that reflect and perpetuate that sense of superiority. Much of my own research over the last 20 years has been on subtle, implicit, or covert forms of prejudice— the prejudice of people who don't believe they are prejudiced, or know they are prejudiced but attempt to conceal it. This is in contrast to the prejudice of overt, obvious, and explicit bigots—members of hate groups, for example. One's sense of entitlement resides mostly in the unconscious. If you ask an entitled person if they feel entitled, they will probably say no and may not even know what you are talking about. Entitlement develops incrementally and imperceptibly in those who have it. But entitlement has tremendous power over how one sees the world and one's place in it. By the time entitlement manifests in behavior and habits, it feels normal and reasonable to those who are propelled by it.

Because entitlement operates implicitly and not explicitly it can be difficult to study. Of course, scholars in any field of the humanities and social sciences might study inequality, but it is my contention that the field of social psychology is particularly well-suited to study prejudice in general, and entitlement in particular. More than other disciplines, social psychology relies on the experimental method. The experimental method allows researchers to re-create real-life situations in controlled laboratory settings. For instance, we can study stereotypes about African Americans by asking research participants to rate the ambiguous behavior of either a White or a Black person behaving in exactly the same way—the only difference in the two people is their race. If respondents evaluate the behavior of the African American individual as suspicious, shifty, even criminal, but evaluate the same behavior of the White individual as neutral, or even positive, we can conclude that the explanation of the different evaluation is respondents' racial biases. These studies can shed light on why, in real life, unarmed African American men are shot by police seven times more often than unarmed White men.[11]

In another example, this one considering gender, experimenters might ask research participants to work on a challenging task for a specific amount of time. At the conclusion of the task, participants can pay themselves whatever they feel they deserve for completing the task. If men pay themselves more than women do for the same performance, we can gain insight into why men feel they deserve more pay than women do. A laboratory study like this can help us understand why men in real life feel more comfortable asking for a raise than women do and why employers pay men more than women in the same job.

I am interested in exploring how phenomena such as racism and sexism—that are rooted in larger societal structures—become internalized by members of groups considered superior. This book explores the relationship between the individual-level processing of psychological deservingness and macro-level problems that impede equality.

Outline of This Book

Across the United States in 2018 there was a slew of emergency calls on African Americans who were engaged in mundane, everyday behaviors that somehow sparked annoyance, fear, or outrage in the mostly White women who called 911. Police were called on a young Black girl who was selling bottled water in front of her house; a White college student called the police when a Black student was napping in her dorm's common area; four African American women were checking out of their Airbnb rental when a White woman called the police about a possible burglary; a White resident of an apartment building called 911 and attempted to physically block the entry of an African American man entering his apartment. Most infamously, a White woman walking her dog in New York's Central Park called the police when a Black man asked her to leash her dog, a requirement in that area of the park. Cashing in her entitlement like it's a Starbucks gift card, the White woman told the man, "I'm gonna tell them there's an African American man threatening my life."[12] And she did just that.

What motivates these individuals to call an emergency number for these actions? Why did they feel entitled to invoke a state apparatus—the legal system—to punish the Black people who offended, scared, or annoyed them?

Chapter 1, *Power, Privilege, and Entitlement*, situates entitlement among related terms that help explain inequality. We start with defining power and then privilege. Power is based on access to resources and the ability to influence others, as well as based on social identity (e.g., gender, race, and sexual orientation). These powers produce unearned advantages—privileges—that are not enjoyed by groups that lack power. When a group is viewed as the ideal or normal group, that group develops feelings of deservingness or entitlement.

How does entitlement relate to power and privilege? Power is about *position*, or one's social location in a system of hierarchies: one's access to influence as a result of having cultural value or having status and resources. Privilege is about the unearned tangible *advantages* that come from power: certain benefits given to someone based on power. Entitlement is about *expectations*—a sense of deservingness. Entitlement keeps us from moving toward a more equal and fair society because it adds another layer of psychological investment of the dominant group to maintain the status quo at any cost, in order to maintain their sense of (unmerited) deservingness.

Chapter 1 defines *entitlement* and details the ways entitlement is measured. Experiments that assess entitlement find reliable differences in women's and men's sense of entitlement. Men tend to have an inflated sense of entitlement relative to women. White individuals tend to have a higher sense of entitlement compared to people of color. In addition to entitlement to pay, research on academic entitlement is examined as well.

Chapter 1 offers an initial glimpse into later chapters that cover what happens when entitled people are blocked from attaining benefits they feel they deserve unquestioningly.

Chapter 2, *Entitlement's Cruel Cousins*, surveys the psychological correlates of entitlement. What attitudes coincide with entitlement that perpetuate inequality? For example, entitlement is associated with overconfidence and immodesty. That is, those who have a sense of entitlement tend to have an outsized belief in their abilities—beliefs that do not match their actual performance. Entitlement is also associated with individualism and the belief in the myth of meritocracy. The entitled tend to explain others' successes and failures as one's own doing. From poverty to sexual assault, those who value individualism and meritocracy tend to see bad things happening to people as their own fault. Entitlement is linked to narcissism as well. Narcissism has been a popular topic in recent years because of supposed generational differences in narcissism.[13] In addition, narcissism has been newsworthy as both clinicians and pundits described former president Donald Trump as a narcissist.[14]

Entitlement is also correlated with dangerous worldviews such as authoritarianism and social dominance orientation—both of which are necessary to examine given trends toward increased authoritarian political tactics in the United States and globally. The authoritarian worldview represents an inflexible personality marked by blind adherence to authority figures. Both authoritarian leaders and followers see the world as a dangerous and threatening place and therefore place high value on "law and order" and quashing dissent. Individual authoritarian attitudes are receptive to the fascist political tactics now common in many countries, including the United States. Those with a social dominance orientation see the world as a competitive jungle in which the strong are justifiably on top and the weak are justifiably on the bottom. Those on top oppose equality and feel entitled to be on top.

Chapter 2 explores entitlement's relationship to hostile and benevolent sexism—two sets of contemporary attitudes toward women that reward traditional women for conforming to gender roles and punish nontraditional women for not. Hostile and benevolent sexism help explain a wide range of behavior—from men who feel entitled to tell women to smile in public, to people blaming victims of sexual assault.

Chapter 3, *Entitlement's Enablers: Parents and Teachers*, explores the development of entitlement in individuals. In March 2019, indictments were issued implicating 50 people in a college admissions cheating scam. Code named "Operation Varsity Blues" by prosecutors, the brazen scheme involved wealthy parents paying, in one case $80,000, to test-takers to take college admissions exams for their children who couldn't gain admission on their own merit.[15] In other cases, parents paid university athletic directors to designate their child as an athletic recruit—including creating phony photos to make them appear to be a star athlete in a sport they did not play. These wealthy and famous parents went to great lengths to get their children into elite colleges using a most antimeritocratic strategy—bribery.

What facilitates the sense of deservingness that some people have relative to others? Continuing where Chapter 2 left off, Chapter 3 begins with the role parents play in producing a child with a social dominance orientation or authoritarian tendencies—two ideologies that are associated with entitlement. Parents who are cold and unaffectionate with their children may lead to children who come to see the world as a competitive jungle in which each person must look out for themselves and attain dominance over others.[16]

Parents' ideas about race and gender are significant in how their child will think about their place in the world. Racially-normative White children will develop an implicit understanding of their value and their normative position in society. They learn to be entitled to fair and positive representation in media and popular culture, and to fair or even preferential treatment by the legal system, even if this sense of entitlement is not conscious. Children of color cannot make these same assumptions about mass media representing them accurately or the legal system treating them fairly. Parents of children of color then are tasked with shepherding their children into adulthood with a sense of racial pride despite messages that might undermine that pride.

Globally, boys are the preferred gender, and this preference is due to the fact that in most cultures, men have more status and power than women. Boys and men cannot help but internalize the value society places on them relative to girls and women. Thus, Chapter 3 explores the gendered treatment of children by caregivers beginning with parents' attitudes toward their newborn daughters and sons.

Chapter 3 next examines teachers' role in facilitating entitlement. Teachers' expectations and treatment of students unintentionally influences entitlement in boys relative to girls, and in White students relative to students of color. Even as early as preschool, teachers' perceptions of a child's academic skills during the fall are associated with their academic achievement the following spring.[17] If teachers' expectations (and biases) can have a measurable impact over the course of one school year, imagine the consequences over a student's entire academic career.

Being the normative racial category allows one to be given the benefit of the doubt when it comes to school discipline. Chapter 3 also looks at the criminalization of Black and Brown girls and boys inside schools that results in a school-to-prison pipeline setting children of color on a trajectory of life-long criminalization. Unlike students of color, the school experience allows White kids to feel entitled to impartial, or even preferential, treatment by law enforcement and the criminal legal system.

Chapter 4, *Entitlement's Enablers: Peers and Popular Culture*, continues to explore the development of entitlement. This chapter is divided into two parts as it considers two areas of developmental influence: the peer group and mass media. Chapter 4 begins with a look at the impact of social dominance goals (e.g., establishing power) of the peer group and the degree to which these goals affect peer interaction and disruptive classroom behavior. Compared to girls, boys' status among peers will be determined by competition and hierarchy. The extent to which boys feel pressure to adhere to traditional masculinity will affect their academic performance and their ability to recognize their need for accepting feedback for improvement. Some boys trade academic effort and success for dominance and status.[18]

Homophobic bullying and gender policing are also addressed in this chapter. Homophobic bullying keeps boys and men from veering into the forbidden and despised femininity—it keeps boys from acting like girls. What keeps men entitled is their power *as* men. Staying powerful and feeling entitled to things you shouldn't necessarily feel entitled to results from one's status as a member of a dominant group. The price for entitlement is the all-out avoidance of femininity and all-in conformity to male norms. Boys and men may come to see conforming to rigid gender rules as a relatively small price to pay for privilege and entitlement.

Sexualized violence is then examined through the lens of entitlement. In some male peer groups, the mistreatment of girls and women is not condemned but actually helps men gain status within that group. Some men perform masculinity for the benefit of other men, and this script may include elevating themselves by denigrating and debasing women.[19] Men have learned to feel entitled to treat women in sexist and misogynist ways. The power of the bystander in these situations is considered as well. If expectations of how men are supposed to treat women changed, men's behavior toward women would change.

Chapter 4 next considers the impact of media and popular culture on the valuing of dominant groups over subordinated groups. Mass media plays a critical role in both reflecting the disparate value attached to various groups and perpetuating inequality. Dominant group members are entitled to, first, representation. Their stories are told; we see the world through their eyes. Second, dominant groups are entitled to a wide range of representation, whereas subordinated groups are globally underrepresented yet overrepresented in negative portrayals.

Finally, the impact of media is explored with a review of experimental and correlational research on how media messages impact viewers. For example, when White research participants are exposed to a news story that varies to include either a Black, White, or race-unknown criminal suspect, White suspects are assumed to be less guilty than the other two groups—even when their conduct is identical.[20] So Whites are given a benefit of the doubt that people of color are not. For boys, repeated exposure to stereotypical portrayals of women and men may increase the adoption and endorsement of the view that men are sex-driven and women are sex objects, and in turn they are more likely to objectify women's bodies.[21]

Anti-intellectualism introduces Chapter 5, *Entitlement Makes People Ignorant, Egocentric, and Mean.* The denial of climate change, the rejection of evolution, and support for failed abstinence-only education, in addition to absurd conspiracy theories, have become mainstream positions inside the Republican Party.

Chapter 5 explores the way entitled people process information that facilitates ignorance, egocentrism, and inconsiderateness. Power and privilege entitle the person to behave in other unfortunate ways because entitled individuals tend to engage in shoddy information processing. Chapter 5 explores the empirical research on power. Compared to those who are marginalized, dominant group members think in shortcuts, inconsiderately, egocentrically, and unempathically.

Power entitles people conveniently and self-servingly to assume they know *more* than they actually do when it comes to telling women and people of color how to think about sexism and racism (e.g., *mansplaining* and *whitesplaining*). At the same time, power entitles people to claim they know *less* than they actually do when they are called to account for sexual violence. There are real-world implications of these dynamics. Some men claim to know very little about women when they want to avoid responsibility for mistreating them. At the height of the #MeToo reckoning in 2017, we saw example after example of the naively ignorant man (as opposed to the cynical sexual predator). Men reported not being able to read women's confusing "signals," which some men claimed led to interactions later characterized as sexual harassment and sexual assault. The suggestion is that women are so subtle or contradictory in their interactions with men that any man could innocently interpret a *no* as a *yes*. Chapter 5 reviews empirical research studies finding that, in fact, men are just as capable as reading social signals as are women.[22] It's just that some men feel entitled to disregard those signals.

At the same time that there is the innocently ignorant man, there are politicians, almost exclusively men, who make decisions about women's reproductive rights as if women are incapable of making basic decisions about their own lives. Combining these patronizing and controlling policies about issues that should be for women to decide, with the anti-science, anti-expertise political moment of late, results in the move away from progress and toward a primitive era that will take decades to reverse.

In the case of climate change, we may be missing a critical window.

In the case of the global COVID-19 pandemic, we missed a critical window.

Entitlement's role in dehumanizing the Other and ignoring others' suffering is also explored in Chapter 5. Because entitled people think their perspective is more important than others', and their thinking and their lives are more valuable, they are also hypersensitive to being challenged and dismissed. Therefore, the latter part of Chapter 5 considers US honor culture and blind patriotism. These two concepts help explain how White men hold onto their power and privilege but become desperate and panicky when their manhood is challenged.

Chapter 6, *Enraged, Rattled, and Wronged*, presents the backlash to social progress by the entitled. Dominant group members are not accustomed to being bossed around. They tend to be ill-equipped to adapt to changing circumstances, and their resistance to change comes in many forms with a range of consequences to themselves and others. Dominant group members are both highly sensitive to criticism but also object to being sidelined. Those used to being the norm, the center, the ideal, the legitimate, feel entitled to take up space, to have their worldview validated, and to not modify their behavior or adapt to others. At the same time, they can feel ignored and decentered.

The history of divide and rule by elites toward poor and working people begins Chapter 6. In the early years of the colonies, before there was a United States, African and European indentured servants shared a common position relative to the European elites who exploited their labor. Indentured servants had much in common with each other. They were exploited and marginalized by rich people. In order to prevent uprisings by the many more marginalized Africans and Europeans compared to the few elites, and in order to maintain a cheap labor force, colonial legislatures began building a racial strategy to split off poor Europeans from Africans. African indenture became lifelong enslavement, whereas White indenture ended after a period of time. Laws were passed preventing Africans and Native Americans from voting, whereas White men could. In most tangible ways, poor Europeans were not treated much better than Africans and Native Americans. However, Whites were assigned *symbolic* status that amounted to a racial bribe—a public and psychological wage of whiteness.[23] This history contextualizes why a less-educated working- or middle-class White person would share a sense of alignment to that of wealthy and influential Whites, rather than working- or middle-class people of color.

Some White people have so internalized their superiority over people of color, that even Whites who are in economic distress support legislation and politicians that have no intention of aiding them. They reject government assistance they desperately need, they refuse to sign up for the Affordable Care Act ("Obamacare") because they believe these initiatives help undeserving minorities. These White people are dying of whiteness,[24] and politicians capitalize on this White racial resentment.

Experimental research on implicit bias finds that White Americans tend to think that only White people are real Americans. Even Native Americans are viewed as less American than White Americans.[25] Therefore, to the extent that ethnic minorities agitate for more fairness and better treatment, they are viewed by some Whites as illegitimate interlopers who don't have any business complaining. Certainly, Donald Trump capitalized on this "American = White" perceptual bias when he flamed the phony "birther" conspiracy theory about President Obama not being born in the United States. Trump then dusted off the same racist trope when Kamala Harris, a woman of color born in Oakland, California, ran for vice president of the United States.

The entitled resentment of those who feel their superior status is undermined manifests in various ways. Experimental research finds that men who are outperformed by a woman on a competitive task attempt to re-instate their status by sexualizing the woman.[26] Women and people of color who dare to demonstrate confidence and competence experience a hubris[27] or dominance[28] penalty compared to White men who behave in similar ways.

Revenge porn, trolling, doxing, and domestic violence represent the rage of the disrespected partner, an ignored suitor, or a stranger enraged by an article a woman writes. These strategies for dealing with the loss of romantic gratification, or the ability to exact power, are used by men who feel entitled to influence their partners to the point of owning them. Contrary to what one might believe, relatively few men who are domestic violence perpetrators are actually "rageaholics"—about 25%.[29] Instead perpetrators feel entitled to treat their partners and their children in controlling and abusive ways, while treating coworkers and strangers in respectful ways.

Entitlement makes people cognitively inflexible and politically unable to adapt to change. Whereas marginalized groups have to be resilient and flex-ible, whether it is in interacting with dominant group members or adapting to a changing job market, members of dominant groups are used to things going their way. When they are sidelined or disrupted, they react emotion-ally. Backlash entails entitled people presenting themselves as victims when they are not: victims of "political correctness," victims of "cancel culture," victims of affirmative action.

This book concludes with a discussion of the consequences of entitlement among those who have it. There are not only psychological and individual consequences of entitlement, but also consequences to our planet and to our democracy. Key concepts discussed in this book regarding entitlement help explain why Americans and the US government have stayed so far be-hind in dealing with climate change. Some of the concepts that are pressed into service to understand climate change denial are individualism, anti-intellectualism, and fragile masculinity.

Republican positions on a host of issues are unpopular among most Americans. The Republican positions on tax cuts for the rich,[30] gun control,[31] the Affordable Care Act,[32] Medicare-for-All,[33] immigration,[34] reproduc-tive rights,[35] and climate change[36] are unpopular with voters. And thus, the only way for Republicans to win is by kicking loose some of the fundamental pillars of democracy. Propping up dominant-group status and the entitlement it produces requires sweeping voter disfranchisement because the more people who vote, the more Republicans lose. Republican legislators have made it more and more difficult for specific groups of people to vote.[37]

Economically struggling White voters cast their lot, not with economic allies, but with wealthy White politicians who enrich wealthy elites, and do little for the working-class and middle-class White people who vote for them. Politicians cynically tap into entitled resentment among some White voters who are willing to accept a psychological wage of whiteness rather than actual wages that will economically lift up themselves, their families, and their communities. Working- and middle-class White voters vote against their economic interests in favor of their racial interests in order to maintain their sense of superiority. That is, they vote for politicians that stoke fear of immigrants, refugees, and Muslims, which reinforces White supremacy. They do so because their often-unconscious loss of majority status is too painful.

Notes

1. Mutz, D. C. (2018). Status threat, not economic hardship, explains the 2016 presidential vote. *Proceedings of the National Academy of Sciences, 115*(19).

2. Rothwell & Diego-Rosell (2016), cited in: Pettigrew, T. F. (2017). Social psychological perspectives on Trump supporters. *Journal of Social and Political Psychology, 5*(1), 107–116. https://doi.org/10.5964/jspp.v5i1.750.

3. Rothwell & Diego-Rosell (2016), cited in: Pettigrew, T. F. (2017). Social psychological perspectives on Trump supporters. *Journal of Social and Political Psychology, 5*(1), 107–116. https://doi.org/10.5964/jspp.v5i1.750.

4. Schaeffer, K. (2020, February 7). 6 facts about economic inequality in the U.S. *Pew Research Center.* https://www.pewresearch.org/fact-tank/2020/02/07/6-facts-about-economic-inequality-in-the-u-s/.

5. Carnes, N., & Lupu, N. (2017, June 5). It's time to bust the myth: Most Trump voters were not working class. *The Washington Post.* https://www.washingtonpost.com/news/monkey-cage/wp/2017/06/05/its-time-to-bust-the-myth-most-trump-voters-were-not-working-class/.

6. Coates, T. (2017, October). The first white president. *The Atlantic.* https://www.theatlantic.com/magazine/archive/2017/10/the-first-white-president-ta-nehisi-coates/537909/.

7. Sargent, G. (2016, March 23). Paul Ryan regrets that "makers and takers" stuff. Sort of, anyway. *The Washington Post.* https://www.washingtonpost.com/blogs/plum-line/wp/2016/03/23/paul-ryan-regrets-that-makers-and-takers-stuff-sort-of-anyway/.

8. Chideya, F. (2015, October 2). Most Americans get "free stuff" from the government. *FiveThirtyEight*. https://fivethirtyeight.com/features/most-americans-get-free-stuff-from-the-government/.

9. Parks, M. (2020, April 7). Fact check: Is mail ballot fraud as rampant as President Trump says it is? *NPR*. https://www.npr.org/sections/coronavirus-live-updates/2020/04/07/829323152/fact-check-is-mail-ballot-fraud-as-rampant-as-president-trump-says-it-is. Trump referred to those who vote by mail as "cheaters" (even though he has voted by mail). He has acknowledged in other places that those who vote by mail are more likely to vote for Democrats. Those who vote by mail are more likely to be members of marginalized groups.

10. Schaeffer, K. (2020, February 7). 6 facts about economic inequality in the U.S. *Pew Research Center*. https://www.pewresearch.org/fact-tank/2020/02/07/6-facts-about-economic-inequality-in-the-u-s/.

11. Kindy, K., & Elliott, K. (2015, December 26). 990 people were shot and killed by police this year. *The Washington Post*. https://www.washingtonpost.com/graphics/national/police-shootings-year-end/?itid=sf_.

12. The Associated Press (2020, May 27). Video shows white woman calling police on black man in Central Park. *The New York Times*. https://www.nytimes.com/video/us/100000007159234/amy-cooper-dog-central-park-police-video.html.

13. Twenge, J. M., & Campbell, W. K. (2009). *The Narcissism epidemic: Living in the age of entitlement*. Atria Books.

14. Malkin, C. (2017). Pathological narcissism and politics: A lethal mix. In B. Lee (Ed.), *The dangerous case of Donald Trump* (pp. 51–68). St. Martin's Press.

15. Pascus, B. (2019, June 3). Every charge and accusation facing the 33 parents in the college admissions scandal. *CBS News*. https://www.cbsnews.com/news/college-admissions-scandal-list-operation-varsity-blues-every-charge-plea-accusation-facing-parents-2019-05-16/.

16. Duckitt, J. (2001). A dual-process cognitive-motivational theory of ideology and prejudice. In M. P. Zanna (Ed.), *Advances in experimental social psychology*, Vol. 33 (pp. 41–113). Academic Press. https://doi.org/10.1016/S0065-2601(01)80004-6.

17. Baker, C. N., Tichovolsky, M. H., Kupersmidt, J. B., Voegler-Lee, M. E., & Arnold, D. H. (2015). Teacher (mis)perceptions of preschoolers' academic skills: Predictors and associations with longitudinal outcomes. *Journal of Educational Psychology*, *107*(3), 805–820. https://doi.org/10.1037/edu0000008.

18. Santos, C. E., Galligan, K., Pahlke, E., & Fabes, R. A. (2013). Gender-typed behaviors, achievement, and adjustment among racially and ethnically diverse boys during early adolescence. *American Journal of Orthopsychiatry*, *83*(2–3), 252–264. https://doi.org/10.1111/ajop.12036.

19. Snyder, R. L. (2019). *No visible bruises: What we don't know about domestic violence can kill us*. Bloomsbury.

20. Mastro, D., Lapinski, M. K., Kopacz, M. A., & Behm-Morawitz, E. (2009). The influence of exposure to depictions of race and crime in TV news on viewer's social

judgments. *Journal of Broadcasting & Electronic Media, 53*(4), 615–635. https://doi.org/10.1080/08838150903310534.

21. Rousseau, A., Rodgers, R. F., & Eggermont, S. (2019). A short-term longitudinal exploration of the impact of TV exposure on objectifying attitudes toward women in early adolescent boys. *Sex Roles, 80*(3–4), 186–199. https://doi.org/10.1007/s11199-018-0925-5.

22. O'Byrne, R., Rapley, M., & Hansen, S. (2006). "You couldn't say 'No', could you?": Young men's understandings of sexual refusal. *Feminism & Psychology, 16*(2), 133–154. https://doi-org.10.1177/0959-353506062970.

23. Du Bois, W. E. B. (1935). *Black reconstruction in America.* Harcourt, Brace and Co.

24. Metzl, J. M. (2019). *Dying of whiteness: How the politics of racial resentment is killing America's heartland.* Basic Books.

25. Devos, T., & Mohamed, H. (2014). Shades of American identity: Implicit relations between ethnic and national identities. *Social and Personality Psychology Compass, 8*(12), 739–754. https://doi.org/10.1111/spc3.12149.

26. Dahl, J., Vescio, T., Weaver, K. (2015). How threats to masculinity sequentially cause public discomfort, anger, and ideological dominance over women. *Social Psychology, 46*(4), 242–254. https://doi.org/10.1027/1864-9335/a000248.

27. Hall, E. V., & Livingston, R. W. (2012). The hubris penalty: Biased responses to "Celebration" displays of Black football players. *Journal of Experimental Social Psychology, 48*(4), 899–904. https://doi.org/10.1016/j.jesp.2012.02.004.

28. Heilman, M. E., Wallen, A. S., Fuchs, D., & Tamkins, M. M. (2004). Penalties for success: Reactions to women who succeed at male gender-typed tasks. *Journal of Applied Psychology, 89*(3), 416–427. https://doi.org/10.1037/0021-9010.89.3.416.

29. Page 153 in: Snyder, R. L. (2019). *No visible bruises: What we don't know about domestic violence can kill us.* Bloomsbury.

30. Sides, J. (2017, November 18). Here's the incredibly unpopular GOP tax reform plan in – one graph. *The Washington Post.* https://www.washingtonpost.com/news/monkey-cage/wp/2017/11/18/heres-the-incredibly-unpopular-gop-tax-reform-plan-in-one-graph/.

31. Montanaro, D. (2019, August 10). Americans largely support gun restrictions to "do something" about gun violence. *NPR.* https://www.npr.org/2019/08/10/749792493/americans-largely-support-gun-restrictions-to-do-something-about-gun-violence.

32. Younis, M. (2020, March 9). Americans' approval of ACA holds steady. *Gallup.* https://news.gallup.com/poll/287297/americans-approval-aca-holds-steady.aspx.

33. Weixel, N. (2020, January 30). Poll: Narrow majority favors "Medicare for All." *The Hill.* https://thehill.com/policy/healthcare/480719-poll-narrow-majority-favors-medicare-for-all.

34. Newport, F. (2018, June 20). Americans oppose border walls, favor dealing with DACA. *Gallup.* https://news.gallup.com/poll/235775/americans-oppose-border-walls-favor-dealing-daca.aspx.

35. Pew Research Center. (2019, August 29). Public opinion on abortion. *Pew Research Center*. https://www.pewforum.org/fact-sheet/public-opinion-on-abortion/.

36. Pew Research Center. (2019, November 25). U.S. public views on climate and energy. *Pew Research Center*. https://www.pewresearch.org/science/2019/11/25/u-s-public-views-on-climate-and-energy/.

37. Anderson, C. (2018). *One person, no vote: How voter suppression is destroying our democracy*. Bloomsbury.

 Berman, A. (2015). *Give us the ballot: The modern struggle for voting rights in America*. Farrar, Straus, and Giroux.

1

Power, Privilege, and Entitlement

*Racists: They're the reason that 911 now has to answer calls with, "Is
this a real emergency or is there just a Black person nearby."*
—Comedian John Oliver[1]

In 2018, a pattern of events started to garner much attention on social media.
The overly zealous White woman who calls the police on a person of color. In
San Francisco, California, a White woman called the police because a young
Black girl was selling bottled water in front of her house without a permit.
White children have sold lemonade from pop-up stands for decades without
a permit. What could this person have been thinking to bring police action
upon an 8-year-old child? Similar instances include a White college stu-
dent calling the police on an African American student napping in her Yale
dorm's common area and a White woman calling the police because some
African Americans were barbecuing at a park in Oakland, California. Two
Black men were removed by police from a Philadelphia Starbucks when the
White woman manager called 911 because they hadn't ordered anything. In
Rialto, California, four African American women were checking out of their
Airbnb rental, luggage in tow, when a neighbor called the police about the
women possibly burglarizing the home. A White resident of an apartment
building called 911 and attempted to physically block the entry of an African
American man entering an apartment complex in St. Louis, Missouri. She
followed him into the elevator and to his apartment to confirm he lived there.

What motivates these individuals to pick up the phone and call the police
on these every day, harmless behaviors? In understanding these callers, we
could think about them in terms of *implicit bias*—that is, automatic and unconscious bias that tells some people to think of Black people as criminals.
These callers likely hold implicit and/or more overt explicit bias against
African Americans. We could think about these events in the context of
the institutional and structural criminalization of Black life so powerfully
described in books such as *The New Jim Crow*. What is also pertinent to understanding these instances of discrimination is the underlying *entitlement*

Enraged, Rattled, and Wronged. Kristin J. Anderson, Oxford University Press. © Oxford University Press 2021.
DOI: 10.1093/oso/9780197578438.003.0002

reflected in these actions. The women making these calls to the police felt entitled to be outraged over something a Black person was doing. They felt entitled to utilize a state apparatus (i.e., the legal system) to threaten and punish the Black person who offended them. This latter fact is particularly noteworthy because it is widely documented that African Americans' interactions with police can end in arrest, a criminal record, and even death. When 12-year-old Tamir Rice was playing with a toy gun in a park (in an open-carry state), someone called the police. Within 2 seconds of arriving at the scene, a police officer had shot and killed the child.[2] Amy Cooper seemed to understand the historical legacy of the predatory-Black-man-pursuing-the-vulnerable-White-woman-victim trope when she called the police after a Black man in New York's Central Park asked her to leash her dog. "I'm gonna tell them there's an African American man threatening my life."[3] And she did.

This book explores how members of socially-preferred groups (i.e., dominant group members) internalize the message of superiority offered by our culture and then act in ways that reflect and perpetuate that sense of superiority by marginalizing those considered inferior (i.e., subordinated or marginalized groups). Entitlement is a psychological loop that keeps us from moving toward a more equal and fair society because it keeps the dominant group locked into their privilege through their sense of unmerited deservingness. This chapter examines the relationship between power, privilege, and entitlement. Specifically, we will consider how unequal power predicts privilege and then entitlement. But first, let's define the key terms: *power*, *privilege*, and *entitlement*.

What Is Power?

They know not to break the rule. And they know we do break the rule.
—CEO of the tech company on the television show *Devs*[4]

Status and Cultural Power

Power is the ability to influence others. It is the capacity to affect the conduct of others through the real, perceived, or threatened use of rewards and punishments.[5] Power can be reflected in one's control over resources. Power holders can be in powerful positions meaning they make the laws that govern a society (e.g., legislators, judges), enforce the laws (e.g., the police), or run powerful organizations (e.g., CEOs of corporations). Their power is based on achieving recognized status that allows them influence.

A different kind of power is cultural power that is simply due to the group to which one belongs (e.g., racial, gender, religious category). This type of power is not based on what one has achieved but instead is based on group identity. Being White, a man, cisgender, heterosexual, and Christian confers power relative to those not possessing these identities. In the United States, as in other Western cultures, White people have more power and status relative to people of color. Whites are the dominant racial group; people of color are the subordinated racial group. In patriarchal societies like the United States, men have more power than women. Cisgender and heterosexual people have more power and higher status than queer people. Cisgender and heterosexual people are the dominant gender-sexuality group. Those who are able-bodied have higher status and more power than those with a physical disability. Your cultural group provides or deprives you of power.

What are the implications of a certain group holding more power and status? First, dominant groups tend to have greater access to resources relative to those who are marginalized by their subordinate status. Men make more money than women do;[6] White people have more accumulated wealth than people of color do;[7] and cisgender people are more likely than transgender people to find employment.[8] History is replete with examples of women being viewed as property, thus being deprived of agency and the ability to exercise power. As late as the 1970s, wives needed their husbands' permission to apply for a credit card. Husbands did not need their wives' permission. Remnants of this ownership relationship today include heterosexual women changing their name to their husband's when they get married. His name and identity matter, but hers does not. And even in the twenty-first century, college students endorse the idea of a woman changing her last name to her husband's,[9] and women who do not change their name when they marry are suspected of not being committed to the relationship.[10] Conversely, no one questions a man's commitment when he fails to take his wife's name.

A second point about the meaning of power is that groups with more power and status are viewed as the normal, natural, ideal identity in a category. Patriarchal societies such as the United States are based on the belief in male superiority; men are viewed as the default gender. Women are seen as "the second sex," "the fairer sex," and more complicated and thus the less normal gender. Gender nonbinary people are considered exceptions, deviates from the norm in societies that have constructed a two-gender system.

The notion of men as the default gender is confirmed by ubiquitous examples. We use language such as *mankind* to refer to women and men, and *he* as a "generic" pronoun meant to apply to both women and men. The typical person represented in a biology or anatomy textbook is usually one with a penis, not one with a vagina. The examples of men as the typical and ideal human are endless. The underlying assumption of that structure is that men are seen as better than and more normal than women. This assumption is further manifested in the profound insult it is to men to be referred to as women or girls. *Cultural power* then refers to certain groups being viewed as the ideal, normal, default identity in a social category. One can have cultural power without having personal wealth or much explicit political influence.

The powerful are more influential than the powerless if they have the resources to influence. However, those who have cultural power but not actual resources in the form of wealth and direct influence are powerful relative to those without cultural power. For example, a White working-class heterosexual man has cultural power even if not actual economic power. His gender, race, and sexual orientation make him the cultural default in three ways—he's a normal guy, heck, he's a normal *person*. A Latinx working-class heterosexual man will not be considered the cultural default in terms of his ethnicity or class status, but his heterosexual maleness confers power. The fact that the White working-class heterosexual man has more power than a Latinx man does not necessarily mean that this White man *feels* powerful any or all of the time. He may not walk around thinking, "I feel so much more powerful than *that* guy." He might not feel powerful when he is passed over for a promotion or hollered at by the driver in the car next to him. He may experience many challenges in his life. However, he will not experience challenges due to his gender, race, and sexual orientation. His demographic status will not prevent him from living in some neighborhoods or being passed over for a promotion. His competence will not be questioned because of his gender, race, or sexual orientation.

Institutional Power

Whereas for most whites racism is prejudice, for most people of color racism is systemic or institutionalized.

—Eduardo Bonilla-Silva[11]

Institutional power is the ability of institutions such as governments, churches, schools, the military, television networks, the legal system, and corporations to influence individuals' lives. Institutions have the power to control people through the use of rewards, such as the allocations of resources and punishments. Institutions get their power because people on the ground, for the most part, agree that their power is legitimate. Of course, marginalized people can rise up and reject institutional power and rearrange the system, but that rarely happens. It's important to note, however, that it could and has.

Curiously, even though institutions profoundly influence our lives, the relative invisibility and normality of institutional influence leads many people to think that institutions do not play a role in inequality. Take racism for example. For some people, when they think of racism, they think only about individual racists—those who hold overt and consciously negative attitudes or engage in deliberately discriminatory behavior toward people of color. While racists certainly exist and are a danger to society, the problem of overt racists is only part of the problem of racism. Racism is a system of inequality based on the presumption of White superiority. This definition is relevant to North America and Europe; racism is likely conceptualized in different ways in other nations and cultures. Racism is embedded in our institutions and is supported and perpetuated by laws, policies, and practices in history and in the present. When you hear people talk about racism as *structural* or *systemic*, they are speaking about prejudice and discrimination against people of color that is supported by institutions often with long histories of White supremacy. If I personally do not have any malice toward people of color, racism does just fine because it is so deeply and historically baked into our institutions. Racism does not simply refer to individual prejudice, but to discrimination against non-Whites at the level of institutions. Therefore, because the term *racism* captures institutional discrimination based on the assumption of White superiority, there is no such thing as "reverse racism" (i.e., racism directed at White people). If you don't like White people, you might be ethnically prejudiced, but you are not a racist.

Appreciating that inequality is created and maintained by institutions teaches us that groups with power create laws, and those laws primarily benefit the powerful. For example, schools were formally and legally segregated by race for most of US history, formalizing and normalizing the belief that one group is socially preferable, is worthy of more resources and societal investment, and should not have to interact with the lower-status group.

Therefore, racism is embedded in the institution of education as is the case with other institutions such as the legal system, health care, and voting.

Institutional power can also reflect uses of power that are less formal than laws and policies. For example, through institutional practices in the form of rituals we can see who has the higher-status identity in a social category. The example earlier of heterosexual women changing their last name to their husband's when they marry is an example of institutional inequality that is not required by law, but is an influential tradition, nonetheless. In addition, in many heterosexual weddings in the United States, the bride is "given away" by her father to another man—as if the nuptials are an economic exchange. The father was responsible for the daughter, and now the husband is responsible for the wife. There is no vice-versa equivalent, and there wouldn't be because men have never been owned by women except for enslaved men. There is nothing about marriage law that makes women and men who get married in the twenty-first century carry on such a demeaning and nakedly transactional tradition. However, it makes sense to those involved in this marriage ritual and it is even freighted with sentimentality. Additionally, the giving away of the bride by the father to the husband is not done by some idiosyncratic subculture in the United States, but it is a ritual that most Americans are familiar with. Therefore, this ritual is *systemic* in that it is deeply embedded in the institution of marriage.

Power by Proximity

In addition to cultural and institutional power, some individuals feel a sense of power because of their proximity to someone else who has one of those types of power. Consider working-class White men without a college degree. They voted for Donald Trump in significant numbers.[12] Why? What do they have in common with someone who has never experienced poverty and in fact has been sued by working people he allegedly exploited?[13] Some White working-class men see themselves in Donald Trump. They see Donald Trump as having more in common with them than that Latinx working-class man described earlier. It is possible that power by proximity explains this relationship. Donald Trump and White heterosexual men are both in the dominant racial, gender, and sexual-orientation group, even if they are not in the same economic group. A White working-class man perhaps has been convinced that he might be in Donald Trump's position and status someday. There is power in proximity. If you see yourself as similar to the powerful—perhaps similar in gender or race if not wealth—that's good enough maybe to even vote against your economic interest. As we see later, this is a trick White working-class voters are susceptible to—Black and Brown working-class voters not so much.

There's some empirical evidence supporting the notion that men are susceptible to an *illusory power transference*. This occurs when people adopt another's power as their own due to their association with that powerful other person. In one research experiment, Noah J. Goldstein and Nicholas A. Hays randomly assigned college students to be paired with another student who was in a high-power or low-power role.[14] The students knew that their power assignment was random. Each student was later put into a negotiation task with a third student. The authors hypothesized that those students who had temporarily been assigned a high-power partner might feel more powerful and confident during their later unrelated negotiation task. The authors indeed found this pattern but only for the men, not the women, in the study. That is, men who were paired with a partner who temporarily had a high-power role in an unrelated task were more confident about their own performance in a later negotiation task. This occurred even though the partner's power was randomly assigned, extremely short-lived, and there was no way for the men to actually leverage their previous partner's power. Furthermore, men assigned to a high-power partner were more optimistic about their future life events that would happen long after the study concluded.

This is the illusory power transference, *illusory* because these individuals are not actually able to draw on the other person's power for anything, but they *felt* powerful because of the association. Goldstein and Hays found evidence consistent with the idea that men's greater orientation toward feeling powerful leads them to psychologically latch onto powerful others with whom they are cooperating in order to feel powerful themselves. And this can occur no matter how weak and ephemeral the association with those others might be. If Goldstein and Hays' findings generalize, women are less likely than men to be susceptible to this influence. Women seem to recognize that the power of their associates is in no way diagnostic of their own power.

How Power Holders Process Information

Power is enacted at the level of the state or institutions, and it is enacted interpersonally—between people. As we know from earlier power is about the ability to influence others, but it is also about the ability to be free from the influence of others. Power does more than insulate one from the influence of others. It actually affects one's thinking. Research in social and cognitive psychology finds that one's sense of power affects how one processes information: that is, what information is noticed and remembered. Personal power tends to engender a sense of entitlement in those who have it, which manifests in various ways. I will briefly highlight a few of these ways in this chapter, and Chapter 5 expands this discussion, linking it to several negative outcomes.

Experimental research finds that people primed to feeling powerful make sense of information and see the world differently from those without power. Power holders experience fewer constraints and challenges to how they think and behave. Think about that sentence for a moment. Consider how powerful people think and make their way through the world. Powerful people are viewed with less suspicion than those without power—the way they think and the things they do tend not to be questioned. Their authority is not challenged. No one asks if they belong. They can get through their day relatively unhindered. In her comprehensive review of how power influences thinking, Ana Guinote finds several patterns of how power affects our thinking and interactions with the world.[15] For example, power holders trust their default ways of processing information, such as being guided by their feelings. They generally do not question the conclusions they make. They do not have the need to second guess themselves. Power holders are not motivated to attend to individual attributes of subordinates, so they are quick to stereotype and are confident in their assessments. Power increases the propensity to engage in opportunistic cognition, which means that those with power rely on ideas that come to mind easily. They conform less to others' opinions and tend to seek out information that confirms their past decisions.

Power orients people toward agency, toward those with influence, and toward the status quo. Powerful people tend not to be distracted by things that do not matter to them. Dominant group members know little about subordinate group members, but subordinate group members tend to know a lot about dominant group members. Because dominant groups are more likely to control the lives of subordinate group members, they have the luxury of not having to know or care much about those perceived to be inferior to themselves. Two overarching points about how power holders process information are important. First, whereas powerful people can be careful processers of information when they are motivated, they are often not very deliberative (i.e., they trust their instincts), meaning they are more likely to stereotype than those without power. They process information in a way that serves them. And especially when dealing with subordinates—those with less power—power holders can be quick to judgment and sloppy in their thinking. They do not feel hindered by their ignorance. Second, research studies suggest that powerful people can be less caring and empathic toward the suffering of others. Because powerful people tend to be self-serving, if they are not in distress, suffering doesn't matter much to them. We explore this more in Chapter 5.

What Is Privilege?

Unearned Advantages Versus Undeserved Disadvantages

In recent decades, the academic and public consciousness about dominant-group privilege has massively expanded. There is little point in examining the impact of inequality on those who experience it without also studying those who benefit from the same cultural arrangements that produce inequality. Those who are members of powerful groups (i.e., groups that are the cultural default and the more valued members of a social category) are granted privileges based on their higher-status group position. These privileges exist regardless of whether the recipients want them and seek them out. So what is meant by privilege? *Privilege* refers to the unearned benefits, opportunities, advantages, protections, and benefits-of-the-doubt granted to dominant group members simply because of their group membership. Many of these advantages should be given to everyone, but they are not. In fact, these benefits are so regularly and automatically given to dominant group members, they often do not realize they have them. And because these benefits are so taken for granted by dominant group members, they may either naively assume everyone gets them or come to believe they deserve the unearned privileges.

As I write this in a coffee shop, a young woman walks in holding her keys and dangling from them is a small pink canister. It is pepper spray. Whereas seeing pepper spray on a man's key may be surprising, pepper spray on a woman's key chain is a routine occurrence; it is also a reminder that women spend a fair amount of time concerning themselves with how to be safe from men's violence. Men generally do not consider whether a parking garage is safe to park in or question whether they can leave their drink unsupervised at a bar while they use the restroom. But women must. The freedom to move without concern for one's safety against sexualized violence is an example of male privilege. We should all feel safe as we make our way through the world, but women—not because of anything they have done or not done—do not. Of course, not all men feel safe in the world. Queer men, men with physical disabilities, and men of color may organize their lives around safety compared to cisgender men, heterosexual men, white men, and men without disabilities .

In her groundbreaking articulation of White privilege, Peggy McIntosh catalogs the myriad unearned advantages of being a White person.[16] For example, for the most part, White people can wander around a store without being followed by security. The credit card they use for payment will not be scrutinized. If a White person is loud or incompetent, it is unlikely to be attributed to their race. White people can rent an apartment without worrying that neighbors will smear feces on their car door handles after they move in—as one colleague of mine recently experienced. If neighbors are unfriendly, they can be pretty sure the bad treatment is not due to their race. McIntosh describes White privilege as an invisible weightless backpack of benefits that White people carry around with them. And because these tend to be invisible advantages, White people may not realize they have them. Ta-Nehisi Coates describes White privilege as a "bloody heirloom" that doesn't ensure automatic success for White people but works as a "tailwind for most of them."[17] In her book, *White Fragility*, Robin DiAngelo[18] describes privilege in terms of belonging. She writes that as a White person, there are very few places in which she feels she does not belong:

> In virtually every situation or context deemed normal, neutral or prestigious in society, I belong racially. This belonging is a deep and ever-present feeling that has always been with me. Belonging has settled deep into my consciousness; it shapes my daily thoughts and concerns, what I reach for in life, and what I expect to find. The experience of belonging is so natural that I do not have to think about it. The rare moments in which I don't belong racially come as a surprise—a surprise that I can either enjoy for its novelty or easily avoid if I find it unsettling.[19]

Being a member of a dominant group means you are rarely questioned on your legitimacy across multiple settings—where you live, where you dine, where you shop, where you walk, who you love, why you succeed or fail. And if your legitimacy is questioned, it is not because of your dominant-group status. When a White person fails, it's not attributed to their race; if a man stumbles, it's not because of his gender. Michael Harriot speaks of the *privilege of individuality* for dominant group members.[20] Regarding race, he states, "It is because we know that the color black is always plural. It is collective. The act of one black person stains us all. Black people's actions are transferrable and contagious. Blackness is never individual." Harriot's point here is that dominant group members do not have to answer for members of their own group. Their privilege entitles them to individuality. When a White man commits a mass shooting at a mall, all White people are not asked to answer for that one man's crimes.[21] Yet when a Muslim man commits an act of violence, Muslims are asked to apologize on behalf of that individual; they are expected to explain how and why the person was radicalized, and they even become targets of retaliatory violence for an act they had nothing to do with.

Examples of heterosexual privilege include the expectation that one's place of worship will host their wedding ceremony. Heterosexuals can teach children or coach kids without parents complaining they are attempting to recruit children into their "lifestyle." They will not be told their identity is a phase. Cisgender privilege means cis people do not get asked invasive questions about their genitalia or their "real name." Cisgender people can use the restroom that matches their gender without having politicians pass laws that prevent them from doing so.

Privilege is not an either/or; it's not simply you have it or don't. If you are a White person, you have White privilege. Even if you had a terrible upbringing. Even if you work 80 hours a week. And even if you are targeted in other ways. If you are White and transgender, you still benefit from White privilege, even though you do not benefit from cisgender privilege. If you are a White woman, you benefit from White privilege even though you do not benefit from male privilege. Your privilege is not cancelled out by a marginalized status. In fact, most people have both privileged and marginal identities. And one's privileged status can change. A White heterosexual cisgender man will spend his life reaping the unearned advantages of White, heterosexual, cisgender, and male privilege. But if he becomes disabled, then he no longer has ability privilege. It doesn't mean he no longer benefits from those other privileges.

In my classes and other settings, I talk to people about prejudice, stereotyping, and discrimination. If they are reasonably open-minded, they can be convinced that inequality exists, that some people are not treated fairly based on a status over which they have no control. However, when I explain that those of us in dominant groups benefit from others' subordination, many people hit a psychological wall. Because now it's about us and our unearned advantages relative to others' undeserved disadvantages. In his discussion of privilege, Tim Wise notes that if there are people who are "underprivileged," there are others who are "overprivileged."[22] You cannot have a down without an up. This revelation can be threatening to those of who feel they have earned what they have fair-and-square, and they have never discriminated against anyone. These feelings falsely lead people to believe that they have no part to play in eradicating oppression. However, the failure to acknowledge privilege functions to keep it in place as one benefits from unearned advantages that others do not enjoy.

What Is Entitlement?

Dear White People: you are not deputized in public spaces. If other people are doing things you don't approve of mind your own business or complain on Twitter like a normal person. It's not for you to adjudicate.

—Roxane Gay[23]

Entitlement is the topic of this book. Those who are valued get special privileges that those who are not valued do not get. When a group is viewed as the ideal or normal group, those in that group develop feelings of entitlement. There is a range of definitions of entitlement. You may be familiar with the term *entitlements* used by politicians to refer to government-funded services. In the United States, conservative politicians view such entitlements as free stuff from the government that lazy people don't deserve. In this book, I am using *entitlement* to refer to one's sense of deservingness. Entitlement captures something psychological. It's one's *belief* or *sense* of what one deserves. Entitlement is about expectations. It is not about concrete things such as a paycheck or benefits from the government such as healthcare. It is not even the unearned advantages of privilege, although the two concepts are related. Privileged people tend to have an inflated sense of entitlement.

How does entitlement relate to power and privilege? Power is about *position* (or social location): one's ability to influence due to having resources or being a member of a dominant group—or one's proximity to those with status, resources, or cultural value. Privilege is about unearned *advantages*: certain benefits or protections given to someone based on power or proximity to power. Entitlement is about *expectations*: the inflated sense of deservingness one has as a result of power and the benefits of privilege. This is the definition of entitlement I will use going forward.

Entitlement: How It Is Measured and What Entitled People Are Like

I wish that girls could fail as bad as men do and be ok. Because let me tell you, watching men fail up? It is frustrating. It is frustrating to see a lot of men blow it and win.

—Michelle Obama[24]

Entitled people tend to think they deserve good things to happen to them regardless of how deserving they really are. Entitled people tend to define their own deservingness based less on what things they have accomplished, such as education or work experience, and more on simply who they are.[25] Entitlement is a slippery phenomenon because those who feel entitled do not usually recognize their sometimes-breathtaking sense of entitlement. They are accustomed to an environment that quietly and seamlessly moves in their direction. Entitled people cut in line at the grocery store without seeming to notice those they have displaced. Entitled people believe they should get out of a ticket at a traffic stop because they were rushing to an important meeting. Entitled people believe they shouldn't have to cooperate with public health laws that require wearing a mask during a global pandemic. Entitled people call the police on African Americans barbequing in a park or selling water or leaving an Airbnb.

Because they are used to things more or less going their way, entitled people can get rattled by obstacles: from not getting a promotion they expected, to not being treated politely by the person serving their food, to having to wait in line, to being judged as suspicious by law enforcement, or to being asked to wear a mask at Walmart. Their sense of entitlement can lead them to become enraged at routine inconveniences. Not surprisingly, entitled people can be self-centered. Entitlement is the opposite of humility.[26] Entitled people tend to take credit for positive events and blame others for negative ones.[27]

Entitled people tend to disregard information that contradicts their world-view and they avoid situations that challenge their positive self-image.[28] Entitled people report thinking they deserve more than their peers and they are greedier than less entitled people.[29] Those in romantic relationships tend to be more selfish, less accommodating to their partner, and less em-pathic than less entitled people.[30] And entitled people are more likely than unentitled people to respond to criticism with aggression.[31]

Consider the 2018 confirmation of Supreme Court nominee Brett Kavanaugh. After testimony from Dr. Christine Blasey Ford, who alleged Kavanaugh sexually assaulted her when they were teenagers, Kavanaugh's public testimony epitomized the entitled resentment of those who are not used to being criticized, critiqued, or questioned. Blasey Ford's testimony was careful and deferential, cautious, and polite. In contrast, Kavanaugh barked and cried his response. He spat and sputtered as he called the hearings a "sham" and a "circus," a "farce," and a "joke."[32] When asked about his own references to binge drinking, he answered with, "Senator, I was at the top of my class academically, busted my butt in school. Captain of the varsity bas-ketball team. Got in Yale College." That was his answer to a question about excessive drinking. Kavanaugh seemed to assume his good grades should exempt him from scrutiny. One of Kavanaugh's many defenders, Senator Lindsey Graham, described the questions about the event as "crap" and "the most unethical sham"—improper queries that would "destroy this guy's life." He offered: "I cannot imagine what you and your family have gone through" and "Would you say you've been through hell?" To be clear, Senator Graham's hyperbolic descriptions were about the victimization of *Kavanaugh*, the al-leged perpetrator of sexual misconduct, not of Blasey Ford, the alleged victim of his sexual misconduct.

Entitlement is typically measured in two ways. One way to measure en-titlement is through self-report: asking people whether they agree with statements that reflect a self-centered and expectant point of view. For ex-ample, those who would agree with the following statements would be cat-egorized by researchers as entitled: "I honestly feel I'm just more deserving than others," "Great things should come to me," and "People like me deserve an extra break now and then." On self-report measures, men tend to show higher levels of entitlement than women.[33] Unfortunately, most of the re-search on gender and entitlement has examined only White respondents; therefore, we know little about the interaction of gender and other social cat-egories such as ethnicity and social class. In one study of US college students where half of the participants were White and the others were Latinx or other people of color, similar gendered patterns of entitlement occurred.[34] A recent study on self-reported entitlement with White, African American, and Latinx college students found the usual gender differences but no ethnic differences.[35] We can expect that any group associated with power would have a stronger sense of entitlement than those with less power. For example, heterosexuals feel entitled to hire a baker for their wedding cake without being refused service because the baker doesn't approve of their "lifestyle." Similarly, many White people feel entitled to fair and impartial, if not preferential, treatment by law enforcement.

Even though there are survey instruments that measure entitlement with items like those described above, entitlement is a thorny concept to capture because it is psychological and not directly behavioral. It is one's *sense* of deservingness. The nature of entitlement is that those who have it operate from it but often do not see themselves as entitled and acting from a position of expectation. Therefore, from a research measurement perspective, when assessing someone's sense of entitlement it is not fruitful to ask someone directly, "Are you entitled?" or "Do you feel a sense of entitlement?" This is because most people who should answer "yes," will not—not because they are lying—they just do not see themselves as entitled. Just as the unearned advantages of privilege received by dominant group members are often invisible to them, the exaggerated sense of deservingness of those groups tend to go unrecognized by them.

The discussion of entitlement thus far is based on research using self-report measures in the form of people agreeing or disagreeing with statements that measure entitled attitudes. Like all self-report measures, these measures depend on respondents having access to their thoughts and feelings and the ability to report them accurately and honestly. In addition to using self-reports as a measure, a second way to measure entitlement is by compensation and valuation of one's labor. When women and men are compared in terms of how much they feel they deserve for completing a task, studies consistently find that men have a stronger sense of entitlement than do women.[36] In a typical study, Lisa Barron[37] conducted simulated job interviews with MBA students. When students were asked about their expected salary, men's salary requests were higher than women's, even though women and men did not differ in grade point average, age, previous salary, or negotiation training. Men were more likely than women to report having a strong sense of what they are worth, and they expected the company to pay them what they believed they are worth. In contrast, women were less likely to report having a sense of what they were worth and they expected the company to determine their worth. Women tended to think they would prove their value only once they got on the job. Men actually reported that they are entitled to a higher salary than their similarly situated peers, whereas women were more likely to believe they were entitled to the same salary as their peers.[38] In another study, researchers gave college students a task to complete followed by instructions to pay themselves what they thought their work was worth. Although independent raters who judged the quality of the work perceived no gender differences in performance, self-ratings indicated that women and men evaluated and paid themselves differently. On average, men paid themselves 18% more than did women for the same amount and quality of work.[39] Notice the pattern here. These studies never ask directly about entitlement; they don't even use the word. Nonetheless, the researchers' measures capture people's sense of deservingness. More specifically, they reveal a consistent pattern of greater entitlement among men than women.

Gendered Entitlement and Its Implications. So how do we account for the gender difference in entitlement? Do many men think they deserve more because they believe they do better work? They might *think* they do better work, but they do not—at least not in these studies. And even if they know they did not perform well, they think they should be paid as much as if they did perform well. In one classic experiment, Brenda Major and her colleagues had college students complete a task.[40] When they finished the students could pay themselves what they considered fair for the work they completed. Like other studies, women paid themselves significantly less than what men paid themselves. This pattern held even when women outperformed men.[41] When Major and her colleagues[42] paid students a *fixed* amount of money to perform a task in a follow-up study, women were more likely than men to work longer, to complete more of the work, to be more accurate, and to be more efficient. Later in the study, participants were asked to provide evaluations of their own performances. Despite the fact that women worked longer than men, completed more work, and worked more accurately and efficiently, women and men did not differ in their self-rated performance evaluations. These experiments capture the nature of entitlement—feeling deserving because of, well, what exactly? It's not because of what they did or how they performed, but who they think they are.

Gender differences in entitlement have often been framed as a problem of women having a deflated or inappropriately low sense of entitlement. In fact, these studies reveal that men tend to have an inflated sense of entitlement, whereas women's entitlement is more analytical and performance-based. Brett Pelham and John Hetts[43] asked American college students to solve easy, moderate, or difficult anagrams of scrambled words. Participants were asked to evaluate their own performance and then pay themselves for their work. You might guess that those who performed poorly would pay themselves less than those who performed well. This was the case for women, but not for men. Specifically, women paid themselves less when they had performed poorly—when they solved fewer anagrams. Men paid themselves well even when they performed poorly. The men in these studies seem to think that their personal feelings of worth entitle them to a certain level of payment, regardless of the quality of their performance. The women in these studies based their level of self-pay on their *work* rather than their subjective sense of *worth*. Taken together, these studies show that women's sense of entitlement isn't deflated, rather men's sense of entitlement is inflated.

Perhaps it is not surprising that men believe they are worth more than what women believe women are worth. Society rewards them accordingly. In controlled experiments in which respondents are asked to allocate salaries to job candidates with exactly the same experience, people allocate higher salaries to men than to women.[44] Jobs arbitrarily labeled as "male" are viewed as higher valued and therefore meriting a higher salary than jobs with the exact same characteristics labeled "female."[45] So people think that men should be paid more than women for doing the same work and that "men's" jobs deserve more pay than "women's" jobs.

When women and men have been asked about what they deserve, how they compare to others, and what information should be used in hiring and salary decisions, there are interesting differences there too. One study found that women's investment in work is not determined by the financial rewards they receive: they invest as much as they can in work regardless of pay. Men, on the other hand, admit to doing more work when pay is higher and less work when pay is lower.[46] Mary Hogue and her colleagues asked individuals about the important characteristics in determining pay.[47] The following characteristics are typically cited: *work output* (quality and quantity of work), *specific status characteristics* (worker education and job experience), *job attributes* (responsibility, working conditions, impact of job, and complexity), and *ascribed status characteristics* (age, race, and gender). When setting a salary, men placed greater importance on ascribed status characteristics than did women. Women placed greater importance on work output, specific status characteristics, and job attributes. In terms of determinants of salary, men feel comfortable relying on *who they are*, whereas women rely on *what they have done*. Again, like most studies on entitlement, the majority of respondents in Hogue's study were White. The results from her study are particularly striking because White men tend to believe that affirmative action and other attempts at leveling the unequal employment field violates notions of meritocracy and allows people to be hired because of who they are and not what they have accomplished.[48] Yet in these studies, White men are comfortable feeling entitled to something regardless of whether they actually deserve it.

Both women and men seem to go along with men's inflated sense of entitlement; consequently, men are led to see their level of deservingness as fair and equal even when, objectively, it is not. For example, in one study,[49] participants were asked to play a bargaining game in which one person offers an amount of money to another and the responder decides whether or not the offered amount is acceptable. As such, each side in the negotiation is motivated to obtain the most amount of money: the proposer is motivated to give up as little as possible, and the responder is motivated to obtain as much as possible. Women made higher offers overall than did men. Men were offered more than women, and less was demanded of men than women. So more was offered to men even when they did not demand more. It is not surprising that some men feel entitled to things they have not earned. How could they not? People reward them accordingly. Consider these patterns in the context of the debate about affirmative action. Again, White men are less likely to support affirmative action than are other groups.[50] And yet, White men are more likely than other groups to feel entitled to pay even when their performance is weak. There is some degree of hypocrisy in White men's objection of strategies to support underrepresented groups and yet some seem to expect to get a break themselves.

Academic Entitlement: Some Implications of Feeling Entitled. One phenomenon where you can see attitudes of entitlement is at the university among some college students. Academic entitlement refers to the expectation that a student should receive more from one's academic experience than they put in, that they deserve more than one's peers, and that they deserve special treatment from instructors. Academic entitlement is typically measured by agreements with statements such as, "Professors must be entertaining to be good," and "My professors should curve my grade if I am close to the next grade." There is individual variation on academic entitlement indicating that some students have it but many do not. The next chapter will address some of the individual variations on entitlement. There are also consistent average gender differences in academic entitlement. Karolyn Chowning and her colleagues find that on some dimensions of academic entitlement, women and men score similarly: for instance on the statements above, women and men are likely to agree with them at the same rates.[51] However, men are more likely than women to agree with statements measuring *externalized responsibility* such as, "It is unnecessary for me to participate in class when the professor is paid for teaching, not for asking questions" and "For group assignments, it is acceptable to take a back seat and let others do most of the work if I am busy." And men more than women are likely to agree with statements such as, "Instructors should bend the rules for me" and "If I felt I deserved a higher grade, I would tell the instructor."[52]

Dealing with entitled students can be annoying and frustrating for teachers. But in addition, there are consequences for the student. Those who attribute their performance to their courses or instructors rather than to themselves may fail to self-correct or develop adaptive strategies for success in college. Entitlement has similarly been found to be associated with academic disengagement, such as not attending class and not asking questions.[53] Entitled students are more likely to cheat in college[54] and are less likely to view cheating as unethical.[55] As students, men are more likely to endorse cheating in college than are women.[56] Academically entitled students are more likely than the unentitled to complain about professors who aren't entertaining or who drink a beverage in class.[57] Academic entitlement is a significant predictor of classroom incivility, such as students using their phones in class, arriving late, and working on other coursework. It is a significant predictor of consumerist attitudes toward education: a college degree is something one can buy, and professors work for students.[58] Academic entitlement is similarly linked to anti-intellectualism,[59] a topic we explore in Chapter 5. Overall, any student can hold attitudes of academic entitlement, but men are particularly prone to externalized responsibility—a specific form of academic entitlement that undermines a personal sense of responsibility over performance. In Chapter 3 we consider the role that overconfidence and lack of humility associated with entitlement plays in boys' academic performance.[60]

Conclusion

This chapter situates entitlement in the context of the study of inequality. Entitlement, the psychological sense of deservingness, is a powerful perpetuator of inequality. In understanding resistance to social progress we must understand how members of advantaged groups come to understand their beliefs in their own worthiness relative to those in disadvantaged groups. We began the chapter by presenting institutional power, interpersonal power, and power by proximity. Power dictates who is valued and who is not. Power produces privilege—the unearned advantages that come with being dominant group members. Those who are valued get special privileges. Those who are not valued, do not. When a group is viewed as the ideal or normal group, that group develops feelings of deservingness, or entitlement. How does entitlement relate to power and privilege? Power is about *position*, or one's social location in a system of hierarchies: one's access to influence as a result of having cultural value or having status and resources. Privilege is about the unearned *advantages* that come from power: certain benefits given to someone based on power. Entitlement is about *expectations*: a sense of deservingness.

We can expect that any dominant group member (i.e., people who are members of preferred groups) will have an outsized sense of entitlement. This is what power and privilege produces. Unfortunately, most of the psychological research studies on entitlement only consider gender patterns in entitlement. Less direct measures of entitlement suggest that any dominant group member may show similar patterns to findings associated with men. Several research studies find that men tend to have an inflated sense of entitlement whether it is entitlement to reward through pay or academic entitlement.

In 2019 a widespread college admissions cheating racket was exposed in the US, revealing wealthy and famous parents having bribed test takers, athletic directors, and admissions personnel in order to gain entry to elite colleges for their children.[61] These rich parents apparently were dubious of their child's ability to gain acceptance on their own merit, yet they still felt their child was entitled to entry.

Men's entitlement prevents them from adjusting their expectations of reward based on their performance. Men tend to believe they deserve a reward regardless of how successful their completion of it is. In contrast, women's pay expectations tend to be based on their performance. What are the implications of these gendered patterns of entitlement for salaries? Obviously, if women ask for less and are offered less, as the research described earlier indicates, they will earn less than men who ask for more and are offered more. Pay raises are often based on a percentage of the worker's salary. If men start out earning more than women, they will get higher and higher raises over their careers that can amount to hundreds of thousands of dollars of difference. Also, the mere recognition of a pay difference associated with group membership is enough to make people believe that a higher-paid group is more competent and worthy than a lower-paid group.[62] In other words, if people notice that men make more money than women, they infer that men deserve more and are worth more; therefore, the pay inequity is perceived as justified even when it is not.

Entitlement is not only about gender. Where there are power differences, there is privilege, and where there is privilege, there is entitlement. Social inequality causes some people from disadvantaged backgrounds to see themselves as deserving of lesser or equal outcomes. Others feel quite deserving but understand the system to be rigged against them. In considering gender, women do not have diminished entitlement. Rather, they have a reasonable sense of entitlement, whereas men tend to have an inflated sense of entitlement. Inflated entitlement is incompatible with promoting fairness and equality. For instance, one study found that the disadvantage associated with lower social class promotes interdependence, which enhances egalitarianism and diminishes entitlement.[63] Consistent with this idea, studies have found that upper-class individuals tend to exhibit more self-oriented emotions, such as pride and contentment, whereas lower-class individuals exhibit more other-oriented feelings of compassion and love.[64] Compared to upper-class individuals, lower-class individuals are more generous, charitable, trusting, and helpful. They seem to be motivated by a greater commitment to egalitarianism and compassion.[65] Upper-class compared to lower-class people report increased entitlement and narcissistic tendencies, and they are more likely to behave in a narcissistic fashion, such as time spent looking at themselves in the mirror.[66] Their narcissistic behavior is attributable to their sense of entitlement. We will explore some of these patterns in the next chapters. In the Chapter 2, we look at attitudes, orientations, and ideologies that come with feelings of entitlement.

Notes

1. Oliver, J. (Host). (2018, August 12). Astroturfing (Season 5, Episode 20). [TV series episode]. In T. Carvell, J. Thoday, & J. Taylor (Executive Producers), *Last week tonight with John Oliver*. HBO.

2. Westbrook, L. (2014, November 27). Tamir Rice shot "within two seconds" of police arrival. *BBC.* https://www.bbc.com/news/av/world-us-canada-30220700.

3. The Associated Press. (2020, May 27). Video shows white woman calling police on black man in Central Park. *The New York Times.* https://www.nytimes.com/video/us/100000007159234/amy-cooper-dog-central-park-police-video.html.

4. Garland, A. (Writer & Director). (2020, March 19). (Season 1, Episode 4) [TV series episode]. In A. Garland, A. Macdonald, A. Reich, E. Bush, S. Rudin, & G. Basch (Executive Producers), *Devs.* FX on Hulu.

5. Harrison, B. C. (2017). *Power & society: An introduction to the social sciences.* Cengage Learning.

6. Graf, N., Brown, A., & Patten, E. (2019, March 22). The narrowing, but persistent, gender gap in pay. *Pew Research Center.* https://www.pewresearch.org/fact-tank/2019/03/22/gender-pay-gap-facts/.

7. Thompson, B. (2018, February 18). The racial wealth gap: Addressing America's most pressing epidemic. *Forbes.* https://www.forbes.com/sites/brianthompson1/2018/02/18/the-racial-wealth-gap-addressing-americas-most-pressing-epidemic/#3732d5a57a48.

8. James, S. E., Herman, J. L., Rankin, S., Keisling, M., Mottet, L., & Anafi, M. (2016). Executive summary of the report of the 2015 U.S. Transgender Survey. *National Center for Transgender Equality.* https://transequality.org/sites/default/files/docs/usts/USTS-Executive-Summary-Dec17.pdf.

9. Robnett, R. D., & Leaper, C. (2013). "Girls don't propose! Ew.": A mixed-methods examination of marriage tradition preferences and benevolent sexism in emerging adults. *Journal of Adolescent Research, 28*(1), 96–121. https://doi.org/10.1177/0743558412447871.

10. Robnett, R. D., Underwood, C. R., Nelson, P. A., & Anderson, K. J. (2016). "She might be afraid of commitment": Perceptions of women who retain their surname after marriage. *Sex Roles, 75*(9–10), 500–513. https://doi.org/10.1007/s11199-016-0634-x.

11. Page 18 in: Bonilla-Silva, E. (2014). *Racism without racists: Color-blind racism and the persistence of racial inequality in America.* Rowman & Littlefield.

12. Sims, A., & Buncombe, A. (2016, November 9). Who voted for Donald Trump? Mostly white men and women, voting data reveals. *Independent.* https://www.independent.co.uk/news/world/americas/us-elections/who-voted-for-donald-trump-white-men-and-women-most-responsible-for-new-president-elect-voting-data-a7407996.html.

13. Berzon, A. (2016, 9 June). Donald Trump's business plan left a trail of unpaid bills. *The Wall Street Journal.* https://www.wsj.com/articles/donald-trumps-business-plan-left-a-trail-of-unpaid-bills-1465504454.

14. Goldstein, N. J., & Hays, N. A. (2011). Illusory power transference: The vicarious experience of power. *Administrative Science Quarter, 56,* 593–621. https://doi.org/10.1177/0001839212440972.

15. Pages 547–569 in: Guinote, A. (2015). Social cognition of power. *APA handbook of personality and social psychology, volume 1: Attitudes and social cognition.* https://doi.org/10.1037/14341-017.

16. McIntosh, P. (1989). White Privilege: Unpacking the invisible knapsack. *Wellesley Centers for women*. https://www.wcwonline.org/images/pdf/Knapsack_plus_Notes-Peggy_McIntosh.pdf.

17. Coates, T. (2017, October). The first White President. *The Atlantic*. https://www.theatlantic.com/magazine/archive/2017/10/the-first-white-president-ta-nehisi-coates/537909/.

18. DiAngelo, R. (2018). *White fragility: Why it's so hard for white people to talk about race*. Beacon Press.

19. Page 53 in: DiAngelo, R. (2018). *White fragility: Why it's so hard for white people to talk about race*. Beacon Press.

20. Harriot, M. (2017, November 5). The privilege of White individuality. *The Root*. https://www.theroot.com/the-privilege-of-white-individuality-1819184476.

21. See, for instance: King, S. (2017, 2 October). The White privilege of the "lone wolf" shooter. *The Intercept*. https://theintercept.com/2017/10/02/lone-wolf-white-privlege-las-vegas-stephen-paddock/.

22. Jhally, S. (Producer & Editor). (2008). *Tim Wise: On White privilege. Racism, White denial & the costs of inequality*. [Film]. Media Education Foundation.

23. Gay, R. [@rgay]. (2019, July 7). *Dear White People: you are not deputized in public spaces. If other people are doing things you don't approve of* [Tweet]. Twitter. https://twitter.com/rgay/status/1147998811257790464?lang=en

24. 2018 Summit: The United State of Women. Los Angeles, May 5–6, 2018. https://www.youtube.com/watch?v=boB9modnMYQ.

25. For a review of definitions of entitlement, see: Major, B. (1994). From social inequality to personal entitlement: The role of social comparisons, legitimacy appraisals, and group membership. In M. P. Zanna (Ed.), *Advances in experimental social psychology* (pp. 293–355). Academic Press.

26. Kesebir, P. (2014). A quiet ego quiets death anxiety: Humility as an existential anxiety buffer. *Journal of Personality and Social Psychology, 106*(4), 610–623. https://doi.org/10.1037/a0035814.

27. Harvey, P., & Martinko, M. J. (2009). An empirical examination of the role of attributions in psychological entitlement and its outcomes. *Journal of Organizational Behavior, 30*, 459–476. https://doi.org/10.1002/job.549.

28. Harvey, P., & Martinko, M. J. (2009). An empirical examination of the role of attributions in psychological entitlement and its outcomes. *Journal of Organizational Behavior, 30*, 459–476. https://doi.org/10.1002/job.549.

29. Campbell, W. K., Bonacci, A. M., Shelton, J., Exline, J. J., & Bushman, B. J. (2004). Psychological entitlement: Interpersonal consequences and validation of a self-report measure. *Journal of Personality Assessment, 83*, 29–45. https://doi.org/10.1207/s15327752jpa8301_04.

30. Campbell, W. K., Bonacci, A. M., Shelton, J., Exline, J. J., & Bushman, B. J. (2004). Psychological entitlement: Interpersonal consequences and validation of a self-report measure. *Journal of Personality Assessment, 83*, 29–45. https://doi.org/10.1207/s15327752jpa8301_04.

31. Campbell, W. K., Bonacci, A. M., Shelton, J., Exline, J. J., & Bushman, B. J. (2004). Psychological entitlement: Interpersonal consequences and validation of a self-report measure. *Journal of Personality Assessment, 83*, 29–45. https://doi.org/10.1207/s15327752jpa8301_04.

32. Kavanaugh hearing transcript. *Washington Post*. https://www.washingtonpost.com/news/national/wp/2018/09/27/kavanaugh-hearing-transcript/?utm_term=.d73de1dde1e3.

33. See, for instance: Crone, T. S., Babb, S., & Torres, F. (2020). Assessing the relationship between nontraditional factors and academic entitlement. *Adult Education Quarterly, 57*(2), 141–158. https://doi.org/10.1177/0741713620905270.

34. O'Brien, L. T., Major, B. N., & Gilbert, P. N. (2012). Gender differences in entitlement: The role of system-justifying beliefs. *Basic and Applied Social Psychology, 34*, 136–145. https://doi.org/10.1080/01973533.2012.655630.

35. Crone, T. S., Babb, S., & Torres, F. (2020). Assessing the relationship between nontraditional factors and academic entitlement. *Adult Education Quarterly, 57*(2), 141–158. https://doi.org/10.1177/0741713620905270.

36. O'Brien, L. T., Major, B. N., & Gilbert, P. N. (2012). Gender differences in entitlement: The role of system-justifying beliefs. *Basic and Applied Social Psychology, 34*, 136–145. https://doi.org/10.1080/01973533.2012.655630.

37. Barron, L. A. (2003). Ask and you shall receive? Gender differences in negotiators' beliefs about requests for a higher salary. *Human Relations, 56*, 635–662. https://doi.org/10.1177/00187267030566001.

38. Barron, L. A. (2003). Ask and you shall receive? Gender differences in negotiators' beliefs about requests for a higher salary. *Human Relations, 56*, 635–662. https://doi.org/10.1177/00187267030566001.

39. Jost, J. T. (1997). An experimental replication of the depressed-entitlement effect among women. *Psychology of Women Quarterly, 21*, 387–393. https://doi.org/10.1111/j.1471-6402.1997.tb00120.x.

40. O'Brien, L. T., Major, B. N., & Gilbert, P. N. (2012). Gender differences in entitlement: The role of system-justifying beliefs. *Basic and Applied Social Psychology, 34*, 136–145. https://doi.org/10.1080/01973533.2012.655630.

    Major, B., McFarlin, D. B., & Gagnon, D. (1984). Overworked and underpaid: On the nature of gender differences in personal entitlement. *Journal of Personality and Social Psychology, 47*, 1399–1412. https://doi.org/10.1037/0022-3514.47.6.1399.

41. O'Brien, L. T., Major, B. N., & Gilbert, P. N. (2012). Gender differences in entitlement: The role of system-justifying beliefs. *Basic and Applied Social Psychology, 34*, 136–145. https://doi.org/10.1080/01973533.2012.655630.

42. Experiment 2: Major, B., McFarlin, D. B., & Gagnon, D. (1984). Overworked and underpaid: On the nature of gender differences in personal entitlement. *Journal of Personality and Social Psychology, 47*, 1399–1412. https://doi.org/10.1037/0022-3514.47.6.1399.

43. Pelham, B. W., & Hetts, J. J. (2001). Underworked and overpaid: Elevated entitlement in men's self-pay. *Journal of Experimental Social Psychology, 37*, 93–103. https://doi.org/10.1006/jesp.2000.1429.

44. Williams, M. J., Paluck, E. L., & Spencer-Rodgers, J. (2010). The masculinity of money: Automatic stereotypes predict gender differences in estimated salaries. *Psychology of Women Quarterly, 34,* 7–20. https://doi.org/10.1111/j.1471-6402.2009.01537.x.

45. Alksnis, C., Desmarais, S., & Curtis, J. (2008). Workforce segregation and the gender wage gap: Is "women's" work valued as highly as "men's"? *Journal of Applied Social Psychology, 38,* 1416–1441. https://doi.org/10.1111/j.1559-1816.2008.00354.x.

46. Moore, D. (1991). Entitlement and justice evaluations: Who should get more, and why. *Social Psychology Quarterly, 54,* 208–223. https://doi.org/10.2307/2786651.

47. Hogue, M., Fox-Cardamone, L., & DuBois, C. L. Z. (2011). Justifying the pay system through status: Gender differences in reports of what should be important in pay decisions. *Journal of Applied Social Psychology, 41,* 823–849. https://doi.org/10.1111/j.1559-1816.2011.00737.x.

48. Kane, E. W., & Whipkey, K. J. (2009). Predictors of public support for gender-related affirmative action: Interests, gender attitudes, and stratification beliefs. *Public Opinion Quarterly, 73*(2), 233–254. https://doi.org/10.1093/poq/nfp019.

Wellman, J. D., Liu, X., & Wilkins, C. L. (2016). Priming status-legitimizing beliefs: Examining the impact on perceived anti-White bias, zero-sum beliefs, and support for affirmative Action among White people. *British Journal of Social Psychology, 55*(3), 426–437. https://doi.org/10.1111/bjso.12133.

49. Solnick, S. J., & Schweitzer, M. E. (1999). The influence of physical attractiveness and gender on ultimatum game decisions. *Organizational Behavior and Human Decision Processes, 79,* 199–215. https://doi.org/10.1006/obhd.1999.2843.

50. Pew Research Center. (2003, May 14). *Conflicted views of affirmative action. Summary of findings.* https://www.people-press.org/2003/05/14/conflicted-views-of-affirmative-action/.

51. Chowning, K., & Campbell, N. (2009). Development and validation of a measure of academic entitlement: Individual differences in students' externalized responsibility and entitled expectations. *Journal of Educational Psychology, 101,* 982–997. https://doi.org/10.1037/a0016351.

52. Fletcher, K. L., Pierson, E. E., Spears Neumeister, K. L., & Finch, W. H. (2020). Overparenting and perfectionistic concerns predict academic entitlement in in young adults. *Journal of Child and Family Studies, 29,* 348–357. https://doi.org/10.1007/s10826-019-01663-7.

53. Holtzman, N. S., Vazire, S., & Mehl, M. R. (2010). Sounds like a narcissist: Behavioral manifestations of narcissism in everyday life. *Journal of Research in Personality, 44*(4), 478–484. https://doi.org/10.1016/j.jrp.2010.06.001.

Knepp, M. M. (2016). Academic entitlement and right-wing authoritarianism are associated with decreased student engagement and increased perceptions of faculty incivility. *Scholarship of Teaching and Learning in Psychology, 2,* 261–272. http://dx.doi.org/10.1037/stl0000072.

54. Stiles, B. L., Pan, M., LaBeff, E. E., & Wong, N. (2019). The role of academic entitlement in college cheating: A comparison between China and the United States. *Research in Higher Education Journal, 33.* https://www.researchgate.net/publication/333323943.

55. Elias, R. Z. (2017). Academic entitlement and its relationship with perception of cheating ethics. *Journal of Education for Business, 92*(4), 194–199. https://doi.org/10.1080/08832323.2017.1328383.

56. Fletcher, K. L., Pierson, E. E., Spears Neumeister, K. L., & Finch, W. H. (2020). Overparenting and perfectionistic concerns predict academic entitlement in in young adults. *Journal of Child and Family Studies, 29*, 348–357. https://doi.org/10.1007/s10826-019-01663-7.

57. Knepp, M. M. (2016). Academic entitlement and right-wing authoritarianism are associated with decreased student engagement and increased perceptions of faculty incivility. *Scholarship of Teaching and Learning in Psychology, 2*, 261–272. http://dx.doi.org/10.1037/stl0000072.

58. Laverghetta, A. (2018). The relationship between student anti-intellectualism, academic entitlement, student consumerism, and classroom incivility in a sample of college students. *College Student Journal, 52*, 278–282.

59. Laverghetta, A. (2018). The relationship between student anti-intellectualism, academic entitlement, student consumerism, and classroom incivility in a sample of college students. *College Student Journal, 52*, 278–282.

60. Nietfeld, J. L., Shores, L. R., & Hoffmann, K. F. (2014). Self-regulation and gender within a game-based learning environment. *Journal of Educational Psychology, 106*(4), 961–973. https://doi.org/10.1037/a0037116.

61. Pascus, B. (2019, June 3). Every charge and accusation facing the 33 parents in the college admissions scandal. *CBS News.* https://www.cbsnews.com/news/college-admissions-scandal-list-operation-varsity-blues-every-charge-plea-accusation-facing-parents-2019-05-16/.

62. Ridgeway, 1991; 2001, cited in: O'Brien, L. T., & Major, B. (2009). Group status and feelings of personal entitlement: The roles of social comparison and system-justifying beliefs. In J. T. Jost, A. C. Kay, & H. Thorisdottir (Eds.), *Social and psychological bases of ideology and system justification* (pp. 427–443). Oxford University Press Online.

63. Piff, P. K. (2014). Wealth and inflated self: class, entitlement, and narcissism. *Personality and Social Psychology Bulletin, 40*, 34–43. https://doi.org/10.1177/014616721350699.

64. Piff, P. K., & Moskowitz, J. P. (2017). Wealth, poverty, and happiness: Social class is differentially associated with positive emotions. *Emotion, 18*(6), 902–905. https://doi.org/10.1037/emo0000387.

65. Piff, P. K., Kraus, M. W., Côté, S., Cheng, B. H., & Keltner, D. (2010). Having less, giving more: The influence of social class on prosocial behavior. *Journal of Personality and Social Psychology, 99*(5), 771–784. https://doi.org/10.1037/a0020092.

66. Piff, P. K. (2014). Wealth and inflated self: Class, entitlement, and narcissism. *Personality and Social Psychology Bulletin, 40*, 34–43. https://doi.org/10.1177/0146167213501699.

2

Entitlement's Cruel Cousins

It would reach a point where anger, the frustration, the anxiety, the poor self-image, feeling cheated, wronged, insecure, [he] decides upon young attractive women being his victims.

—Serial killer Ted Bundy[1]

In Chapter 1 entitlement is situated among other phenomena that support and maintain inequality: unequal power and privilege. This chapter examines the psychological correlates of entitlement. What attitudes coincide with entitlement that perpetuate inequality? For example, entitlement is associated with not only overconfidence and immodesty, as we saw in the last chapter, but also narcissism, hostility toward marginalized others, individualism, and belief in the myth of meritocracy. Entitlement is also correlated with dangerous worldviews such as authoritarianism and social dominance orientation, both of which are necessary to examine given trends toward increased authoritarian political tactics in the United States and globally. Finally, we will explore entitlement's relationship to hostile and benevolent sexism, two sets of contemporary attitudes toward women that reward traditional women for conforming to gender roles and punish nontraditional women for not.

Overconfidence and Arrogance

Let me interrupt your expertise with my confidence.

—New Yorker Cartoon[2]

One of entitlement's manifestations is in exaggerated confidence. Men tend to give higher estimates of their abilities than women do and, notably, men's self-estimates tend to be disconnected from their actual abilities.[3] Men's overconfidence permeates a variety of domains. On cognitive tests of performance, for instance, men give themselves higher ratings than their actual

Enraged, Rattled, and Wronged. Kristin J. Anderson, Oxford University Press. © Oxford University Press 2021.
DOI: 10.1093/oso/9780197578438.003.0003

performance merits, whereas women tend to have a more realistic appraisal of their own performance.[4] When researchers asked graduate students in business about their performance on a task they completed, both women and men overestimated their performance, but men did so to a significantly greater degree—their overestimations were further from the mark.[5] Swedish men, but not Swedish women, judged their performance on their college entrance exam to be higher than it actually was.[6] When runners in a Polish marathon estimated their running times, men were more overconfident than women, and younger men were the most wrong about their time.[7] In a study that asked people to rate their own and others' attractiveness, African Americans and White men overestimated their attractiveness compared to how others rated them, whereas White women more accurately rated their own attractiveness.[8] Interestingly, in this particular study, men (Black and White) were relatively accurate in assessing how others view them but they nonetheless persisted in holding enhanced views of themselves. In other words, they persisted in believing they were more attractive even when knowing others did not think so.

Unrealistic attractiveness assessments aside, men's overconfidence can manifest in dangerous behavior—for themselves and others. For example, men, but not women, think they are better drivers than their peers and think they are less likely to be impaired by sleep loss or texting while driving.[9] Compared to women drivers, men are more likely to run red lights,[10] to change lanes without signaling,[11] and to drive drunk.[12] This inaccurate self-image likely plays a significant role in men's high rates of traffic collisions, including fatal crashes.[13]

Based on the above, it is not surprising that men tend to be less humble than women.[14] Entitlement is the antithesis of humility.[15] A *Washington Post* headline captures this problem in one area, academia: "New study finds that men are often their own favorite experts on any given subject."[16] The article describes a research study that calculated the number of times academics cite their own prior work in their current work. In academia, article citations like these are a marker of authority and influence: If your work gets cited by others, that is a good indicator you're making a mark on your field. Universities sometimes factor in citation counts when making decisions about hiring, tenure, and salary, so it is easy to see how *self*-promotion can lead to *actual* promotion in the academic workplace. Molly M. King and her colleagues set out to find how often this so-called self-citation happens. They did so by examining a massive database of academic work: 1.5 million papers published between 1779 and 2011. They found a substantial difference in self-citation patterns between women and men. Overall, men cited their own papers 56% more than women did, and in recent decades, men self-cited 70% more than women.[17] This self-citation gap held true across every major academic field the authors studied, including biology, sociology, philosophy, and law.

Why do men feel entitled to cite themselves? In addition to men having a higher opinion of their own abilities compared with women, they face fewer social penalties for self-promotion. Women face a *dominance penalty* for confidence and assertiveness. Men do not. That is, women who behave assertively and confidently are judged more harshly than men with the same personality profile. In my book *Modern Misogyny* (and yes, I realize I am self-citing here) I review a number of studies that find that competent, ambitious women tend to be disliked by both women and men, compared to competent and ambitious men.[18] King did not look at ethnic patterns of self-citations, but other studies reveal that overconfidence yields benefits and penalties differently across racial lines. African American men, compared to White men, face what has been described as a *hubris penalty* (i.e., being viewed as arrogant and punished for the same behavior that White men engage in without judgment).[19] Observers and evaluators are comfortable with confident White men, whereas the exact same behavior in African American men is regarded as "uppity." In fact, the term *uppity* has historically and presently been reserved almost exclusively for members of marginalized groups who have the nerve to be self-confident. And it is not a compliment.

Entitlement, Narcissism, and Hostility Toward Others

You girls have never been attracted to me. I don't know why you girls aren't attracted to me but I will punish you all for it. It's an injustice, a crime because I don't know what you don't see in me, I'm the perfect guy and yet you throw yourselves at all these obnoxious men instead of me, the supreme gentleman. I will punish all of you for it.
—Elliot Rodger, Isla Vista shooter[20]

Numerous headlines have addressed narcissism in recent years. Some psychologists have tracked changes in levels of narcissism in the last several decades to conclude that children born around the turn of the twenty-first century are more self-centered than earlier generations.[21] One could argue that a little bit of narcissism is psychologically healthy and that a slightly un-realistic positive self-image provides a psychological boost.[22] However, true narcissism is a form of extreme self-centeredness and self-absorption. The clinical diagnosis of narcissistic personality disorder has received increased attention primarily due to Donald Trump's manner of campaigning and ul-timate governing style—both of which feature some of the ugliest aspects of narcissism.[23] Not surprisingly, entitlement has some overlap with nar-cissism. In fact, professional clinicians view psychological entitlement as one aspect of narcissism. Drawing on what we know about entitlement, we can expect, and we do find, that men are more likely than women to be narcissists.[24] Seventy-five percent of those diagnosed with narcissistic per-sonality disorder are men.[25] Narcissists crave admiration; they tend to have a grandiose view of their own talents and significance. They also have callous, adversarial, and hostile approaches to interpersonal relationships. There is a high incidence of narcissism in perpetrators of intimate partner violence.[26] Arrogance, grandiosity, excessive need for admiration from others, feeling entitled to special privileges, and deficits in empathy are all hallmarks of nar-cissism. These elements help us see how narcissism—particularly in concert with power, privilege, and entitlement—can be pretty terrible.

When we consider entitlement through the lens of narcissism, we can see how toxic entitlement can be. Entitled people can be dismissive and disregarding of others, but why? Perhaps the entitled people fail to notice or think of others and are only aware of their own needs. Maybe the entitled person does notice others but fails to consider their needs. Or perhaps they consider the needs of others but dismiss those needs as less important than their own.

All of the above possibilities see the self as central without necessarily ac-tively disliking others. Phyllis Anastasio and Karen Rose explored whether entitlement produces a sort of passive disregard or a more active hostility to-ward others.[27] Their research finds active and targeted distrust and dislike of others by entitled people. But not *all* others. There is a relationship between psychological entitlement and negative attitudes toward *meaningful* others at the group level. For instance, college students with high levels of entitlement dislike a rival school's student body, but not a nonrival student body. Entitled White people are more likely than less entitled Whites to hold derogatory attitudes toward people of color—a meaningful outgroup. It appears that antagonism toward "the Other" in psychological entitlement does not arise from simply feeling superior. Rather, Anastasio and Rose's research indicates that entitlement also brings with it actively negative attitudes toward others at the group level—but only those perceived as a potential threat. For example, heterosexual men who are narcissists direct more hostility toward heterosexual women—a meaningful group to them—than toward lesbians and gay men.[28] The authors reason that perhaps these men do not find lesbians as threats to heterosexual men's status and power the way they do heterosexual women. Narcissistic hostility seems to be about a group's potential to provide or withhold gratification rather than ideology about a group's sexual orientation or conformity to heterosexual gender roles.[29] Bearing in mind the findings from these two studies, imagine how a cynical politician could capitalize on this link between entitlement and animosity toward targeted groups such as immigrants, Muslims, or feminists.

Looking more closely at animosity toward meaningful others produced by narcissism, consider misogynistic men who have been rejected by women. We can examine their violence through the lens of entitlement: They feel entitled to women and when rebuffed, some turn to violence. Serial killer of women, Ted Bundy, quoted at the beginning of this chapter is one example. Men like Elliot Rodger, the mass shooter who is quoted at the beginning of this section, is a fitting example of this kind of *entitled resentment* (i.e., an extreme or unrealistic sense of deservingness that is unfulfilled and undermined allegedly by people who are perceived to be lower in status and less deserving). Elliot Rodger (and Ted Bundy) may or may not have been narcissists in the psychiatric sense, but their rhetoric reflects the language of self-absorption, insecurity, and grandiosity, that conveys entitled rage. There is a relationship between narcissism and provoked aggression (actually the *perception* of being provoked), and entitlement accounts for that relationship. That is, those narcissists who are likely to aggress against others do so out of a sense of entitlement. Those who have a strong sense of entitlement more easily have their expectations violated when others are perceived to treat them poorly.[30] They experience entitled resentment.

Another feature of narcissism that makes it so toxic is what psychologists describe as *exploitativeness-entitlement*. Individuals with this feature of narcissism believe the world owes them more than it does and that people should bend to their will. They tend to use the people around them to make themselves feel special. Those narcissists with exploitativeness-entitlement agree with statements such as, "I find it easy to manipulate people," and "I will never be satisfied until I get all that I deserve." Exploitativeness-entitlement is more common among men than women.[31] Interestingly, this particular aspect of narcissism is associated with academic disengagement in college students, such as not attending class,[32] and engaging in threats or harassment at work.[33]

Another descriptor for a certain type of narcissism is particularly salient given the existence of Donald Trump. In the book *The Dangerous Case of Donald Trump*, written by mental health professionals, several authors offer the "diagnosis" of Trump as a *malignant narcissist*. I put the term *diagnosis* between quotation marks for two reasons. First, a mental health professional should not diagnose someone without interviewing that person—none of these writers interviewed Trump. Second, malignant narcissism is not an actual diagnosis you will find in the *Diagnostic and Statistical Manual of Mental Disorders*. Instead these authors offer the term to capture a set of characteristics of Trump that made him a unique danger as president. Malignant narcissism captures the blending of pathological narcissism with *psychopathy*: the inability to experience empathy and remorse.[34] So malignant narcissists are self-centered, ruthless manipulators who, when crossed, are vengeful. They engage in projection, imagining the danger they feel inside themselves (anxiety, panic, confusion, and doubt) is coming from outside.[35] Donald Trump engages in projection, for example, accusing "Crooked Hillary" of corruption and "Lying Ted" Cruz of mistruths.

Entitled Ideologies and Worldviews

Individualism and Meritocracy

There is nobody in this country who got rich on his own. Nobody. You built a factory out there? Good for you. But I want to be clear: you moved your goods to market on the roads the rest of us paid for; you hired workers the rest of us paid to educate; you were safe in your factory because of police forces and fire forces that the rest of us paid for. You didn't have to worry that marauding bands would come and seize everything at your factory, and hire someone to protect against this, because of the work the rest of us did. Now look. You built a factory and it turned into something terrific or a great idea, god bless. Keep a big hunk of it. But part of the underlying social contract is you take a hunk of that and pay forward for the next kid who comes along.

—US Senator, Elizabeth Warren[36]

The dominant narrative associated with the United States is *individualism*. Individualism as a value permeates our laws and policies, our popular culture, even advertisements selling everything from automobiles to lipstick. The rugged individual. The cowboy. These are powerful American tropes. If you ask kids from the United States to tell you about themselves, they might tell you their likes and dislikes, or what they are good at. They describe what distinguishes them from others. If you ask kids in other countries, they might describe themselves in terms of who their parents are, their family members; what's salient to their identity is who they are in relation to others. In many ways, being an individual is good. It may mean you are an independent thinker. It may mean you resist mindless conformity. You are not a pushover. The world needs people willing to go against the crowd—especially if the crowd supports an oppressive government or institution that is immoral, cruel, and unjust. We can all think of moments in history when the majority of a community did terrible things and only a few heroes were willing to resist the majority and risk their own peril.

In terms of how individualism as a uniquely US value gets deployed, it too sounds pretty heroic. Americans glorify individuality, self-sufficiency, and personal advancement.[37] Individualism is associated with hard work as the route to achievement, and not depending on others for success. Personal responsibility is a virtue. Dependency is a vice, a moral flaw. Most people would probably agree that young people should learn the value of hard work. In the United States, individualism is tied to the *Protestant work ethic*: the idea that people who work hard and live morally will receive rewards from God both in an afterlife and here on Earth. With support from the Protestant work ethic, individualism produces the myth of *meritocracy*. The United States markets itself as a meritocracy to its citizens. Meritocracy is the belief that those in power are there because of their ability and their own effort. Meritocracy represents the belief that those who are hired for jobs or accepted into prestigious universities get there as a result of individual effort and talent. In a meritocracy, the most competent individuals are at the top.[38] This ideology is so ingrained into the mainstream US consciousness it has been rightly described as the "secular gospel of the United States of America."[39]

These three notions of individualism, the Protestant work ethic, and meritocracy, seem just and fair on their surface. They match up to the appealing idea that hard work and self-reliance bring rewards. However, the underlying assumptions that support these ideas and their implications reveal them to be a trick that benefits the rich and powerful and that justifies inequality. Consider meritocracy. First, the notion of meritocracy assumes that individual achievement happens on a level playing field, a system in which we all start in the same place with the same opportunities, and whoever makes it to the finish line first deserves the medal. This assumption ignores historic and current structural inequality. Recall from Chapter 1 that inequality is systemic and structural and has a historic lineage. Meritocracy ignores the fact that, for instance, it was illegal for enslaved people to learn to read. It ignores centuries of segregation during which African Americans had no access to schooling and then had substandard schools historically and presently. In the education system, individualism and meritocracy tells students of color they can overcome resource-deprived schools with untrained teachers by acquiring "grit" and "zest."[40] Meritocracy ignores the fact that home loans were set aside for White people and not people of color so Whites could accumulate wealth in the form of buying property that could be handed down to descendants (a process intensified by redlining, blockbusting, and restrictive covenants). The myth of meritocracy ignores the fact that Social Security benefits were not given to domestic and farm workers, jobs that went to people of color. "Meritocracy" is based on merit only if we all start in the same position and face the same roadblocks along the path.

A second problem with the myth of meritocracy is that it is too convenient to think that success is one's own making. Again, meritocracy says if you are successful, it is a result of your individual talent and grit. However, people never succeed solely on their own. Some get hundreds of millions of dollars from their rich parents to grow a real estate empire, and then get rescued from financial ruin by those parents—as Donald Trump did.[41] They have spouses and servants who cook for them and keep their houses clean and raise their children so they can concentrate on building a business, getting a raise, and being promoted. They have employees that they pay low enough for them to make a profit off of their labor. They hire inventors and scientists that have been educated with public tax dollars. They have tax incentives provided by the government. They hide their money from the IRS.[42] No one becomes rich on their own. That is a myth. Other individuals have helped you along the way, or structures have been put in place to benefit your group—usually both.

Third, how does the belief in the myth of meritocracy explain those who don't make it? Is their lack of success due to personal failings? Perhaps they haven't tried hard enough? Or they are intellectually deficient, lazy, or immoral? Individualism and the myth of meritocracy justify stereotypes about marginalized groups. These are the stories that some successful people promulgate: People of color are lazy, otherwise they could succeed because America is based on success from individual hard work. Poor people haven't applied themselves. Queer people are immoral. Accordingly, it's understandable that they are shut out of jobs. This logic, besides being untrue, conceals privilege and facilitates victim blaming. These explanations matter because, according to this worldview, those just described should not be entitled to any help.

On a related point, let's consider growing income inequality in the United States. In 1978 the average CEO made thirty times more than their average worker. In 2016, CEOs made 271 times their average worker.[43] With each passing decade, corporate executives make more and more money, while their workers' pay stagnates or decreases. How do we explain this? A meritocratic argument would say that CEOs deserve more pay because they are smarter and have worked harder than CEOs 40 years ago and they work that much harder than their average workers. How can that be? There are only 24 hours in a day. Extreme pay inequality exposes meritocracy as a sham. The myths of individualism and meritocracy serve well people who are in powerful and privileged positions. The way to justify the breathtaking inequality in the United States is to promote the idea that those at the top deserve to be there and those at the bottom deserve their fates as well. And elites have really won if they can convince those workers (who make not even a penny to their dollar) that they deserve their fate, or that all they have to do is work really hard and be smart and they, too, one day, will be as rich as Bill Gates, Jeff Bezos, and Mark Zuckerberg. Furthermore, when marginalized groups endorse the myth of meritocracy, they are likely to blame their own group's struggles on members of their group. For example, a study found that when Latinx individuals and women read about prejudice against their group, those who endorsed the myth of meritocracy blamed their group for its low status more than those who reject the myth meritocracy.[44]

Individuals who are financially well-off tend to feel entitled to their wealth because they imagine they earned it fairly. In fact, the rich are incentivized to deny income inequality. For instance, high-income White people believe that the glaring Black-White wage gap is not as extreme as it actually is. They minimize the racial income gap and the even greater wealth gap. In contrast, low-income people and African Americans, regardless of income, are more accurate in the assessment of the degree of inequality. Conveniently, White people are fairly accurate at assessing *past* inequality. And those who subscribe to the myth of meritocracy are less accurate in assessing present inequality.[45] These findings make sense because if you believe in the myth of meritocracy, you are going to insist that things are fair, and if they are not, then place blame on the victims of that unfairness. And for those doing well, believing that *past* inequality existed isn't a problem for them—they believe they are not benefiting from past inequality according to this mythology, so they are free to acknowledge it. However, if you acknowledge present inequality, then you have to figure out how to explain it.

Social class insulates the rich from the truth about inequality, but it also protects them from the suffering of others. Studies show that affluent individuals are less likely than the less affluent to report feeling compassion toward others. For example, they are less likely to agree with statements such as, "Taking care of others gives me a warm feeling inside," and "It's important to take care of people who are vulnerable."[46] These patterns hold even after controlling for factors we know affect compassionate feelings, such as gender, ethnicity, and spirituality. In addition, when participants watch one of two videos (in one someone is explaining how to build a patio; the other shows children who are suffering from cancer) there are differences in compassion there as well. Participants with less income and parental education, are more likely than those better off to report feeling compassion while watching the video of the cancer patients. In addition, compared to those better off, their heart rates slow down while watching the cancer video—a response that is associated with paying greater attention to the feelings and motivations of others.[47] So why would wealth and status decrease our feelings of compassion for others? The researchers of this study theorize that the answer may have something to do with how wealth and abundance give us a sense of freedom and independence from others. The less we have to rely on others, the less we may care about their feelings. This leads us toward being more self-focused. We will explore the selfishness of the wealthy more in Chapter 5.

Political Conservatism and Rigidity

Political conservatives tend to be prejudiced.[48] Their prejudice seems to be due in large part to their individualist perspective and the way they explain people's success and failure. Because conservatives tend to buy into individualism and the myth of meritocracy, they see people as responsible for the negative outcomes they experience. Accordingly, they see certain groups, such as African Americans or poor people, as violating these norms and values.[49] Political conservatives are cognitively more rigid than political progressives—at least when those on the extreme right and left are compared.[50] Part of that rigidity involves a cognitive *need for closure*: conservatives prefer clear answers rather than ambiguity, and they are more likely than liberals to view things in black and white. Those with a need for closure tend to vote for conservative political candidates.[51] Conservatives tend to be uncomfortable with nuance. They object to women who act outside of traditional feminine norms, they object to queer people for, well, not being heterosexual. Ultimately, conservatives tend to be upset by their expectations being violated.

It is no exaggeration to say that, in recent years, some political conservatives have become obsessed with transgender individuals and where they use the restroom. One study illuminates an aspect of transgender people that upsets conservatives so much—their perceived violation of gender rules. Chadly Stern and Nicholas O. Rule presented people with photos of transgender men at various points in their transition. In some photos the man looks more feminine, in later photos the man looks more masculine.[52] Respondents were asked how positively they felt about the person in the picture. Conservatives but not liberals rated people who looked more gender-typical in their appearance more positively than those who looked more androgynous. In other words, conservatives were more accepting of transgender men who looked like traditional men. In a second study, respondents were asked to categorize the photos according to the target's gender—simply to label the photos as women or men. Although liberals and conservatives took similar amounts of time to categorize the target's gender, conservatives evaluated targets more negatively when it took them longer to categorize them. That is, the more difficult it was to label the photo as that of a woman or a man, the more negative they felt about the person who confused them.[53] Uncertainty is more frightening to conservatives than to liberals.[54] Political conservatives do not like perceived value or norm violators. Men should be men; women should be women. Political conservatives compared to liberals are more likely to reject a woman for a job if she is the primary caregiver of a child whereas they did not express gender bias if that role is not mentioned.[55] Presumably, the rejection is based on the belief that a woman with a young child should be at home taking care of the child rather than working. The studies might help explain why political conservatives feel entitled to interact with people that make sense to them and those who do not pose a cognitive and moral threat for them. Particularly in public spaces, dominant group members, whether they are White people calling the police on African Americans or cisgender people peeping around bathrooms, feel entitled to have their space inhabited by those who do not challenge them cognitively and emotionally. In contrast, marginalized groups do not feel entitled to such verification and validation of their beliefs.

Social Dominance Orientation

One's orientation toward power and group dominance informs the way one views the world and can inform one's sense of entitlement, sometimes with deadly consequences. Social dominance orientation has been studied for decades but has gotten recent attention due to the hard right turn of politics in the United States and globally. In his book, *How Fascism Works: The Politics of Us and Them*, Jason Stanley writes, "The most telling symptom of fascist politics is division. It aims to separate a population into an 'us' and a 'them.'"[56] Those with a social dominance orientation view the world as a competitive jungle in which the strong are on top and the weak are on the bottom. Donald Trump speaks and governed from a social dominance orientation. People oriented toward social dominance agree with statements such as, "Some groups of people are simply inferior to others," and "We should not push for group equality." They think their group should be on the top of the social ladder and other groups at the bottom. So they prize group-based dominance. They actively oppose equality because those with a strong social dominance orientation see group differences in status, power, and wealth as inevitable and even desirable.[57] One can even find a correspondence between people's chosen careers and their social dominance orientation. For instance, police officers have relatively high social dominance scores, while those who work in the public defender's office have lower social dominance scores.[58] Men have higher scores than women,[59] and White people have higher scores than people of color.[60]

Inequality persists in large part because those with power are able to shape social thinking by promoting legitimizing ideologies that protect their privilege. In order to justify the inequality they support, those with a social dominance orientation draw on *legitimizing myths*, which are attitudes and beliefs that justify inequality.[61] So, for instance, the belief that women are compassionate and nurturing, and men are competitive and aggressive, justifies men's superior position in a competitive work environment. People high in social dominance (compared to low) are more suspicious of women who do not take their husband's last name when they marry.[62] The belief that queer people flaunt their sexuality justifies preventing them from adopting children or teaching in schools. Legitimizing myths are insidious because they can be used to deny others equality even while prejudice is socially disapproved of— the unequal treatment seems rational and just. Discrimination reinforces the existing social hierarchy. Dominant groups tend to support and enforce policies that entrench their advantages. And because many of these ideologies mask their function behind reasonable or ethical-seeming notions, many people accept them. Once social institutions that sustain inequality are stabilized in a society, they tend to reinforce and reinvent the social dominance orientations that gave rise to them in the first place.[63]

People with social dominance orientations view the world as competitive and cut-throat—a place where there must be winners and losers. Those with a social dominance orientation tend to be socially and culturally conservative.[64] They object to social policies that help disadvantaged groups such as aid to the poor and sick. Thus, they readily see the world in terms of, and classify people into, ingroups and outgroups. Because of their self-oriented and cynical view of the world, they can be manipulative in their interpersonal relations and lack empathy toward others.[65] When placed in competitive situations in which their chances of winning are threatened, those high in social dominance react to this competitive threat with selfishness and readiness to break rules to win at all costs.[66] Those high in social dominance will support violence against marginalized groups, even as they do not necessarily support violence across the board. They tend to support violence directed at subordinated groups when subordinated groups are perceived as violating group-based status boundaries—when those of lower status do not "stay in their place." And they support violence by dominant groups against subordinated groups but not vice versa.[67]

People with social dominance orientations are motivated to maintain existing hierarchies. Therefore, they do not take complaints about inequality well, especially when complaints come from marginalized groups. One study demonstrates the role that social dominance plays in people's justification of the status quo. Miguel M. Unzueta and his colleagues asked White respondents to evaluate a workplace promotion scenario where a police officer applied for a promotion but another officer got it instead.[68] In one version the police officer was Black and the officer who got the promotion was

White; in the other version, the police officer was White and the officer who got the promotion was Black. In addition to these two versions, the reaction of the nonpromoted officer varied: in one version the officer attributed their rejection to discrimination; in another version they did not. In all there were four versions of the scenario. Respondents read only one version and were asked various questions about the rejected officer. The question for Unzueta and his colleagues was, do respondents evaluate the Black and White officers differently based on whether they attribute their rejection for promotion to discrimination? And does judgment of the officer depend on whether the respondent has a social dominance orientation? There are several findings related to our discussion. When the rejected officer did not attribute his rejection to discrimination, those respondents high in social dominance liked the Black officer more than the White officer. That is, those with social dominance orientations like a Black person who doesn't complain about discrimination. They rewarded the African American officer for not complaining. What about when the rejected officer attributes his rejection to discrimination? White officers who attributed their rejection to discrimination were liked more than Black officers who attributed their rejection to discrimination. Thus, when Black people complain about discrimination, they pay a social cost; White people who complain about discrimination do not.

Unzueta conducted a similar study with both White and Black respondents and found similar patterns among those with social dominance orientations—even among African Americans with dominance orientations. Because claims made by people of color question the legitimacy of racial hierarchy, those with social dominance orientations react negatively whether they are Black or White. However, White complainers are actually liked more by social dominants. These and other studies find that as social dominance levels increase so does perceived racial discrimination—but only for White people, not for people of color.[69] Social dominance causes members of dominant but not subordinate groups to feel victimized. Perceived victimization by dominant group members is used to maintain hierarchy and is key to entitled resentment.

A feature of social dominance revealed in one of the findings described above is that one does not have to be on top to have a social dominance orientation. Researchers have determined that social dominance is not simply the desire to have one's own group dominate socially relevant outgroups; social dominance theory has been refined to reflect the general desire to establish and maintain hierarchically structured intergroup relations regardless of the position of one's own group within that hierarchy.[70] For instance, poor and working-class people with social dominance orientations tend to think their own group deserves its lowly position. This phenomenon could explain in part the support of Donald Trump and other bigoted politicians by the very people they denigrate at their rallies. In recent years in the United States, there appears to be an increase in men of color joining White supremacist hate groups.[71] This phenomenon is paradoxical to be sure. And again, White people are more oriented toward social dominance than are people of color. The hypermasculine, hierarchical worldviews of these groups can appeal to anyone with these attitudes, not only White people. It probably also helps that White supremacist hate groups are misogynist and homophobic, as well as racist,[72] and that may appeal to some men of color who also hold those attitudes.

Authoritarianism

Well I have the ultimate authority . . . President of the United States has the authority to do what the president has the authority to do, which is very powerful. The President of the United States calls the shots . . . When somebody's the President of the United States, the authority is total. And that's the way it's gotta be.
                                        —Former US President Donald Trump[73]

Authoritarianism is an ideology that puts a premium on deference to authority, with an uncritical acceptance of authority figures.[74] The study of authoritarianism captures both politics and psychology. There are authoritarian leaders and governments: for instance, Adolf Hitler in Germany, Benito Mussolini in Italy, and, more recently, Viktor Orbán in Hungary, Jair Bolsonaro in Brazil, Rodrigo Duterte in the Philippines, and Recep Tayyip Erdoğan in Turkey. And there are individuals with an authoritarian personality—the mindset, the lens through which one views the world—whether or not they run a nation. Authoritarians—both leaders and followers—see the world as a dangerous and threatening place, so they place high value on security. Authoritarians agree with statements such as, "Our country will be great if we show respect for authority and obey our leaders" and "This country will flourish if young people stop experimenting with drugs, alcohol, and sex, and pay attention to family values."[75]

Authoritarians are politically conservative and conventional. They do not like people who disrupt traditional roles. They organize the world in terms of ingroups and outgroups: those who are normal and share their values and those who do not. Outsiders threaten the authoritarian's sense of security. Like conservatives, authoritarians tend toward mental inflexibility. They see the world in simple terms, they want definite answers, they have a high need for closure, meaning they want quick, simple answers. Authoritarians tend to be uninterested in experiencing new things so they do not get exposure to perspectives different from their own. In addition, authoritarians tend to be self-righteous. They see themselves as morally superior and therefore justified in looking down on anyone that authority figures define as less moral or less normal. Their self-righteousness can lead to them seeing their own faults in the targets of their disdain. Therefore, like narcissists, authoritarians may engage in projection: accusing people of what they themselves are doing. Authoritarians tend toward conspiracy theories and political paranoia.[76] The racist "birther" conspiracy theory perpetrated by Donald Trump accused President Obama of being a secret Muslim who was born in Kenya. The combination of a Black man being president and one with the name Barack Obama triggered those who fear difference. Of course, Donald Trump may have cynically deployed the birther conspiracy, not necessarily because he believed it but because it drummed up support from authoritarian voters.

Let's take a closer look at how authoritarians are oriented to those in power who share their view of the world, whether those in power are bosses, religious leaders, or presidents.

Authoritarianism is made up of three dimensions.[77] First, we have *authoritarian submission*.[78] Authoritarians submit to authorities who are perceived to be established and legitimate. There was a bumper sticker several years back that said, "God said it. I believe it. That settles it." Second, authoritarians are willing to engage in *authoritarian aggression*.[79] They support violence against people that established authorities marginalize. Think of some Trump supporters' reaction to protesters and even the news media ("the enemy of the people") at Trump rallies. Authoritarian citizens will do the bidding of authority figures. For instance, one study found that authoritarians who believed their boss disliked a certain group were willing to discriminate against members of that group, whereas those who are not authoritarians were not willing to do so.[80] A third dimension of authoritarianism is *conventionalism*: authoritarians adhere to social conventions endorsed by established authorities.[81]

A primary tool used in authoritarianism is bigotry. It is used to amplify condemnation of those on the margins. The authoritarian thinks: I see the world as a threatening place. I'm scared. Let's ban Muslims from the United States because they are terrorists (*simple answers*). Muslims are trying to impose Sharia Law in the United States (*conspiracy thinking*). Muslims are different from me (*outgroup categorizing*). They are not Christians (*they don't share my values*).

How about members of the queer community? The authoritarian thinks: I see the world as a threatening place. Queer people are a threat to the traditional heterosexual nuclear family. They're different from me (*outgroup categorizing*). Their sexual behavior is immoral (*self-righteousness*). And so on. Authoritarian leaders offer followers explanations of their fear with specific targets and bumper-sticker language that followers can easily remember.

There is a warehouse of research on the role that authoritarianism plays in prejudice. Authoritarians justify prejudice against fat people because they believe they are lazy—fatness also violates the Protestant work ethic. They are prejudiced against African Americans because they believe they are lazy *and* dangerous. They are prejudiced against poor people because they believe they are lazy and immoral. They dislike feminists because they deviate from traditional notions of womanhood. These patterns are evident at the individual psychological level, but can also be used as a tool for manipulation by an authoritarian leader.

Authoritarianism and Social Dominance Orientation:
What's the Difference?
It is easy to confuse social dominance orientation and authoritarianism because their members are entitled, intolerant, and punitive, but the two ideologies are distinct. Authoritarians' prejudice is based on fear, moral judgment, and intolerance, whereas those with a social dominance orientation develop their prejudice on the basis of competition, greed, and selfishness. Interestingly, both types of individuals can be prejudiced against the same groups but for different reasons. Those high in social dominance are prejudiced against African Americans, Asian Americans, Native Americans, Muslims, immigrants, queer people, and feminists,[82] not so much because these groups are frightening, immoral, or nontraditional, but because these groups challenge the legitimacy of social inequality as a system. As an example, authoritarians are prejudiced against immigrants who appear to refuse to assimilate—they are strange and different and have different values.

In contrast, those with a social dominance orientation are prejudiced against immigrants who *do* assimilate because now they are potential competitors with nonimmigrants.[83]

Authoritarianism reflects a dogmatic view of the world. Authoritarians are motivated by perceived threat and then the desire for collective security, control, stability, and order (as opposed to individual freedom, autonomy, and self-expression). They are social/cultural conservatives. Authoritarians tend to be concerned with social threats, whereas social dominance is concerned with competitive threats. Social dominance prioritizes self-enhancement (e.g., power, achievement), and a preference for a strong, dominant and unequal social system.[84] For those with social dominance orientations, the world is a ruthless jungle in which the strong and able win, and the weak and unfit lose.

Can People's Authoritarianism and Social Dominance Orientation Change?

Most psychologists who study them agree that authoritarianism and social dominance orientation are relatively stable ideologies or worldviews. But one's levels of either can fluctuate to some degree. Life changes can modify these ideologies, and even studies that prime people for threat and fear show some potential for movement. First, let's look at authoritarianism. Becoming a parent makes authoritarianism increase, presumably because social threats become more relevant.[85] Those who were near and survived the 9/11 terrorist attacks in the United States experienced a shift toward conservatism following the attacks—and the shift occurred with both Democrats and Republicans.[86] Those with high levels of conservatism and authoritarianism were more likely to show symptoms of posttraumatic stress disorder and depression many months after the incident. Even reading about a destabilizing political crisis increases one's susceptibility to authoritarianism.[87] In addition, economic conditions affect authoritarianism. When times are hard, people feel under greater threat.[88] On the other hand, authoritarianism scores can change over the lifespan in the other direction. Whereas parenting tends to increase authoritarianism, experience in higher education decreases it.[89] Education encourages critical thinking, nuance, and learning about people who are different. And just as inducing people to think about fear and threat increases authoritarian attitudes, increasing a participant's feeling of physical safety results in participants expressing less socially conservative views and less resistance to change.[90]

Experiences can shape one's social dominance orientation, and it can change depending on one's circumstances. People who experience more privileges than disadvantages develop stronger orientations toward social dominance than others. The longer people are members of a high-power social group, the higher they score on social dominance measures. One study tracked law students and psychology students and found that law students' social dominance scores increased with years at university, but psychology students' social dominance scores decreased with years.[91] This divergence is likely due to the topics studied and the underlying values of each field: one is a helping profession and the other emphasizes argument and competition. Similar patterns come to light when research participants are assigned to power or lack of power. Experiments that assign people to powerful positions cause an increase in their social dominance scores.[92] Therefore, social power is not simply correlated with social dominance orientation, it can *cause* it. In other words, those who are power seeking will likely be in competitive and aggressive roles, but those put in positions that require competition and aggression will become more oriented toward social dominance.

Ambivalent Sexism

Social dominance orientation and authoritarianism are correlated with feelings of entitlement. So is sexism. Entitled people think about gender and gender equality in certain ways. For example, the more men endorse gender inequality, the more pay they feel entitled to for a job. For women, the more they endorse gender inequality, the less entitled to pay they feel.[93] In other words, to the extent that both women and men endorse gender inequality, men believe *as men*, they are deserving, and women believe *as women*, they are less deserving.

Finally, another ideology that links to entitlement is contemporary beliefs about women. The theory of ambivalent sexism captures people's attitudes toward traditional and nontraditional women. Peter Glick and Susan Fiske[94] find that people's (women's and men's) attitudes toward women can be divided into two kinds of sexist attitudes that make up *ambivalent sexism*: hostile sexism and benevolent sexism. *Hostile sexism* is what most people think of when they think of sexism. It consists of overtly hostile feelings toward women, with particularly negative feelings toward nontraditional women. Hostile sexism seeks to justify men's power, traditional gender roles, and men's exploitation of women as sexual objects through derogatory characterizations of women. Hostile sexists would agree with statements such as, "Most women interpret innocent remarks or acts as being sexist" and "Many women get a kick out of teasing men by seeming sexually available and then refusing male advances." Hostile sexism is correlated with social dominance orientation.[95]

Benevolent sexism is a sneakier form of sexism. It involves attitudes toward women that seem positive on the surface but, in fact, are patronizing and disempowering. Benevolent sexists characterize women as innocent creatures who need protection from men. It reflects the view that women should be adored by men and that women are necessary to make men complete. Benevolent sexism allows men to characterize their privileges as well deserved, even as a responsibility they must bear (similar to the "White man's burden"[96]). Men should be willing to sacrifice their own needs (but not their power) to care for the women in their lives. Benevolent sexists agree with statements such as, "In a disaster, women ought to be rescued before men" and "A good woman should be set on a pedestal by her man." Benevolent sexism is a subtle form of sexism. People do not immediately recognize benevolent sexism as sexist, and many women are even flattered by the attitudes of benevolent sexism,[97] just as some women are flattered by so-called chivalry. But chivalry is a protection racket that comes with a price.[98] Like chivalry, benevolent sexism is disarming because it promises that men's power will be used to women's advantage, as long as they can secure a high-status male protector. Some women (specifically traditional women) are protected to some extent by chivalry, but at great cost. In excluding women from the outside world of work and from positions traditionally held by men, benevolent sexists exclude women from roles that offer more status in society. Thus, women are protected in some fairly meaningless ways, but also patronized and excluded. Benevolent sexism undermines women's resistance to male dominance because it is appealing to some women.

Hostile and benevolent sexism are distinct concepts that reflect two different kinds of sexism; however, people can, and often do, hold hostile and benevolent sexist attitudes simultaneously. In fact, both types work in concert. People tend to direct hostile sexism toward women who violate traditional gender roles (e.g., feminists, sexually-active women, women soldiers, and ambitious women) and benevolent sexism toward conventional women (e.g., homemakers, secretaries). Glick and Fiske describe benevolent sexism as the "carrot," the reward of positive (albeit patronizing) feelings toward, and the promise of protectiveness to, women who embrace traditional roles, and hostile sexism is the "stick," the punishment directed at women who reject traditional roles.[99] Punishment alone (through hostile sexism) is not the most effective means of shaping behavior because that might result in resentment and resistance. However, punishment for women who do *not* cooperate, combined with reinforcement for women who *do*, helps maintain male dominance and the gender status quo.[100] Furthermore, benevolent sexism can quickly turn into hostile sexism if a woman does not conform to gender rules.

Ambivalent sexism is correlated with other concepts discussed in this chapter, such as social dominance orientation and authoritarianism. For example, women with social dominance orientations have to justify their inferior position. They do so by adhering to benevolent sexism. These women justify women's low status as legitimate, which, in turn, makes them seek out protection from men.[101] For men, social dominance orientation is correlated with hostile sexism, whereas authoritarianism is correlated with benevolent sexism.[102] That is, men's authoritarianism is geared toward social conformity, which corresponds to their support of traditional women. In contrast, men with social dominance orientations emphasize competition and the superiority of their group so they hold hostile sexist beliefs that they direct toward nontraditional women—perhaps women who refuse to be subordinated by them or women who might be in direct competition with them for resources.

What is the relationship between ambivalent sexism and entitlement? For men, entitlement and benevolent sexism are correlated in that those men who score high on measures of entitlement are also likely to be benevolent sexists.[103] Perhaps benevolent sexism allows the entitled man to maintain a positive self-image by allowing him to maintain a notion of himself as protector and provider for the weaker sex. For women, the relationship between entitlement and benevolent sexism is even stronger. Women who feel deserving of special treatment are also likely to endorse more paternalistic views of their own gender. Although benevolent sexism is ultimately associated with gender inequality and poorer treatment of women, on the surface it appears to provide preferential treatment for women, such as women having doors opened for them. Entitled women seem to be tempted by the so-called preferential treatment and therefore are likely to endorse attitudes that promote gender inequality.[104] These are short-term (and trivial) gains at the expense of long-term equality. Benevolent sexism entitles men to power over women while not believing themselves to be sexist and discriminatory.

Benevolent sexism offers women protection in name only. The attitudes that view women as soft and nurturing and ladylike are the same attitudes that want to exclude women from all but the most traditional female of workplaces.

Conclusion

This chapter describes several of the harmful effects of entitlement, such as overconfidence and arrogance. Aside from just being wrong about one's capabilities and talents, there are other negative consequences of overconfidence. For example, among adolescents, overconfidence is related to the probability of committing crimes. Overly confident teens are more likely to engage in criminal offenses than those with more reasonable confidence, and the overconfident are more likely to offend unwisely—making mistakes that result in a higher probability of being arrested.[105] Entitlement is linked to narcissism as well. In fact, clinically, entitlement is a subcategory of narcissism. Narcissists can be toxic to interpersonal relationships, organizations, and even nations. Whereas there is not necessarily a direct line from a narcissistic personality disorder to the mistreatment of marginalized individuals, a narcissistic leader's self-centeredness and lack of empathy may influence both the policies they promote and the damaging rhetoric they use normalizing the mistreatment of subordinated groups. A national leader who is oriented toward social dominance and is an authoritarian, or whose followers are authoritarians, is part of a toxic stew of harshness and intolerance of subordinated groups.

Recall that high levels of entitlement are associated with perceived threat and subsequent mistreatment of the object that is the supposed threat. Entitled people see *meaningful* others, not necessarily any random person or group, as a threat. To the extent that a leader can use security or morality threats in their favor, this resonates with followers who feel emboldened and entitled to carry out the logical extensions of their leader's rhetoric. Individuals with these tendencies can justify their mistreatment of marginalized others, while not being violent across the board. Their targets are not random—the perpetrators' attacks are specific and allow them to indulge in a false sense of innocence.

The entitled person targets primarily those thought to violate norms of the Protestant work ethic and the myth of meritocracy promoted by the value of individualism. These ideologies reflect the notion that a person's success or failure is a result of their individual effort (or lack of), intelligence (or lack of), and grit (or lack of), and that one's ultimate success or failure is just, correct, and earned. In his book, *How Fascism Works*, Jason Stanley writes that those who disrupt the patriarchal set up of the cisgender heterosexual patriarchal head of the household (or head of the country) are particular targets of those with fascist politics. Members of the queer community make for obvious targets here, and introducing "bathroom bills" in state legislatures is a method of dehumanization. Women who want to control their reproduction are also threats to patriarchy, and anti-abortion bills are strategies to control women's freedom and independence.

One thread that runs through many of the correlates of entitlement described in this chapter are rigidity and punitiveness. Many of the individuals described here can be mean and unforgiving. Those who have worked with men who are participants in batterer programs find that men convicted of domestic abuse are rigid, black-or-white thinkers. Contrary to the "rageaholic" many people assume these men to be, an inflexible, rigid personality may be even more common.[106] Political conservatives, and those with social dominance orientations, are actually more reluctant to give and receive apologies than are political progressives.[107] Apologies are a rhetorical vehicle for removing power inequities in relationships after a transgression. Conservatives and those oriented toward social dominance seem to be more invested in maintaining power differences, whereas those most likely to offer and reward apologies are those with liberal ideologies.

Hostile and benevolent sexism work in concert. Hostile sexism entitles people to punish women who step out of line; benevolent sexism rewards women who stay in line. Recall that narcissistic heterosexual men tend to direct hostility toward heterosexual women and not lesbians and gay men, as the latter two groups do not present a threat to these men because they will not provide or withhold gratification.[108] We can find repeated examples of the hostile self-centeredness of narcissists combined with contemporary attitudes toward women in Donald Trump's hyperbolic reactions to certain women. Heterosexual women who appear uppity, assertive, or do not cow tow to Trump are targets of his entitled resentment: Hillary Clinton, Megyn Kelly, Alexandria Ocasio-Cortez, Nancy Pelosi, and on and on.

The next chapter explores how these cruel cousins of entitlement are acquired. What kinds of parenting practices promote these attitudes and ideologies? What role do teachers play in perpetuating overconfidence and entitlement? These are among the questions examined in Chapter 3.

Notes

1. Berlinger, J, (Writer & Director). (2019, January 24). One of us. (Season 1, Episode 2) [Netflix series episode]. In J. Berlinger, J. Doran, J. Kamen, & J. Wilkes (Executive Producers), *Conversations with a killer: The Ted Bundy tapes*. Netflix. https://www.netflix.com/title/80226612.
2. Katzenstein, J. (2018). *Let me interrupt your expertise with my confidence* [Cartoon]. Condé Nast. https://condenaststore.com/featured/let-me-interrupt-your-expertise-with-my-confidence-jason-adam-katzenstein.html.
3. Visser, B. A., Ashton, M. C., & Vernon, P. A. (2008). What makes you think you're so smart? Measured abilities, personality, and sex differences in relation to self-estimates of multiple intelligences. *Journal of Individual Differences, 29*(1), 35–44. https://doi.org/10.1027/1614-0001.29.1.35.
4. Pallier, G. (2003). Gender differences in the self-assessment of accuracy on cognitive tasks. *Sex Roles, 48*, 265–276. https://doi.org/10.1023/A:1022877405718.
5. Reuben, E., Rey-Biel, P., Sapienza, P., & Zingales, L. (2012). The emergence of male leadership in competitive environments. *Journal of Economic Behavior & Organization, 83*, 111–117. https://doi.org/10.1016/j.jebo.2011.06.016.
6. Tellhed, U., & Adolfsson, C. (2017). Competence and confusion: How stereotype threat can make you a bad judge of your competence. *European Journal of Social Psychology*. https://doi.org/10.1002/ejsp.2307.
7. Krawczyk, M., & Wilamowski, M. (2017). Are we all overconfident in the long run? Evidence from one million marathon participants. *Journal of Behavioral Decision Making, 30*(3), 719–730. https://doi.org/10.1002/bdm.1984.
8. Yoder, M. S., Ault, L. K., & Mathews, M. A. (2017). Knowing your face: A componential analysis of self-perceived facial attractiveness. *Journal of Social Psychology, 157*(3), 366–381. https://doi.org/10.1080/00224545.2016.1229252.
9. Wohleber, R. W., & Matthews, G. (2016). Multiple facets of overconfidence: Implications for driving safety. *Transportation Research Part F, 43*, 265–278. http://dx.doi.org/10.1016/j.trf.2016.09.011.
10. Insurance Institute for Highway Safety, Highway Loss Data Institute. (2019, May). *Red light running*. https://www.iihs.org/topics/red-light-running.
11. Insurance Journal. (2005, January 25). *Farmers survey: Red light running among top causes of crashes: men more than women feel need to run*. https://www.insurancejournal.com/news/national/2005/01/25/50151.htm.
12. Sunderland, M. (2017, January 13). People think women are worse drivers than men-statistics say otherwise. *Vice*. https://www.vicc.com/en_us/article/qvdpgv/people-think-women-are-worse-drivers-than-menstatistics-say-otherwise.
13. Sunderland, M. (2017, January 13). People think women are worse drivers than men-statistics say otherwise. *Vice*. https://www.vice.com/en_us/article/qvdpgv/people-think-women-are-worse-drivers-than-menstatistics-say-otherwise.
14. Muris, P. Merckelbach, H., Otgaar, H., & Meijer, E. (2017). The malevolent side of human nature: A meta-analysis and critical review of the literature on the dark triad

(narcissism, Machiavellianism, and psychopathy). *Perspectives on Psychological Science, 12*, 183–204. https://doi.org/10.1177/1745691616666070.

15. Kesebir, P. (2014). A quiet ego quiets death anxiety: Humility as an existential anxiety buffer. *Journal of Personality and Social Psychology, 106*(4), 610–623. https://doi.org/10.1037/a0035814.

16. Ingraham, C. (2016, August 1). New study finds that men are often their own favorite experts on any given subject. *The Washington Post.* https://www.washingtonpost.com/news/wonk/wp/2016/08/01/new-study-finds-that-men-are-often-their-own-favorite-experts-on-any-given-subject/?postshare=4581470057910393&tid=ss_tw.

17. King, M. M., Bergstrom, C. T., Correll, S. J., Jacquet, J., & West, J. D. (2017). Men set their own cites high: gender and self-citation across fields and over time. *Socius: Sociological Research for a Dynamic World, 3*(1). https://doi.org/10.1177/2378023117738903.

18. See Chapter 5 in: Anderson, K. J. (2015). *Modern misogyny: Anti-feminism in a post-feminist era.* Oxford University Press.

19. Hall, E. V., & Livingston, R. W. (2012). The hubris penalty: Biased responses to "Celebration" displays of black football players. *Journal of Experimental Social Psychology, 48*(4), 899–904. https://doi.org/10.1016/j.jesp.2012.02.004.

20. Garvey, M. (2014, May 24). Transcript of the disturbing video "Elliot Rodger's retribution." *Los Angeles Times.* https://www.latimes.com/local/lanow/la-me-ln-transcript-ucsb-shootings-video-20140524-story.html.

21. Twenge, J. M., & Campbell, K. W. (2009). *The Narcissism epidemic: Living in the age of entitlement.* Free Press.

22. Malkin, C. (2017). Pathological narcissism and politics: A lethal mix. In B. Lee (Ed.), *The dangerous case of Donald Trump* (pp. 51–68). St. Martin's Press.

23. Malkin, C. (2017). Pathological narcissism and politics: A lethal mix. In B. Lee (Ed.), *The dangerous case of Donald Trump* (pp. 51–68). St. Martin's Press.

24. Grijalva, E., Newman, D. A., Tay, L., Donnellan, M. B., Harms, P. D., Robins, R. W., & Yan, T. (2015). Gender differences in narcissism: A meta-analytic review. *Psychological Bulletin, 141*(2), 261–310. https://doi.org/10.1037/a0038231.

25. Cited in: Keiller, S. W. (2010). Male narcissism and attitudes toward heterosexual women and men, lesbian women, and gay men: Hostility toward heterosexual women most of all. *Sex Roles, 63*, 530–541. See also: Hart, W., Tortoriello, G. K., & Richardson, K. (2019). Deprived and grandiose explanations for psychological entitlement: Implications for theory and measurement. *Journal of Personality Assessment.* https://doi.org/10.1007/s11199-010-9837-8.

26. Snyder, R. L. (2019). *No visible bruises: What we don't know about domestic violence can kill us.* Bloomsbury.

27. Anastasio, P. A., & Rose, K. C. (2013). Beyond deserving more: Psychological entitlement also predicts negative attitudes toward personally relevant outgroups. *Social Psychological and Personality Science, 5*, 593–600. https://doi.org/10.1177/1948550613519683.

28. Keiller, S. W. (2010). Male narcissism and attitudes toward heterosexual women and men, lesbian women, and gay men: Hostility toward heterosexual women most of all. *Sex Roles, 63*, 530–541. https://doi.org/10.1007/s11199-010-9837-8.
29. Keiller, S. W. (2010). Male narcissism and attitudes toward heterosexual women and men, lesbian women, and gay men: Hostility toward heterosexual women most of all. *Sex Roles, 63*(7–8), 530–541. https://doi.org/10.1007/s11199-010-9837-8.
30. Rasmussen, K. (2015). Entitled vengeance: A meta-analysis relating narcissism to provoked aggression. *Aggressive Behavior, 42*(4), 362–379. https://doi.org/10.1002/ab.21632.
31. Grijalva, E., Newman, D. A., Tay, L., Donnellan, M. B., Harms, P. D., Robins, R. W., & Yan, T. (2015). Gender differences in narcissism: A meta-analytic review. *Psychological Bulletin, 141*(2), 261–310. http://dx.doi.org/10.1037/a0038231.
32. Holtzman, N. S., Vazire, S., & Mehl, M. R. (2010). Sounds like a narcissist: Behavioral manifestations of narcissism in everyday life. *Journal of Research in Personality, 44,* 478–484. https://doi.org/10.1016/j.jrp.2010.06.001.
33. Grijalva, E., Newman, D. A., Tay, L., Donnellan, M. B., Harms, P. D., Robins, R. W., & Yan, T. (2015). Gender differences in narcissism: A meta-analytic review. *Psychological Bulletin, 141*(2), 261–310. http://dx.doi.org/10.1037/a0038231.
34. Malkin, C. (2017). Pathological narcissism and politics: A lethal mix. In B. Lee (Ed.), *The dangerous case of Donald Trump* (pp. 51–68). St. Martin's Press.
35. Malkin, C. (2017). Pathological narcissism and politics: A lethal mix. In B. Lee (Ed.), *The dangerous case of Donald Trump* (pp. 51–68). St. Martin's Press.
36. Madison, L. (2011, September 22). Elizabeth Warren: "There is nobody in this country who got rich on his own." *CBS News.* https://www.cbsnews.com/news/elizabeth-warren-there-is-nobody-in-this-country-who-got-rich-on-his-own/.
37. Goodman, D. J. (2011). *Promoting diversity and social justice: Educating people from privileged groups.* Routledge.
38. For a debunking of the myth of meritocracy, see Chapter 6 in: Anderson, K. J. (2010). *Benign bigotry: The psychology of subtle prejudice.* Cambridge University Press.
39. Wise, T. ([Host]. 2018, October 23). Episode 50: Donald Trump, the myth of meritocracy and building solidarity through radical humility [Audio podcast episode]. *In Speak Out with Tim Wise.* https://www.podomatic.com/podcasts/speakoutwithtimwise/episodes/2018-10-23T12_17_39-07_00.
40. Love, B. L. (2019). *We want to do more than survive: abolitionist teaching and the pursuit of educational freedom.* Beacon Press.
41. Barstow, D., Craig, S., & Buettner, R. (2018, October 2). Trump engaged in suspect tax schemes as he reaped riches from his father. *The New York Times.* https://www.nytimes.com/interactive/2018/10/02/us/politics/donald-trump-tax-schemes-fred-trump.html.
42. Smith, A. (2018, October 2). New York Times report says that Trump engaged in "outright fraud" to avoid taxes as he inherited father's wealth-worth more than $400 million in today's dollars. *Business Insider.* https://www.businessinsider.com/new-york-times-trump-tax-fraud-father-fred-inheritance-2018-10.

43. Umoh, R. (2018, January 22). CEOs make $15.6 million on average-here's how much their pay has increased compared to yours over the year. *CNBC*. https://www.cnbc.com/2018/01/22/heres-how-much-ceo-pay-has-increased-compared-to-yours-over-the-years.html.

44. Major, B., Kaiser, C. R., O'Brien, L. T., & McCoy, S. K. (2007). Perceived discrimination as worldview threat or worldview confirmation: Implications for self-esteem. *Journal of Personality and Social Psychology*, *92*(6), 1068–1086. https://doi.org / 10.1037/0022-3514.92.6.1068.

45. Kraus, M. W., Rucker, J. M., & Richeson, J. A. (2017). Americans misperceive racial economic equality. *Proceedings of the National Academy of Sciences of the United States of America*, *114*(39), 10324–10331. https://doi.org/10.1073/pnas.1707719114.

46. Study 1: Stellar, J. E., Manzo, V. M., Kraus, M. W., Keltner, D. (2012). Class and compassion: Socioeconomic factors predict responses to suffering. *Emotion*, *12*(3), 449–459. https://doi.org/10.1037/a0026508.

47. Study 2: Stellar, J. E., Manzo, V. M., Kraus, M. W., Keltner, D. (2012). Class and compassion: Socioeconomic factors predict responses to suffering. *Emotion*, *12*(3), 449–459. https://doi.org/10.1037/a0026508.

48. Mendoza, S. A., & DiMaria, M. G. (2019). Not "with her": How gendered political slogans affect conservative women's perceptions of female leaders. *Sex Roles*, *80*(1/2), 1–10. https://doi.org/10.1007/s11199-018-0910-z.

Erhart, R. (2016). A cross-national examination of prejudice toward immigrants: The role of education and political ideology. *Journal of Aggression, Conflict and Peace Research*, *8*(4), 279–289. https://doi.org/10.1108/JACPR-02-2016-0212.

49. Mendoza, S. A., & DiMaria, M. G. (2019). Not "with her": How gendered political slogans affect conservative women's perceptions of female leaders. *Sex Roles*, *80*(1–2), 1–10. https://doi.org/10.1007/s11199-018-0910-z.

50. Jost, J. T., Glaser, J., Kruglanski, A. W., & Sulloway, F. J. (2003). Political conservatism as motivated social cognition. *Psychological Bulletin*, *129*(3), 339–375. https://doi.org/ 10.1037/0033-2909.129.3.339.

51. Chirumbolo, A., & Leone, L. (2008). Individual differences in need for closure and voting behaviour. *Personality and Individual Differences*, *44*(5), 1279–1288. https://doi.org/10.1016/j.paid.2007.11.012.

52. Stern, C., & Rule, N. O. (2017). Physical androgyny and categorization difficulty shape political conservatives' attitudes toward transgender people. *Social Psychological and Personality Science*, *9*(1), 1–8. https://doi.org/10.1177/1948550617703172.

53. Stern, C., & Rule, N. O. (2017). Physical androgyny and categorization difficulty shape political conservatives' attitudes toward transgender people. *Social Psychological and Personality Science*, *9*(1), 1–8. https://doi.org/10.1177/1948550617703172.

54. Jost, J. T., Stern, C., Rule, N. O., & Sterling, J. (2017). The politics of fear: Is there an ideological asymmetry in existential motivation? *Social Cognition*, *35*(4), 324–353. https://doi.org/10.1521/soco.2017.35.4.324.

Stern, C., West, T. V., & Rule, N. O. (2015). Conservatives negatively evaluate counterstereotypical people to maintain a sense of certainty. *Proceedings of the*

National Academy of Sciences of the United States of America, 112(50), 15337–15342. https://doi.org/10.1073/pnas.1517662112.

55. Hoyt, C. L. (2012). Gender bias in employment contexts: A closer examination of the role incongruity principle. *Journal of Experimental Social Psychology, 48*(1), 86–96. https://doi.org/10.1016/j.jesp.2011.08.004.

56. Page xvi in: Stanley, J. (2018). *How fascism works: The politics of us and them.* Random House.

57. Sidanius, J., Cotterill, S., Sheehy-Skeffington, J., Kteily, N., & Carvacho, H. (2018). Social dominance theory: Explorations in the psychology of oppression. In F. K. Barlow, & C. G. Sibley (Eds.), *The Cambridge handbook of the psychology of prejudice: Concise student edition* (pp. 102–143). Cambridge University Press.

58. For a review, see: Sidanius, J., Cotterill, S., Sheehy-Skeffington, Kteily, N., & Carvacho, H. (2017). Social dominance theory: Explorations in the psychology of oppression. In C. G. Sibley & F. K. Barlow (Eds.), *The Cambridge handbook of the psychology of prejudice* (pp. 149–187). Cambridge University Press.

59. Rosenthal, L., Levy, S. R., & Earnshaw, V. A. (2012). Social dominance orientation relates to believing men should dominate sexually, sexual self-efficacy, and taking free female condoms among undergraduate women and men. *Sex Roles: A Journal of Research, 67*(11–12), 659–669. https://doi.org/10.1007/s11199-012-0207-6.

60. Thomsen, L., Green, E. G. T., Ho, A. K., Levin, S., van Laar, C., Sinclair, S., & Sidanius, J. (2010). Wolves in sheep's clothing: SDO asymmetrically predicts perceived ethnic victimization among White and Latino students across three years. *Personality and Social Psychology Bulletin, 36*(2), 225–238. https://doi.org/10.1177/0146167209348617.

61. For a discussion of legitimizing beliefs, see: Sidanius, J., Cotterill, S., Sheehy-Skeffington, J., Kteily, N., & Carvacho, H. (2018). Social dominance theory: Explorations in the psychology of oppression. In F. K. Barlow, & C. G. Sibley (Eds.), *The Cambridge handbook of the psychology of prejudice: Concise student edition* (pp. 102–143). Cambridge University Press.

62. Robnett, R. D., Underwood, C. R., Nelson, P. A., & Anderson, K. J. (2016). "She might be afraid of commitment": Perceptions of women who retain their surname after marriage. *Sex Roles, 75*(9–10), 500–513. https://doi.org/10.1007/s11199-016-0634-x.

63. Jackson, L. M. (2011). *The psychology of prejudice: From attitudes to social action.* American Psychological Association.

64. Duckitt, J., & Sibley, C. G. (2017). The dual process motivational model of ideology and prejudice. In C. G. Sibley & F. K. Barlow (Eds.), *The Cambridge handbook of the psychology of prejudice* (pp. 188–221). Cambridge University Press. https://doi.org/10.1017/9781316161579.009.

65. For a review of the literature, see Chapter 6 in Kite, M. E., & Whitley Jr., B. E. (2016). *Psychology of prejudice and discrimination* (3rd edition). Routledge.

66. Duckitt, J., & Sibley, C. G. (2017). The dual process motivational model of ideology and prejudice. In C. G. Sibley & F. K. Barlow (Eds.), *The Cambridge handbook of the psychology of prejudice* (pp. 188–221). Cambridge University Press. https://doi.org/10.1017/9781316161579.009.

67. For a discussion of social dominance theory see: Sidanius, J., Cotterill, S., Sheehy-Skeffington, J., Kteily, N., & Carvacho, H. (2018). Social dominance theory: Explorations in the psychology of oppression. In F. K. Barlow, & C. G. Sibley (Eds.), *The Cambridge handbook of the psychology of prejudice: Concise student edition* (pp. 102–143). Cambridge University Press.

68. Unzueta, M. M., Everyly, B. A., & Gutiérrez, A. S. (2014). Social dominance orientation moderates reactions to Black and White discrimination claimants. *Journal of Experimental Social Psychology, 54,* 81–88. https://doi.org/10.1016/j.jesp.2014.04.005.

69. Thomsen, L., Green, E. G. T., Ho, A. K., Levin, S., Laar, C. van, Sinclair, S., & Sidanius, J. (2010). Wolves in sheep's clothing: SDO asymmetrically predicts perceived ethnic victimization among White and Latino students across three years. *Personality and Social Psychology Bulletin, 36,* 225–238. https://doi.org/10.1177/0146167209348617.

70. Sidanius, J., Cotterill, S., Sheehy-Skeffington, J., Kteily, N., & Carvacho, H. (2018). Social dominance theory: Explorations in the psychology of oppression. In F. K. Barlow, & C. G. Sibley (Eds.), *The Cambridge handbook of the psychology of prejudice: Concise student edition* (pp. 102–143). Cambridge University Press.

71. Gupta, A. (2018, September 6). Why young men of color are joining White-supremacist groups. *Daily Beast.* https://www.thedailybeast.com/why-young-men-of-color-are-joining-white-supremacist-groups.

72. Oppenheim, M. (2018, July 25). Misogyny is a key element of White supremacy, Anti-Defamation League report finds. *The Independent.* https://www.independent.co.uk/news/world/americas/misogyny-white-supremacy-links-alt-right-antidefamation-league-report-incel-a8463611.html.

73. Guardian News (2020, April 14). *Donald Trump: "When somebody is president of the United States, the authority is total."* [video]. YouTube. https://www.youtube.com/watch?v=r3QXrQDTDYo.

74. I'm drawing from Chapter 6 in: Kite, M. E., & Whitley Jr., B. E. (2016). *Psychology of prejudice and discrimination* (3rd edition). Routledge. Theoretically, you can have left-wing authoritarians, but the empirical work on authoritarianism finds that it is most common on the political right. Therefore, my use of *authoritarianism* here refers to right-wing authoritarianism.

75. Duckitt, J., Bizumic, B., Krauss, S. W., & Heled, E. (2010). A tripartite approach to right-wing authoritarianism: The authoritarianism-conservatism-traditionalism model. *Political Psychology, 31*(5), 685–715. https://doi.org/10.1111/j.1467-9221.2010.00781.x.

76. Grzesiak-Feldman, M. (2015). Are the high authoritarians more prone to adopt conspiracy theories? The role of right-wing authoritarianism in conspiratorial thinking. In M. Bilewicz, A. Cichocka, & W. Soral (Eds.), *The psychology of conspiracy* (pp. 99–121). Routledge/Taylor & Francis Group.

77. Brown, R. (2010). *Prejudice: Its social psychology.* Wiley-Blackwell.

78. Duckitt, J., Bizumic, B., Krauss, S. W., & Heled, E. (2010). A tripartite approach to right-wing authoritarianism: The authoritarianism-conservatism-traditionalism model. *Political Psychology, 31*(5), 685–715. https://doi.org/10.1111/j.1467-9221.2010.00781.x.

79. Duckitt, J., Bizumic, B., Krauss, S. W., & Heled, E. (2010). A tripartite approach to right-wing authoritarianism: The authoritarianism-conservatism-traditionalism model. *Political Psychology*, *31*(5), 685–715. https://doi.org/10.1111/j.1467-9221.2010.00781.x.

80. Petersen, L.-E., & Dietz, J. (2000). Social discrimination in a personnel selection context: The effects of authority's instructions to discriminate and followers' authoritarianism. *Journal of Applied Social Psychology*, *30*, 206–220. https://doi.org/10.1111/j.1559-1816.2000.tb02312.x.

81. Duckitt, J., Bizumic, B., Krauss, S. W., & Heled, E. (2010). A tripartite approach to right-wing authoritarianism: The authoritarianism-conservatism-traditionalism model. *Political Psychology*, *31*(5), 685–715. https://doi.org/10.1111/j.1467-9221.2010.00781.x.

82. Chapter 6 in Kite, M. E., & Whitley Jr., B. E. (2016). *Psychology of prejudice and discrimination* (3rd edition). Routledge.

83. Duckitt, J., & Sibley, C. G. (2018). The dual process motivational model of ideology prejudice. In F. K. Barlow & C. G. Sibley (Eds.), *The Cambridge handbook of the psychology of prejudice: Concise student edition* (pp. 144–181). Cambridge University Press.

84. Duckitt, J., & Sibley, C. G. (2018). The dual process motivational model of ideology prejudice. In F. K. Barlow & C. G. Sibley (Eds.), *The Cambridge handbook of the psychology of prejudice: Concise student edition* (pp. 144–181). Cambridge University Press.

85. Altemeyer, B. (1996). *The authoritarian specter*. Harvard University Press.

86. Bonanno, G. A., & Jost, J. T. (2006). Conservative shift among high-exposure survivors of the September 11th terrorist attacks. *Basic and Applied Social Psychology*, *28*(4), 311–323. https://doi.org/10.1207/s15324834basp2804_4.

87. Altemeyer, B. (1988). *Enemies of freedom: Understanding right-wing authoritarianism*. Jossey-Bass.

88. For a review, see: Brown, R. (2010). *Prejudice: Its social psychology*. Wiley-Blackwell.

89. For a review, see: Brown, R. (2010). *Prejudice: Its social psychology*. Wiley-Blackwell.

90. For a review, see: Duckitt, J., Sibley, C. G. (2017). The dual process motivational model of ideology and prejudice. In C. G. Sibley & F. K. Barlow (Eds.), *The Cambridge handbook of the psychology of prejudice* (pp. 188–221). Cambridge University Press.

91. Guimond, S., Dambrun, M., Michinov, N., & Duarte, S. (2003). Does social dominance generate prejudice? Integrating individual and contextual determinants of intergroup cognitions. *Journal of Personality and Social Psychology*, *84*(4), 697–721. https://doi.org/10.1037/0022-3514.84.4.697.

92. For a review, see: Duckitt, J., Sibley, C. G. (2017). The dual process motivational model of ideology and prejudice. In C. G. Sibley & F. K. Barlow (Eds.), *The Cambridge handbook of the psychology of prejudice* (pp. 188–221). Cambridge University Press.

93. O'Brien, L. T., & Major, B. (2009). Group status and feelings of personal entitlement: The roles of social comparison and system-justifying beliefs. In J. T. Jost, A. C. Kay, & H. Thorisdottir (Eds.), *Social and psychological bases of ideology and system justification* (pp. 427–443). Oxford University Press.

94. Glick, P., & Fiske, S. T. (2001). An ambivalent alliance: Hostile and benevolent sexism as complementary justifications for gender inequality. *American Psychologist, 56*(2), 109–118. https://doi.org/10.1037/0003-066X.56.2.109.

95. Christopher, A. N., & Mull, M. S. (2006). Conservative ideology and ambivalent sexism. *Psychology of Women Quarterly, 30*(2), 223–230. https://search.ebscohost.com/login.aspx?direct=true&db=eric&AN=EJ736486&site=eds-live&scope=site.

96. "White man's burden" is the racist idea that because European people are believed to be superior (e.g., more civilized) to African people, it is Europeans' responsibility to care for (i.e., control) people of African descent. Africans were thought to be so primitive that they were unable to conduct themselves properly—they were more akin to animals or children than adult humans.

97. Barreto, M., & Ellemers, N. (2005). The burden of benevolent sexism: How it contributes to the maintenance of gender inequalities. *European Journal of Social Psychology, 35*(5), 633–642. https://doi.org/10.1002/ejsp.270.

98. Peterson, S. R. (1977). Coercion and rape: The state as a male protection racket. In M. Vetterling-Braggin, F. A. Elliston, & J. English (Eds.), *Feminism and philosophy* (pp. 360–371). Littlefield Adams.

99. Robnett, R. D., Anderson, K. J., & Hunter, L. E. (2012). Predicting feminist identity: Associations between gender-traditional attitudes, feminist stereotyping, and ethnicity. *Sex Roles, 67*(3–4), 143–157. https://doi.org/10.1007/s11199-012-0170-2.

100. Glick, P., & Fiske, S. T. (2001). An ambivalent alliance: Hostile and benevolent sexism as complementary justifications for gender inequality. *American Psychologist, 56*(2), 109–118. https://doi.org/10.1037/0003-066X.56.2.109.

101. Radke, H. R. M., Hornsey, M. J., Sibley, C. G., & Barlow, F. K. (2017). Negotiating the hierarchy: Social dominance orientation among women is associated with the endorsement of benevolent sexism. *Australian Journal of Psychology, 70*(2), 158. https://doi.org/10.1111/ajpy.12176.

102. Sibley, C. G., Wilson, M. S., & Duckitt, J. (2007). Antecedents of men's hostile and benevolent sexism: The dual roles of social dominance orientation and right-wing authoritarianism. *Personality and Social Psychology Bulletin, 33*(2), 160–172. https://doi.org/10.1177/0146167206294745.

103. Grubbs, J. B., Exline, J. J., & Twenge, J. M. (2014). Psychological entitlement and ambivalent sexism: Understanding the role of entitlement in predicting two forms of sexism. *Sex Roles, 70*(5–6), 209–220. https://doi.org/10.1007/s11199-014-0360-1.

104. Grubbs, J. B., Exline, J. J., & Twenge, J. M. (2014). Psychological entitlement and ambivalent sexism: Understanding the role of entitlement in predicting two forms of sexism. *Sex Roles, 70*(5–6), 209–220. https://doi.org/10.1007/s11199-014-0360-1.

105. Loughran, T. A., Paternoster, R., Piquero, A. R., & Fagan, J. (2013). "A good man always knows his limitations": The role of overconfidence in criminal offending. *Journal of Research in Crime and Delinquency, 50*(3), 327–358. https://doi.org/10.1177/0022427812459649.

106. Snyder, R. L. (2019). *No visible bruises: What we don't know about domestic violence can kill us.* Bloomsbury.

107. Hornsey, M. J., et al. (2017). Conservatives are more reluctant to give and receive apologies than liberals. *Social Psychological and Personality Science, 8*(7), 827–835. https://doi.org/10.1177/1948550617691096.

108. Keiller, S. W. (2010). Male narcissism and attitudes toward heterosexual women and men, lesbian women, and gay men: Hostility toward heterosexual women most of all. *Sex Roles, 63*(7–8), 530–541. https://doi.org/10.1007/s11199-010-9837-8.

3

Entitlement's Enablers

Parents and Teachers

The men basically wake up one morning, look in the mirror and say "I'd be a great state legislator" and they just run whereas women need to be recruited. And there is that sense of entitlement that frankly we should all feel, right? We are all entitled to be elected officials. But women have not been raised that way.

—Rutgers University Professor Debbie Walsh[1]

In March 2019, indictments were issued implicating fifty people in a college admissions cheating scam. Code-named "Operation Varsity Blues" by prosecutors, the brazen scheme involved wealthy parents paying, in one case, $80,000 to test-takers to take college admissions exams for their children who couldn't gain admission on their own merit.[2] In other cases, parents paid university athletic directors to designate their child as an athletic recruit—including creating phony photos to make them appear to play a sport they did not play. For example, "A teenage girl who did not play soccer magically became a star soccer recruit at Yale. Cost to her parents: $1.2 million."[3] These parents went to great lengths to get their children into elite colleges using a most antimeritocratic strategy—bribery. Donald Trump's older sister reported that he paid someone to take the SAT for him in order to get into college.[4] How ironic it is that critics complain that affirmative action is unfair because it benefits students of color and "penalizes" White students; in other words, it is not based on merit. This train of thought however ignores the egregious and long-standing history of the way in which the rich are able to subvert merit in the most naked ways. The parents ensnared in the Varsity Blues scandal claimed their children had no knowledge of their parents' crimes. If true, it would seem these privileged students did not know the extent to which they had the wind at their backs—whether through overt misdeeds or more everyday unearned advantages—and erroneously believed the world is fair. The illusion follows that they succeeded solely on their own

Enraged, Rattled, and Wronged. Kristin J. Anderson, Oxford University Press. © Oxford University Press 2021.
DOI: 10.1093/oso/9780197578438.003.0004

merits, and it is affirmative action admittees who are given a benefit they do not deserve and thus they do not belong.

This chapter explores the development of entitlement in individuals: the sense of deservingness that some people have relative to others. As the quotation that begins this chapter suggests, men come to have a sense of entitlement relative to women. What entities surrounding the newborn, the child, and young adult convey the sense of deservingness that some people have relative to others? Continuing where Chapter 2 left off, this chapter begins with the role parents play in producing a child with a social dominance orientation or authoritarian tendencies—two ideologies associated with entitlement. Parents' ideas about race and gender are significant in how their child will think about their place in the world. We explore the gendered treatment of children by caregivers beginning with parents' attitudes toward their newborn daughters and sons. Next, teachers are examined for encouraging entitlement in boys relative to girls, and in White students relative to students of color. For both caregivers and teachers, the expectations they have of children contribute to boys' and White children's sense of deservingness. Being the normative racial category allows one to be given the benefit of the doubt when it comes to school discipline. This chapter looks at the criminalization of Black and Brown girls and boys inside schools that results in a school-to-prison pipeline, setting children of color on a trajectory of lifelong criminalization. The school experience allows White kids to feel entitled to impartial or even preferential treatment by law enforcement and the criminal legal system.

Parents

How do individuals acquire an entitled way of viewing the world? Entitlement is not hereditary in the genetic sense, but it certainly can be passed down from generation to generation. In Chapter 1 we learned that members of dominant groups have power and privilege by virtue of their membership in a preferred group relative to those in subordinated groups. A sense of entitlement can emerge from social position, such as being influential through wealth or politics, or associated with someone who is influential. Are there ways of thinking about the world that facilitate entitlement? Let's start with caregivers. Parents influence children's development in all sorts of ways, especially in the early years when peers and mass media have yet to significantly impact them. Children's attitudes about various groups are influenced by their parents' attitudes toward those groups during childhood, adolescence, and into young adulthood.[5] Children imitate adults' interactions with out-group members, even when the behavior they observe is subtle. For example, White 5-year-olds who watched a video of a White adult who was verbally friendly but nonverbally distant toward an African American imitated the negative nonverbal behavior they saw in the video.[6] Regarding attitudes of prejudice and acceptance, children's attitudes tend to align with their parents' attitudes in general terms, although not necessarily in specific attitudes toward particular groups.[7] General prejudicial attitudes reflect broader value orientations, and children often adopt ideologies similar to their parents.

In addition to shared ideologies, there is some evidence that children cognitively process information in a similar way to their parents. For example, as we saw in Chapter 2, the cognitive need for closure has been linked to prejudice, intolerance, and the dualistic thinking of the entitled. *Need for closure* refers to a person's desire for clear and unambiguous answers and an aversion to ambiguity. People high in a need for closure seek definitive answers that can be made quickly. They are not comfortable with nuance, uncertainty, or doubt. Need for closure is a feature of social dominance orientation, authoritarianism, and conservatism. To the extent that parents have a high need for closure, their children are more likely to as well.[8]

Parents' Role in Social Dominance Orientation and Authoritarianism

His life will never be the one that he dreamed about and worked so hard to achieve. That is a steep price to pay for 20 minutes of action out of his 20 plus years of life.
                    —Dan Turner, father of convicted rapist Brock Turner[9]

Like other attitudes and ideologies, parents play a role in downloading social dominance attitudes onto their children.[10] Recall that social dominance is a view of the world as an ugly struggle for power, and the belief that certain groups belong on top and others belong on the bottom. Certain parenting practices facilitate social dominance in their children. Parents who are cold and unaffectionate with their children may lead to children who come to see the world as a competitive jungle in which each person must look out for themself and attain superiority over others.[11] In contrast, parents who are warm and affectionate toward their children are more likely to influence their children to see the world as cooperative, emphasizing concern for others and an orientation toward social equality. Parents' responsiveness to their offspring, as reported by their adolescent children, is negatively associated with teens' social dominance tendencies. In other words, unresponsive parents are more likely to produce children with high levels of social dominance. In contrast, children of responsive parents have been shown to prefer egalitarian relationships among groups in society.[12] Of course, there are myriad factors that affect how a child will evolve in the way they view the world. Parenting practices do not produce an inevitable and specific destiny for a child. However, cold or warm caregiver practices nudge children toward harsh or generous orientations toward the world, respectively.

Chapter 2 discussed how experiences shape one's social dominance orientation and one's social dominance orientation can change depending on the circumstances. People who experience more advantage than disadvantage develop stronger social dominance orientations than others. Over time, the longer people are members of a high-power social group the higher they tend to score on measures of social dominance. Recall that law students' social dominance scores increase but psychology students' scores decrease with years of study.[13] Thus, in addition to parenting style, the influence parents exert over chosen career paths may also have the potential to increase a person's eventual degree of social dominance and subsequent entitlement.

Like the cold and unaffectionate parenting practices that move children toward social dominance orientations, authoritarian parents who are cold and punitive can also lead to conforming personalities.[14] Children with authoritarian parents learn to see the world as a dangerous and threatening place. These children may tend toward seeking security and conformity as a means of minimizing threats. In contrast, tolerant child-rearing practices lead to an independent and expansive view of the world. Kids with this latter experience are more likely to value personal freedom over conformity and see the world as safe and secure rather than frightening.[15]

Another type of parenting style, *overparenting*, also seems to be a predictor of entitlement. Examples of overparenting include, for instance, buying things the child does not need and doing tasks for the child (e.g., laundry) that they could do themselves, thus creating an unrealistically clear path that deprives the child of appropriate maturation. A study of mostly White 19-year-olds found that their sense of entitlement (measured by statements such as, "I demand the best because I am worth it" and "People like me deserve an extra break now and then") and self-efficacy was related to overparenting.[16] Overparenting was associated with high entitlement but low self-efficacy in these 19-year-olds. Overparenting also predicts academic entitlement (a type of entitlement discussed in Chapter 1). College students with "hovering" parents are more likely to believe that instructors should give them preferential treatment, for example.[17] Parents that excessively impose their will on their children in the form of providing things and doing tasks for their child may raise children with an oversized sense of deservingness and an undersized sense of ability to accomplish things. Overparenting has even shown to be correlated with men's sense of sexual entitlement and coercive sexual tendencies. As we already know, entitled individuals believe they deserve special treatment, believe their wants and desires outweigh those of others, and tend to lack empathy.[18] Hostility between parents is associated with the perpetration of sexual coercion by young men who grow up in that environment. In addition, overparenting, as well as inconsistent parenting (e.g., setting limits with a child and then giving in) are indirectly associated with the perpetration of sexual coercion through feelings of entitlement.[19] In other words, inconsistent rule-setting and overparenting increases men's sense of entitlement and the likelihood of coercive sexual strategies with potential sex partners.

The lenient sentence for rapist Brock Turner, a Stanford University athlete, sparked national outrage in 2016 and is perhaps a lesson in overparenting and runaway entitlement. Turner was convicted of sexually assaulting a young woman behind a dumpster on the campus of Stanford University. Whereas Turner faced 14 years in prison, he actually served only 3 months in a county jail.[20] That Turner was White and an athlete at a prestigious university seemed to entitle him to special treatment by both the media and the sentencing judge. For example, the picture of Turner used by media outlets was not his mugshot, but instead was a picture of him in a suit. This contrasts with how African American criminal suspects are typically portrayed in the media—handcuffed, disheveled, and not fully dressed.[21] In addition, during Turner's sentencing, his father read a letter to the judge requesting that Turner receive leniency in part because:

> Brock always enjoyed certain types of food and is a very good cook himself. I was always excited to buy him a big ribeye steak to grill or to get his favorite snack for him. I had to make sure to hide some of my favorite pretzels

or chips because I knew they wouldn't be around long after Brock walked in from a long swim practice. Now he barely consumes any food and eats only to exist.[22]

The most infamous line from Brock Turner's father's letter begins this section. Dan Turner dismissively describes the sexual assault his son committed as merely "20 minutes of action."[23] Dan Turner epitomizes the tendency of some parents to come to their adult offspring's defense so they do not have to face the consequences of their actions. Perhaps many parents would come to their child's defense in hopes of a more lenient sentence, but describing a sexual assault as "20 minutes of action" reveals how the entitled view the lives of others—as not meriting human regard and humane treatment.

Parents' Ideas About Race in Producing Entitlement

Parents transmit their ideas about race to their children and those ideas impact the child's and then the adult's sense of entitlement. When you are the racial norm, that understanding, even if it is only an implicit understanding, is going to inform what you expect from the world. Beverly Daniel Tatum studies children's racial identity development.[24] Children of color learn early in their lives that their ethnicity is not the norm. They are often in contexts in which they are the only person of color among White people. White children ask them why their skin color is dark or their hair different from theirs. Children of color cannot assume storybooks will show characters who look like them or history will tell stories about people from their community. They do not grow up entitled to seeing themselves depicted in positive ways in popular culture.

For those whose identity is not the norm, they cannot take for granted many aspects of life that those with normative identities can. A developmental task for ethnic minority children then is to make it into and through adulthood with a sense of racial pride despite messages from society that might undermine that pride. According to Tatum, a challenge for parents is to offer counter-stereotyped images of people of color so their children will resist the negative images of their ethnic group. For families of color, racial socialization is a broad class of parental behaviors that transmits attitudes, values, and information regarding their racial group members and inter-group relationships with children. Parents focus on cultural socialization, preparation for bias, and egalitarianism. For example, one study of African American parents with sons between 3 and 8 years old found that parents reported nurturing their sons' individuality—typical for American parents, especially for boys.[25] At the same time, these parents situate their sons' place in the larger group, so parents emphasize communion as well. Unlike parents of White children, the African American parents in this study connected personal achievement to how it benefits African American communities. Parents of color understand their successes can be seen as successes for the community, and their setbacks also impact, not just them as individuals, but everyone in their community. As Michael Harriot argues, White people have the privilege of individuality.[26] Bad acts that an individual White person commits do not attach to all White people. White people are not asked to answer for another White person's crime. In contrast, Arab Americans are routinely asked to account for crimes that some other Arab American commits as if each Arab American knows and is responsible for all other Arab Americans. People of color do not experience the privilege of individuality.

Parents' Racial Colorblindness and the Luxury of Being the Norm

In contrast to parents of color in the United States, parents of White children tend to not discuss race with their kids. If they do speak about race, it may be in hushed tones, even scolding their child for noticing that some people have different skin color. Robin DiAngelo[27] asks us to think about what it means for a parent to shush a White child who sees an African American person and says, "That man's skin is black!" Why is the parent embarrassed by this? Would the parent also shush the child if she pointed out that the man is handsome or strong? Probably not. DiAngelo uses this example to illustrate that White children learn a lot about race from this experience. First, discussions about race are distasteful and should not be openly discussed. Second, having dark skin is taboo, the way that you would not want to point out a large birthmark on someone's face or a person with a visible disability. DiAngelo notes this is why White people sometimes lower their voice in conversations in which they refer to a person's race.

One of the luxuries of being the racial norm is not having to contend with your race. Your life doesn't depend on it. For many White people, racism, and even race, is someone else's issue. In fact, according to Beverly Daniel Tatum, some White people don't have an answer to the question, "What are you?" Or they may answer, "I'm just regular." Racial colorblindness tends to be the main approach of racial socialization by White parents living in the United

States. They tend to believe that if they do not notice or speak about race, they will not be racist, or accused of being racist. And if they do not talk to their children about race, these parents often assume, their children will not grow up to be racist. Even when parents who have participated in research related to ethnicity or race were instructed by researchers to talk to their children about racial issues, the parents tended to avoid the discussion.[28]

I have written in detail about racial colorblindness in my book *Benign Bigotry*[29] and I refer you to that discussion, which details how, in a culture that includes people of different hues, it is impossible to be racially colorblind. Briefly, people automatically encode others' race (and gender), whether they want to or not.[30] In fact, empirical research finds that White people who espouse colorblind beliefs tend to have more awkward and negative interactions with people of color than Whites who do not claim to be colorblind.[31] A colorblind perspective also denies the reality of the potent role racism plays in who is treated fairly and who is not. Finally, Whites' belief in colorblindness prevents them from realizing and acknowledging the unearned privileges they get as the dominant racial group in a White-dominated society. If people believe race is irrelevant, then they can think that race can never be the reason they got a job over someone else or they can assume a person wasn't aggressively thrown out of their vehicle during a traffic stop because of their race.

To give you a sense of how some White parents deal with race with their children, consider a study from Erin Pahlke and her colleagues.[32] They observed and recorded White mothers reading stories to their 4- to 5-year-old children. The stories were created to encourage explicit discussions about race and difference. However, White mothers almost never mentioned race or interracial interactions when reading the stories. Mothers also reported that they infrequently provided race-related messages to their children. In another part of the study, the young children were asked to distinguish between pictures of White and Black people. The mothers predicted their children would not be able to distinguish the pictures according to race, although the children did on eighty-three of eighty-four pictures they were shown. Overall, this study suggests that White parents seem to think that not talking about race is good parenting. The mothers incorrectly assume their young children do not "see" race, when they do. Of course, if White parents do not engage in the topic of race with their children, their children are more likely left to be influenced by the ugly racial messages of society, a society that is very clear on who is valued and who is not.

Tim Wise argues that teaching children colorblindness amounts to intellectual child abuse.[33] How do you explain to your children structural forms of inequality such as segregated neighborhoods? A colorblind approach to understand inequality would be grounded in a false meritocratic explanation (i.e., that those who live in unsafe, resource-deprived neighborhoods live there because of their own personal failings) that they are less capable, less moral, or just plain lazy. Children combine their recognition of inequality with the standard message of their society. Unless parents explain that inequality is the result of systemic and institutionalized oppression, children will fill in the gaps through a lens of individualism. Only thoughtful color consciousness can prepare children to confront the world around them honestly and accurately. Not seeing color (or pretending not to) makes it harder to see the *consequences* of color. White parents who "protect" their children from discussions of racism ensure that Black and Brown children will *not* be protected from racism. Children of color are forced to actively explore their race and ethnicity because of their encounters with racism. The same is not true for White children. They have the luxury of viewing themselves as individuals, not as part of an ethnic or racial group. And if children of color have to understand what color means, shouldn't White children? Preferably, White children would develop a White identity based in reality, not on assumed superiority or the ignorance of White privilege and corresponding entitlement. Such a change would go far in eliminating the negative effects of colorblindness.

Parents' Ideas About Gender and Sexuality in Producing Entitlement

Like children who belong to the normative racial category, children who belong to the normative gender category learn that their gender is superior. Children learn these messages from mass media, teachers, peers, and parents, often in subtle ways. Gender is a central social category from the beginning of a child's life. When a child is born, the first question usually asked is not about the health of the newborn or mother but whether the child is a girl or a boy.[34] We live in a culture in which one's gender is typically believed to determine one's preferred colors, whether or what kinds of sports one will play, one's college major, one's job, and so on. Thus, people believe they need this information in order to know how to think about and interact with the newborn. Because gender is so critical in our interactions with others, some people become upset or even enraged when they cannot immediately identify the gender of an individual. This irrational response to gender ambiguity likely plays a role in the epidemic of murders of transgender people.[35] Why is it so upsetting for some people to not easily categorize someone's gender? Sure, we don't like to be confused or mistaken. However, a chief reason for wanting clear, identifiable boundaries between genders is so we know who confers power and who does not. If we know someone's gender, we think we know whether a person should be a doctor or nurse, the boss or the secretary, leader or support person. In other words, we want to offer the appropriate power to men, and ensure we do not mistakenly bestow power upon women. In terms of children's gender development, if we know the child is a boy, for instance, then certain agentic and aggressive behaviors are tolerated as "boys will be boys." However the same behavior may be chastised in girls.

Globally, boys are the preferred gender, and this preference is due to the fact that in most cultures, men have more power, influence, and higher status than women. You might think this fact is pertinent to faraway places like Saudi Arabia or China, but Western nations value boys over girls even if it manifests in subtler ways. In a Gallup survey with an ethnically diverse sample of potential parents, 36% of respondents reported they wanted a son more than they wanted a daughter. Just 28% said they would rather have a daughter.[36] In fact, Gallup noted that Americans' preference for a boy has not changed significantly since 1941, when 38% preferred a son. American men, compared to women, drive the preference for boys. Furthermore, those who are less educated, political conservatives, and Republicans, tend to prefer sons over daughters.[37]

Parents' preference for sons over daughters is an early building block for men's greater sense of entitlement, relative to women. Boys and then men cannot help but internalize the value society places on them relative to girls and women. Much of this chapter and the next detail this process. Parents have fantasies about what their sons and daughters will be like, and their fantasies can be totally disconnected from what their children are actually like. Their fantasies include the hopes their sons will be big and strong and their daughters will be nurturing and gentle. Parents' gender stereotypes dictate how they orient toward their children and the degree to which they stereotype their children. For example, parents equate becoming a successful man with adhering to traditional male gender stereotypes such as competition and individualism.[38] So to the extent that parents want their

sons to be successful men, they will direct them toward traditional masculine roles.

In a classic study from 1974, Jeffrey Rubin and his colleagues[39] gathered fifteen newborn girls and fifteen newborn boys—all less than 24 hours old. The
infants were matched on Apgar scores, as well on their weight and length—
ensuring there were no actual differences between the size, weight, and health
of the girl and boy newborns. Mothers and fathers of each infant were asked
to, "Describe your baby as you would to a close friend or relative" on several
bipolar dimensions (e.g., noisy-quiet, firm-soft, hardy-delicate). Daughters
compared to sons were rated as soft, fine-featured, and inattentive. Fathers
compared to mothers were more extreme in their ratings of both daughters
and sons. For example, fathers rated sons as firmer, larger-featured, better-
coordinated, more alert, stronger, and hardier than daughters. Fathers rated
daughters as softer, finer-featured, more awkward, less attentive, weaker, and
more delicate than sons. Again these parental assessments were made within
24 hours of their babies' birth—these are tiny babies who did not differ in
alertness, features, strength, softness, and so on. Parents projected onto their
newborns their fantasies about who they hoped their children will be, not
who they were.[40]

Cisgender and heterosexual individuals are entitled to feeling normal
and unchallenged for their gender presentation and their relationship
desires. Transgender and nonheterosexual individuals enjoy no such luxury.
Most parents begin raising their children with the assumption they will be
cisgender and heterosexual. They (usually inadvertently) reinforce this assumption in a variety of ways. Adults sometimes refer to young children
as "flirts" or refer to young boys as "lady killer" or "stud" or even "pimp."
Amazon sells onesies that say "Flirt"[41] and "Stud."[42] Little girls might be
asked by adults if they have a boyfriend. Parents say to children, "Some day
when you are married . . ." with the assumption their partner will be other-
gender. Such gestures reinforce heteronormative behavior beginning early
in a child's life. Thus, children who will identify as queer have to negotiate
their identity in the context of a hostile world. Those with queer identities are
confronted with challenges to their identities whether it's comments such as,
"What's your real name?" or "Maybe this is a stage." These comments amount
to the questioning of a person's very essence. Like youth of color, for queer
youth, it is necessary to actively explore their identity in adolescence in a way
that heterosexual and cisgender youth, White kids, boys, and kids without a
disability need not. Certainly growing up can be difficult for any child, but

the difficulties that kids in the dominant group face will not be due to their dominant group membership. Sometimes hostility comes from their own parents if parents react negatively toward a child's gender identity or sexual orientation. Even when parents are supportive, kids may face criticism from relatives, peers, and school personnel.

Parents' Differential Treatment of Daughters and Sons Produces Entitlement in Boys

Caregivers treat girls and boys differently. We know this going back to a classic study on how we project our gender stereotypes onto unwitting children. Researchers dressed up a 6-month-old infant as either a girl and called her Beth or a boy and called him Adam.[43] They asked women to interact with the child and supplied a number of objects and toys. Keep in mind, a 6 month old is still very small—no walking, no talking. But that did not stop the women from gender socializing the babies. Participants more often handed a doll to "Beth" and handed a train to "Adam." They also smiled more at "Beth" than Adam. These differences may seem trivial. However, if children are consistently treated in gender-stereotyped ways—not just for a few minutes in a research lab but for days, weeks, months, and years—that treatment is going to constrain that child's environment. Gender-stereotyped treatment results in narrowing one's behavioral repertoire. Children will learn to behave according to half the human experience. The seemingly minor detail of smiling more at girls than boys teaches girls that smiling is part of the appropriate behavioral repertoire for girls.[44] When girls become women, they are expected to smile in public, even for strangers, and if they do not, some men feel entitled to demand smiles from women reflected in the routine experience of women being told to "smile" by random strangers. It is difficult to come up with an example of a similar strategy of social control directed at men by women.

The different rules about women and men smiling reflect the different assumptions about emotionality regarding gender. We falsely assume that women are the emotional gender (i.e., moody and expressive), and men are nonemotional (with the exception of anger), stoic, and steady. This is a lie.[45] But many people are entrenched in their belief that women are inextricably tied to their emotions and men barely have any. Caregivers engage in emotion socialization without even realizing it. First of all, mothers have been found to engage in more emotion talk with their children than do fathers[46]—modeling that women are the emotional gender. Fathers have been found to be reluctant to convey fear and sadness—emotions referred to as "submissive" negative emotions in the psychological literature.[47] Parents are more likely to convey that anger is an appropriate emotion for boys, but sadness and happiness are appropriate emotions for girls.[48] In a homophobic, as well as misogynist, culture such as the United States, fathers are particularly concerned with the gender-appropriate behavior of their sons.[49] Many fathers believe that any deviation from traditional masculine behavior is a sign that a son may be gay or targeted as weak—like a girl, and who wants to be a girl? By the time boys become men, they are hesitant to talk in emotionally disclosing ways out of fear of looking weak to other boys. Boys and men may not always speak emotionally, but they are just as capable of emotional expression as girls and women.[50] To believe that women are the emotional gender means you have never heard of a school shooter, spouse-abuser, or road-rager, or been a spectator at a sporting event. That we do not encourage boys to deal with their strong emotions in healthy ways can lead to unhealthy coping behaviors such as using firearms against those who have hurt their feelings or challenged their sense of entitlement.

Of course, gender socialization goes beyond how people talk to children about emotions. Campbell Leaper and Timea Farkas[51] provide a comprehensive review of the role parents play in turning babies into girls and boys and then women and men—women and men with different expectations of what they deserve. One example is play activities, which are important contexts for socialization of gender because they provide opportunities for practicing particular behaviors. So, to the extent that parents encourage sons to engage in masculine-coded activities, they are likely to learn assertiveness, competition, and mastery over objects. If parents encourage daughters to engage in feminine-coded activities, they tend to learn a broader repertoire of skills that includes both assertive and affiliative communication strategies resulting in more collaborative interacting styles. Parents tend to allow daughters more opportunity to play with a wider range of toys, those stereotypically associated with girls and boys, whereas they are more likely to encourage their sons to play with "boy toys" only.[52] This double standard leads girls to practice flexible interaction styles, whereas it teaches boys at least two lessons: (1) boys should have less accommodating and more rigid interaction styles, and (2) activities associated with girls and women should be avoided. Flexible learning styles will make it easy for women to modify their communication depending on the audience, whereas men will not feel the same pressure to modify and show flexibility with interaction partners.

Even household chores are gendered and set the stage for entitlement for boys compared to girls. Girls tend to have more demands on them for chores and help with younger siblings than do boys, and girls spend more time than boys on household chores.[53] In her review of research on children's chores, Virginia Valian found that girls tend to be given toys that turn into unpaid household chores when they get older such as cooking, childcare, and cleaning toys. Boys' toys are more likely to turn into adult men's toys (e.g., cars, videogames), occasionally adult men's paid work (e.g., police officer, firefighter), or finally and less likely, unpaid occasional household chores (e.g., yard work).[54] Not only do daughters tend to do more chores than sons, when parents offer children payment for chores, boys tend to earn significantly more money than girls for doing chores.[55] Interestingly, boys tend to spend the money on themselves more than girls do, and girls tend to give more of their money to charities than boys do.[56]

Gendered Treatment Becomes Gendered Entitlement

The gendered patterns related to chores teach children important lessons about entitlement. Boys learn their labor has monetary value—that men are entitled to pay. Girls learn their labor does not necessarily deserve monetary compensation. These early patterns predict adult chore performance. For instance, one study found in Great Britain that the chores boys did at age 16 years predicted the chores they did at age 29.[57] A nationally representative study of US couples found that heterosexual men with partners who work outside the home as much as they do report that their women partners do more housework than they do. However, these men also report that the inequality is fair.[58] Heterosexual men, relative to women, tend to have a sense of domestic entitlement—they feel justified doing less domestic labor than their spouse.[59] In contrast to men, some women feel guilty when they believe they are not doing enough housework, even when they are doing the majority of the work and both partners work.[60] Women also tend to experience guilt when they work long hours outside the home that might make them neglect domestic chores, but men in the same circumstances do not.[61] Women seem to learn the lesson that ultimately household chores are their responsibility, whereas men seem to learn that they should do chores, but housework is not a priority for them.

These early gendered parenting practices encourage different levels of entitlement in girls and boys and then, subsequently, women and men. Again, girls learn that it's unfeminine and selfish to ask for too much; boys learn their work has value that deserves payment.[62] These patterns, combined with the fact that boys are more valued in our society, make it unsurprising that parents overestimate their sons' abilities in a number of domains compared to their daughters'. For example, parents (and boys themselves) overestimate their sons' intelligence relative to their actual intelligence. Parents of daughters (and girls themselves) tend to underestimate their intelligence.[63] Parents' ideas about their child's abilities can influence a child's sense of their own abilities. For instance, one study found that whereas girls' and boys' math grades were not different, girls had lower self-concepts about math relative to boys. This was particularly true if girls' parents believed that boys have higher ability than girls.[64] Boys are more likely than girls to overestimate their abilities[65] and their performance on tasks.[66]

Not only do boys have stronger ability beliefs than girls, despite the lack of average differences in performance, they also have higher confidence in their physical appearance and social competence. This is so even when peers rate girls as more competent in these domains (with the exception of athletic performance).[67] We can find similar patterns at the college level, with men having higher academic self-esteem than women, even when there are no actual gender differences in academic ability.[68] Importantly, overconfidence can hinder performance—particularly for boys. For example, in one study with an ethnically diverse sample of eighth graders, overconfidence in one's performance negatively impacted it—especially for boys.[69] The study found that boys who were underconfident performed significantly better than boys who were overconfident. As we know from the previous chapter, men overestimate their abilities in all kinds of domains: driving, marathon running, physical attractiveness, and SAT scores. We know that overconfidence and entitlement are linked.

Teachers, Education, and Schooling

I tried not to feel intimidated when classroom conversation was dominated by male students, which it often was. Hearing them, I realized that they weren't at all smarter than the rest of us. They were simply

emboldened, floating on an ancient tide of superiority, buoyed by the
fact that history had never told them anything different.

—Michelle Obama[70]

Parents and caregivers are not the only adults in children's lives who socialize them. Teachers' potential to influence their students is made obvious by the number of hours they spend with kids each day. Years of interactions with teachers make them mega-influencers on how children come to view the world and their role in it. We can look at teachers as facilitators of students' level of entitlement.

Teachers' Differential Treatment of Students

Research going back decades finds that teachers pay more attention to boys in class. Some have argued that teachers pay more attention to boys because boys initiate more interactions and are more disruptive and attention demanding. However, beyond this difference, teachers still attend more to boys than girls. What does the attention look like? Boys receive both more positive and negative attention from teachers.[71] Some studies find that boys receive more criticism of their behavior than girls do; however, they also receive more intellectual criticism—and intellectual support—than girls.[72] The positive and negative intellect-related interactions boys have with teachers reveal that teachers take boys seriously as intellectual beings and reinforce them for critical thinking. This differential treatment also suggests that more intellectual advances are expected of boys than girls, and that boys are more valued than girls for their intellect. Boys, relative to girls, then come to believe that they are entitled to be heard and attended to in the academic context.

Teachers have different intellectual and social expectations of girls and boys in their classrooms, resulting in differential treatment of their students. Teacher expectations affect students' academic performance, and school performance influences a person's later opportunities. Even as early as preschool, teachers' perceptions of a preschooler's academic skills during the fall are associated with their academic achievement the following spring.[73] If teachers' expectations (and biases) can have a measurable impact over the course of one school year, imagine the consequences over a student's entire academic career.

Teachers' expectations about their students' motivation in school affects students' grades throughout their academic career—especially for students of color.[74] Compared to White students, teachers tend to underestimate ethnic minority students' motivation and achievement relative to their actual motivation and achievement.[75] And these perceptions matter. When teachers overestimate their motivation, students of color perform better compared to when they are underestimated, in which case, their performance suffers.[76] Regarding gender-related expectations, teachers seem to believe that girls are motivated to perform well and try hard but are limited in their ability.[77] Teachers tend to overrate boys' math ability relative to girls.[78] These expectations are not confined to primary schooling. College faculty show gender bias against women. One study found that when science professors were presented with the prospect of hiring a woman or a man as a lab manager, they exhibited bias against women undergraduates.[79] Professors judged the woman to be less competent and less worthy of being hired than a man with identical qualifications. They also offered her a smaller starting salary and less career mentoring. Faculty reported liking the woman more than the man, but that liking didn't translate into getting the job, and in fact, probably worked against the woman.[80] For women and not men, work-related competence is negatively associated with likeability, and likeability is negatively associated with perceived competence.[81] Accordingly the perceived "benefit" of likeability for women is a two-edge sword, resulting in the assumption of incompetence.

Boys Falling Behind?

Gentleman, our way of life is under attack. Society is trying to erase boys! They give us drugs that make us do girly things like pay attention!
—Milhouse Van Houten in *The Simpsons*[82]

Pundits and academics have decried lower average grades among boys than girls, as well as lower rates of college graduation for men than women. This gender pattern has been described as a "boy crisis" and a feminist takeover of the academy.[83] Examining underachievement in the United Kingdom, Susan Jones and Debra Myhill find that the current student underachievement discussion is not a discussion about all children who are struggling academically.[84] Rather, discussions typically center on boys. Underachieving girls are invisible. Girls' underachievement is ignored or not important enough to focus resources on. Why is this? Aside from boys' accomplishments just mattering more than girls', the underlying assumptions of girls' and boys' motivation, personalities, and talents are reflected in the attributions people make about girls' and boys' successes and failures. Jones and Myhill find that boys' achievement is viewed as the result of intrinsic potential and natural brilliance, whereas girls' achievement is seen as the result of diligence and hard work (*not* ability). Boys are constructed as curious, disruptive, and questioning, whereas girls are constructed as diligent, conformist, and rule following. Superiority underlies everything boys do (even when they "fail"). Framed in this way, the good behavior (hard work) from a girl becomes a negative, and the poor behavior (disruptive) from a boy is a quality. Teachers report to Jones and Myhill that boys are more difficult to teach but infer this is, in fact, a strength. Boys underachieve in a loud way. In contrast, girls are perceived as easier to teach, and this is a weakness. Some girls underachieve in a quiet way.

What are the implications of these assumptions? When boys are identified as underachievers, one still sees their potential; however, there is no potential in underachieving girls. In Jones and Myhill's study, boys themselves saw natural abilities as more desirable than achievement through hard work. They aspired to exhibit "effortless achievement": that is, getting results without making an effort (or appearing not to). For boys, lack of engagement may be the result of the desire for effortless achievement and may contribute to their actual lack of achievement. Jones and Myhill question whether any boy actually achieves without effort and why this myth persists. Regardless, achievement without effort is the height of entitlement because boys are given the benefit of the doubt in a way that girls are not. The fact that people believe boys are more likely to have inherent brilliance allows them to coast in a way girls cannot. Jones and Myhill observe that boys have underachieved for decades if not longer, but their failures have been protected from public scrutiny by the myth of boys' intrinsic potential.

One variant of the "effortless achievement" found by Jones and Myhill is the pressure for boys to avoid appearing academic or too "nerdy." Campbell Leaper and Timea Farkas find that the endorsement of traditional masculine ideology may undermine engagement and success in school.[85] Boys who are concerned about appearing tough may be reluctant to comply with teachers' authority or to seek help. For boys, school culture centers on opposing school authority, acting tough, and rejecting femininity. So when boys experience a lot of pressure from peers to uphold masculine norms, their educational functioning tends to suffer.[86] A study of 12-year-old Belgian students found that pressure to conform to masculine gender norms negatively impacted boys' academic self-efficacy, but pressure to conform to feminine gender norms positively impacted girls' academic self-efficacy.[87] This same study found that boys scored higher on perceived gender-conformity pressure. In other words, compared to girls, boys feel more pressure to conform to masculine gender roles, and those gender roles can be incompatible with academic success.

School Discipline: Entitlement for Some, Criminalization for Others

Right-wing pundits and politicians who have declared that there is a "war against boys" in schools see White boys as victims of feminism and multiculturalism.[88] Racial discrimination does not feature into their discussions of the supposed "boy crisis." This fact is a missed opportunity because a worthy area of concern for boys is the treatment of ethnic minority boys in school settings. Instead, "boy crisis" authors seem to want to recenter White boys and men back to their position as patriarchal leaders.

Teachers hold more positive expectations for White and Asian American students than African American and Latinx students. Teachers also tend to make more positive comments to White students than African American and Latinx students.[89] Unfortunately, schools mirror the general society that criminalizes and pathologizes girls and boys of color. Some teachers and administrators view Black and Brown girls and boys through a criminalized lens, viewing mischief, "attitude," and disruption as criminal offenses worthy of involving law enforcement. Black and Brown youth are more likely to be disciplined for the same infractions as White youth.[90] School principals are more likely to discipline African American students and to see them as "troublemakers" for the exact same infractions as White students.[91]

Starting in preschool, African American children are four times more likely to be suspended than White children.[92] So what has been described as a school-to-prison pipeline for youth of color could be characterized as a *preschool*-to-prison pipeline. Black boys are disciplined around five times as often as White boys. White people inaccurately read the facial expressions of grown Black men as hostile when their faces are neutral,[93] and similar patterns of misinterpretation also harm African American children. The ambiguous behavior of sixth graders is interpreted as aggressive when the children are Black,[94] revealing just how early Black boys are associated with aggression and criminality. Incidents such as fights in school that could be handled by counseling, a trip to the principal's office, or even academic suspension are instead routed to the criminal legal system for children of color. And once a person of any age gets caught in the machinery of the criminal legal system, it is very hard to get out. It is well established that African Americans are more likely to be cited for low-level infractions than Whites who commit infractions at the same rates. Furthermore, African Americans are more likely to be indicted, less likely to be offered bail, more likely to be convicted, and serve longer sentences than Whites for the same crimes.[95]

At the same time, in an erasure of girls and women, girls of color are pathologized and criminalized in similar ways to boys of color, yet this racial difference in girls is understudied.[96] Girls of color are often left out of any examination of racism or sexism in schools, amounting to what Kimberlé Crenshaw calls an intersectional failure.[97] In fact, Crenshaw finds that the differential treatment of Black and White girls is more extreme than the bias against Black boys relative to White boys. Crenshaw and her colleagues note that Black girls are disciplined around ten times more often than White girls.[98] Black girls are especially likely to be targets for harsh discipline. Risk for suspension is higher for Black girls when compared to White girls, and higher than it is for Black boys compared to White boys. In other words, in terms of bias in discipline, these racial disparities are even more dramatic when we look at girls.

In many schools, there is simultaneously "zero-tolerance" for aggression and violence but also an implicit tolerance of sexual harassment and homophobic bullying. Campus sexual harassment is sometimes ignored, trivialized, or even dismissed as an adorable aspect of young heterosexual courtship. Studies on antiqueer bullying find similar dismissing by teachers. One study of sex education teachers exposed how ill-equipped these teachers were to deal with gender- and sexuality-related harassment.[99] These teachers denied the very existence of queer students in their classrooms. They also tended to dismiss the seriousness of bullying of queer kids by labeling the bullying as immature and, therefore, insignificant when it did occur. When the teachers did engage the topic of bullying, they tended to view it as an individual bully-victim problem as opposed to anti-queer harassment being part of gender policing of heteronormative structures.[100] The minimizing of anti-queer bullying renders queer experiences invisible and silences the possibility of queer existence for students. That is, queer kids learn that their identity targets them for mistreatment. In contrast, heterosexuality is reinforced as what is normal.

When girls, especially girls of color, defend themselves from harassment, they can be penalized, making them more vulnerable to school discipline than kids who do not defend themselves. Some people might assume that because of stereotypes of them as fragile and emotional, girls and women are treated more delicately by those in power. Kimberlé Crenshaw's research finds this is not the case for girls and women of color. Furthermore, a recent exposé[101] of treatment of women prisoners finds that women, regardless of their race and ethnicity, are treated more harshly for minor infractions by prison staff than prisoners who are men. For example, women in prison are more likely to be disciplined than men in prison—for all kinds of infractions, but notably minor ones. For example, consider this: Women are much more likely to be disciplined for "disrespect," for "derogatory comments" about corrections officers or other inmates, "disobedience," and for being "disruptive." They are also described in ways such as, "They won't take no for an answer." In other words, women are punished for sass. And while they are more likely than men to be punished for these minor infractions, their punishment is hardly minor. One woman inmate was put in solitary confinement for "reckless eye-balling" (rolling her eyes). They lose good conduct credit, which can then add years to their sentences. They can lose access to pads and tampons, visitation, and phone privileges.[102] One prison warden acknowledged that women are disciplined based on emotion rather than on safety and security. The corrections officers, who are mostly men, do not like being mouthed off to by women.[103] And finally, while the prison population for men is decreasing somewhat, it is increasing for women—750% since 1980. So while boys of color are overdisciplined and criminalized relative to White boys, girls and women are punished for not being lady-like, even while they are incarcerated. Girls and women of color seem to get the worst of it as they are criminalized as people of color and are perceived to violate gendered expectations about how girls are supposed to behave. This disparate treatment of marginalized groups leads them to feel unprotected and overinspected. They learn they are not entitled to fair treatment, nor to the freedom of existence and movement that the entitled have.

Conclusion

Parents and caregivers are significant socializers of children, especially be-fore children begin in school to be influenced by teachers, peers, and popular culture. Parents' ideologies and parenting practices influence how their chil-dren will view the world and their own sense of deservingness. Even parents' ways of processing information, such as their flexibility and tolerance of nu-ance, measured by their need for closure, are correlated with their children's flexibility. In subtle ways, parents of White children teach them that they are the normative racial category, that race is irrelevant to their lives, and discus-sion of anything racial is unseemly and taboo. White children are thereby ill-equipped to understand the reality of racism, especially its structural and institutional nature. White children learn that, to the extent that they are ever treated badly, it will not be due to their race.

Parents' attitudes tend to mirror popular culture's enchantment with boys and men. Boys and men learn they are the normative gender that is com-petent and "gets stuff done." Boys also learn that anything associated with girls and women would be degrading for them to adopt, so feminine things should be avoided. Girls learn different lessons. They learn they should be passive and accommodating. Their toys and learning styles tend to be more flexible than that of boys. Flexible learning styles make it easier for women to modify their communication depending on the audience and adapt to chan-ging circumstances. Boys learn they do not have to adapt and they do not require flexibility in interaction styles. Thus men will not feel the same pres-sure to modify and show flexibility with interaction partners or change their positions and surroundings, which ultimately increases the expectation that the world will conform to them.

Both parents and teachers view boys as more competent than they are, and, correspondingly, boys themselves tend to think they are better performers than they actually are. For girls, there is less likely to be a disconnect between confidence and performance. Teachers pay more attention to boys than to girls, offering boys more intellectual feedback under the assumption that boys are inherently able. Girls? Well, they are seen as "hard workers."

If you consider this flexibility of girls with their relative lack of entitlement versus boys' rigidity and sense of entitlement, you can see potential for boys' and then men's entitled resentment. Men come to feel entitled to recogni-tion, to jobs, and to success in a way women may not. And when environ-ments change, men are less equipped to deal with changes. They feel entitled to have their surroundings adapt to them rather than vice versa. Feelings of entitlement can lead to entitled resentment when the economy changes or the demography of the country changes or even when changes occur in their household. Some men are left confused and angry. They feel entitled to have things go their way because they haven't had to change and adapt.

For girls and boys of color, not only are they not attended to by teachers the way White boys are, their experience in schools includes criminalization by teachers and administrators who seem to think that bad behavior in school is a precursor to felonious behavior. The disciplinary problems of children of color are viewed through a lens of criminalization and pathology as their bad behavior is more likely to be routed through the criminal legal system than the same bad behavior of White children. Girls of color are at even greater risk of criminalization. The disparate disciplinary treatment of girls of color compared to White girls, is greater than the disparate treatment between boys of color and White boys. And yet, when the racial disparity in discipline is acknowledged and addressed, the attention tends to be on boys of color (e.g., former President Obama's My Brother's Keeper Alliance).[104] Nathaniel Bryan writes about teachers' role in perpetuating the school-to-prison pipeline.[105] He argues that White teachers influence White children's perception of African American boys, as they disproportionately target and discipline Black boys for minor and subjective infractions. Bryan argues that White children inherit the intergenerational lineage and socialization about African American boys—that they are inherently and uniquely criminally inclined.[106] Deficit messages about girls and boys of color are passed down from one generation to the next, from White teachers to White children. Bryan's message then is not simply about how teachers treat marginalized kids, but how kids in the dominant group also absorb the message of their superiority. If White children observe over years of schooling the disproportionate disciplining of children of color, they too will come to associate color with criminality. Moreover, those White children will come to believe they are entitled to fair or preferential treatment by adults and by the criminal legal system and that different rules apply to children of color.

Notes

1. Connolly, N., Freeman, J., & Balogh, B. (Hosts). (2019, May 10). The year of the woman. A history of women in Congress (No. 278) [Audio podcast episode].

Backstory. Virginia Humanities. https://www.backstoryradio.org/shows/the-year-of-the-woman/.

2. Pascus, B. (2019, June 3). Every charge and accusation facing the 33 parents in the college admissions scandal. *CBSNEWS*. https://www.cbsnews.com/news/college-admissions-scandal-list-operation-varsity-blues-every-charge-plea-accusation-facing-parents-2019-05-16/.

3. Medina, J., Benner, K., & Taylor, K. (2019, March 12). Actresses, business leaders and other wealthy parents charged in U.S. college entry fraud. *The New York Times*. https://www.nytimes.com/2019/03/12/us/college-admissions-cheating-scandal.html.

4. Mena, K., Diamond, J., & Bohn, K. (2020, August 23). Trump's sister bitterly criticizes him in conversations secretly recorded by her nice Mary Trump. *CNN*. https://www.cnn.com/2020/08/22/politics/maryanne-trump-barry-donald-trump-mary-trump/index.html.

5. Degner, J., & Dalege, J. (2013). The apple does not fall far from the tree, or does it? A meta-analysis of parent–child similarity in intergroup attitudes. *Psychological Bulletin*, *139*(6), 1270–1304. https://doi.org/10.1037/a0031436.

6. Castelli, L., De Dea, C., & Nesdale, D. (2008). Learning social attitudes: Children's sensitivity to the nonverbal behaviors of adult models during interracial interactions. *Personality & Social Psychology Bulletin*, *34*(11), 1504–1513. https://doi.org/10.1177/0146167208322769.

7. Degner, J., & Dalege, J. (2013). The apple does not fall far from the tree, or does it? A meta-analysis of parent–child similarity in intergroup attitudes. *Psychological Bulletin*, *139*(6), 1270–1304. https://doi.org/10.1037/a0031436.

   Meeusen, C., & Dhont, K. (2015). Parent-child similarity in common and specific components of prejudice: The role of ideological attitudes and political discussion. *European Journal of Personality*, *29*(6), 585–598. https://doi.org/10.1002/per.2011.

8. Dhont, K., Roets, A., & Hiel, A. V. (2013). The intergenerational transmission of need for closure underlies the transmission of authoritarianism and anti-immigrant prejudice. *Personality and Individual Differences*, *54*(6), 779–784. https://doi.org/10.1016/j.paid.2012.12.016.

9. Miller, M. E. (2016, June 6). "A steep price to pay for 20 minutes of action": Dad defends Stanford sex offender. *The Washington Post*. https://www.washingtonpost.com/news/morning-mix/wp/2016/06/06/a-steep-price-to-pay-for-20-minutes-of-action-dad-defends-stanford-sex-offender/.

10. For a comprehensive review of parents' role in children's attitudes, see: Degner, J., & Dalege, J. (2013). The apple does not fall far from the tree, or does it? A meta-analysis of parent–child similarity in intergroup attitudes. *Psychological Bulletin*, *139*(6), 1270–1304. https://doi.org/10.1037/a0031436.

11. Duckitt, J. (2001). A dual-process cognitive-motivational theory of ideology and prejudice. In M. P. Zanna (Ed.), *Advances in experimental social psychology*, Vol. 33 (pp. 41–113). Academic Press.

12. Cross, J. R., & Fletcher, K. L. (2011). Associations of parental and peer characteristics with adolescents' social dominance orientation. *Journal of Youth and Adolescence*, *40*(6), 694–706. https://doi.org/10.1007/s10964-010-9585-7.

13. Guimond, S., Dambrun, M., Michinov, N., & Duarte, S. (2003). Does social dominance generate prejudice? Integrating individual and contextual determinants of intergroup cognitions. *Journal of Personality and Social Psychology, 84*(4), 697–721. https://doi.org/10.1037/0022-3514.84.4.697.

14. Duckitt, J. (2001). A dual-process cognitive-motivational theory of ideology and prejudice. In M. P. Zanna (Ed.), *Advances in experimental social psychology*, Vol. 33 (pp. 41–113). Academic Press.

15. Duckitt, J. (2001). A dual-process cognitive-motivational theory of ideology and prejudice. In M. P. Zanna (Ed.), *Advances in experimental social psychology*, Vol. 33 (pp. 41–113). Academic Press.

16. Givertz, M., & Segrin, C. (2014). The association between overinvolved parenting and young adults' self-efficacy, psychological entitlement, and family communication. *Communication Research, 41*(8), 1111–1136. https://doi.org/10.1177/0093650212456392.

17. Fletcher, K. L., Pierson, E. E., Spears Neumeister, K. L., & Finch, W. H. (2020). Overparenting and perfectionistic concerns predict academic entitlement in in young adults. *Journal of Child and Family Studies, 29*, 348–357. https://doi.org/10.1007/s10826-019-01663-7.

18. Capron, E. W. (2004). Types of pampering and the narcissistic personality trait. *Journal of Individual Psychology, 60*(1), 76–93.

19. Richardson, E. W., Simons, L. G., & Futris, T. G. (2017). Linking family-of-origin experiences and perpetration of sexual coercion: College males' sense of entitlement. *Journal of Child and Family Studies, 26*, 781–791. https://doi.org/10.1007/s10826-016-0592-5.

20. Grinberg, E., & Shoichet, C. E. (2016, September 3). Brock Turner released after 3 months in jail. *CNN*. https://www.cnn.com/2016/09/02/us/brock-turner-release-jail/index.html.

21. Oliver, M. B. (2003). African American men as "criminal and dangerous": Implications of media portrayals of crime on the "criminalization" of African American men. *Journal of African American Studies, 7*(2), 3–18. https://doi.org/10.1007/s12111-003-1006-5.

22. Xu, V. (2016, June 8). The full letter read by Brock Turner's father at his sentencing hearing. *Stanford Daily*. https://www.stanforddaily.com/2016/06/08/the-full-letter-read-by-brock-turners-father-at-his-sentencing-hearing/.

23. Koren, M. (2016, June 6). Telling the story of the Stanford rape case. *The Atlantic*. https://www.theatlantic.com/news/archive/2016/06/stanford-sexual-assault-letters/485837/.

24. Tatum, B. D. (2017). *Why are all the black kids sitting together in the cafeteria?* Basic Books.

25. Howard, L. C., Rose, J. C., & Barbarin, O. A. (2013). Raising African American boys: An exploration of gender and racial socialization practices. *American Journal of Orthopsychiatry, 83*(2), 218–230. https://10.1111/ajop.12031.

26. Harriot, M. (2017, October 5). The privilege of White individuality. *The Root*. https://www.theroot.com/the-privilege-of-white-individuality-1819184476.

27. DiAngleo, R. (2018). *White fragility: Why it's so hard for white people to talk about racism*. Beacon Press.

28. Vittrup, B., & Holden, G. W. (2011). Exploring the impact of educational television and parent–child discussions on children's racial attitudes. *Analyses of Social Issues and Public Policy, 11*(1), 82–104. https://doi.org/10.1111/j.1530-2415.2010.01223.x.

29. Anderson, K. J. (2010). *Benign bigotry: The psychology of subtle prejudice*. Cambridge University Press.

30. Norton, M. I., Sommers, S. R., Apfelbaum, E. P., Pura, N., & Ariely, D. (2006). Color blindness and interracial interaction: Playing the political correctness game. *Psychological Science, 17*(11), 949–953. https://doi.org/10.1111/j.1467-9280.2006.01810.x.

31. Norton, M. I., Sommers, S. R., Apfelbaum, E. P., Pura, N., & Ariely, D. (2006). Color blindness and interracial interaction: Playing the political correctness game. *Psychological Science, 17*(11), 949–953. https://doi.org/10.1111/j.1467-9280.2006.01810.x.

32. Pahlke, E., Bigler, R. S., & Suizzo, M-A. (2012). Relations between colorblind socialization and children's racial bias: Evidence from European American mothers and their preschool children. *Child Development, 83*(4), 1164–1179. https://doi.org/10.1111/j.1467-8624.2012.01770.x.

33. Wise, T. (2018, March 9). Color-blindness as intellectual child abuse: Raising anti-racist kids in an unequal society. *Medium*. https://medium.com/@timjwise/color-blindness-as-intellectual-child-abuse-raising-anti-racist-kids-in-an-unequal-society-cc5e3278a40.

34. Intons-Peterson, M. J., & Reddel, M. (1984). What do people ask about a neonate? *Developmental Psychology, 20*(3), 358–359. https://doi.org/10.1037/0012-1649.20.3.358.

35. Human Rights Campaign. (n.d.). Violence against the transgender community in 2018. https://www.hrc.org/resources/violence-against-the-transgender-community-in-2018.

36. Newport, F. (2018, July 5). Slight preference for having boy children persists in the U.S. *Gallup*. https://news.gallup.com/poll/236513/slight-preference-having-boy-children-persists.aspx.

37. Newport, F. (2011, June 23). Americans prefer boys to girls, just as they did in 1941. *Gallup*. https://news.gallup.com/poll/148187/americans-prefer-boys-girls-1941.aspx.

38. Howard, L. C., Rose, J. C., & Barbarin, O. A. (2013). Raising African American boys: An exploration of gender and racial socialization practices. *American Journal of Orthopsychiatry, 83*(2–3), 218–230. https://doi.org/10.1111/ajop.12031.

39. Rubin, J. Z., Provenzano, F. J., & Luria, Z. (1974). The eye of the beholder: Parents' view on sex of newborns. *American Journal of Orthopsychiatry, 44*(4), 512–519. https://doi.org/10.1111/j.1939-0025.1974.tb00905.x.

40. For a replication of Rubin's classic study, see: Karraker, K. H., Vogel, D. A., & Lake, M. A. (1995). Parents' gender-stereotyped perceptions of newborns: The eye of the beholder revisited. *Sex Roles, 33*, 687–700.

41. Amazon.com.   https://www.amazon.com/Piece-FLIRT-Onesie-Beautiful-Organza/ dp/B00YF2O8H0.

42. https://www.amazon.com/Stud-Muffin-Current-One-Piece-Bodysuit/dp/ B07RJZG8C9/ref=sr_1_1?dchild=1&keywords=stud+onesie&qid=1587846956&s= apparel&sr=1-1.

43. Will, J. A., Self, P. A., & Datan, N. (1976). Maternal behavior and perceived sex of infant. *American Journal of Orthopsychiatry, 46*(1), 135–139. https://doi.org/10.1111/ j.1939-0025.1976.tb01234.x.

44. Cooley, E., Winslow, H., Vojt, A., Shein, J., & Ho, J. (2018). Bias at the intersection of identity: Conflicting social stereotypes of gender and race augment the perceived femininity and interpersonal warmth of smiling Black women. *Journal of Experimental Social Psychology, 74*, 43–49. https://doi.org/10.1016/j.jesp.2017.08.007.

   Wondergem, T. R., & Friedlmeier, M. (2012). Gender and ethnic differences in smiling: A yearbook photographs analysis from kindergarten through 12th grade. *Sex Roles, 67*(7–8), 403–411. https://doi.org/10.1007/s11199-012-0158-y.

45. See, for instance: McFarlane, J., Martin, C. L., & Williams, T. M. (1988). Mood fluctuations: Women versus men and menstrual versus other cycles. *Psychology of Women Quarterly, 12*(2), 201–223. https://doi.org/10.1111/j.1471-6402.1988. tb00937.x.

   Jarva, J. A., & Oinonen, K. A. (2007). Do oral contraceptives act as mood stabilizers? Evidence of positive affect stabilization. *Archives of Women's Mental Health, 10*, 225–234. https://doi.org/10.1007/s00737-007-0197-5.

46. van der Pol, L. D., Groeneveld, M. G., van Berkel, S. R., Endendijk, J. J., Hallers-Haalboom, E. T., Bakermans-Kranenburg, M. J., & Mesman, J. (2015). Fathers' and mothers' emotion talk with their girls and boys from toddlerhood to preschool age. *Emotion, 15*(6), 854–864. https://doi.org/10.1037/emo0000085.

47. Brown, G. L., Craig, A. B., & Halberstadt, A. G. (2015). Parent gender differences in emotion socialization behaviors vary by ethnicity and child gender. *Parenting: Science and Practice, 15*(3), 135–157. https://doi.org/10.1080/15295192.2015.1053312.

48. van der Pol, L. D., Groeneveld, M. G., van Berkel, S. R., Endendijk, J. J., Hallers-Haalboom, E. T., Bakermans-Kranenburg, M. J., & Mesman, J. (2015). Fathers' and mothers' emotion talk with their girls and boys from toddlerhood to preschool age. *Emotion, 15*(6), 854–864. https://doi.org/10.1037/emo0000085.

49. Endendijk, J. J., Groeneveld, M. G., van der Pol, L. D., van Berkel, S. R., Hallers-Haalboom, E. T., Mesman, J., & Bakermans-Kranenburg, M. J. (2014). Boys don't play with dolls: mothers' and fathers' gender talk during picture book reading. *Parenting: Science & Practice, 14*(3/4), 141–161. https://doi.org/10.1080/ 15295192.2014.972753.

50. Leaper, C., Carson, M., & Baker, C. (1995). Self-disclosure and listener verbal support in same-gender and cross-gender friends' conversations. *Sex Roles, 33*, 387–404. https://doi.org/10.1007/BF01954575.

   Anderson, K. J., & Leaper, C. (1998). Emotion talk between same- and mixed-gender friends: Form and function. *Journal of Language and Social Psychology, 17*(4), 419–448. https://doi.org/10.1177/0261927X980174001.

51. Leaper, C., & Farkas, T. (2015). The socialization of gender during childhood and adolescence. In J. E. Grusec & P. D. Hastings (Eds.), *Handbook of socialization* (2nd Ed.) (pp. 541–565). Guilford.

52. Valian, V. (1998). *Why so slow? The advancement of women.* MIT Press.

53. Research on low income Latinx families: Dodson, L., & Dickert, J. (2004). Girls' family labor in low-income households: A decade of qualitative research. *Journal of Marriage and Family, 66*(2), 318–332. https://doi.org/10.1111/j.1741-3737.2004.00023.x.

    Research on Australian families: Ferrar, K. E., Olds, T. S., & Walters, J. L. (2012). All the stereotypes confirmed: Differences in how Australian boys and girls use their time. *Health Education & Behavior, 39*(5), 589–595. https://doi.org/10.1177/1090198111423942.

54. Valian, V. (1998). *Why so slow? The advancement of women.* MIT Press.

55. BusyKid. (2018, June 29). Gender pay gap starts with kids in America. https://busykid.com/2018/06/gender-pay-gap-starts-with-kids-in-america/.

56. BusyKid. (2018, June 29). Gender pay gap starts with kids in America. https://busykid.com/2018/06/gender-pay-gap-starts-with-kids-in-america/.

57. Anderson, G., & Robson, K. (2006). Male adolescents' contributions to household labor as predictors of later-life participation in housework. *The Journal of Men's Studies, 14*(1), 1–12. https://doi.org/10.3149/jms.1401.1.

58. Pew Research Center. (2015, November 4). Raising kids and running a household: How working parents share the load. https://www.pewsocialtrends.org/2015/11/04/raising-kids-and-running-a-household-how-working-parents-share-the-load/.

59. Fetterolf, J., & Rudman, L. (2014). Gender inequality in the home: The role of relative income, support for traditional gender roles, and perceived entitlement. *Gender Issues, 31*(3/4), 219–237. https://doi.org/10.1007/s12147-014-9126-x.

60. Young, M., Wallace, J. E., Polachek, A. J. (2015). Gender differences in perceived domestic task equity: A study of professionals. *Journal of Family Issues, 36*(13), 1751–1781. https://doi.org/10.1177/0192513X13508403.

61. Young, M., Wallace, J. E., Polachek, A. J. (2015). Gender differences in perceived domestic task equity: A study of professionals. *Journal of Family Issues, 36*(13), 1751–1781. https://doi.org/10.1177/0192513X13508403.

62. Valian, V. (1999). *Why so slow? The advancement of women.* MIT Press.

63. Steinmayr, R., & Spinath, B. (2009). What explains boys' stronger confidence in their intelligence? *Sex Roles, 61*, 736–749. https://doi.org/10.1007/s11199-009-9675-8.

64. Tiedemann, J. (2000). Parents' gender stereotypes and teachers' beliefs as predictors of children's concept of their mathematical ability in elementary school. *Journal of Educational Psychology, 92*(1), 144–151. https://doi.org/10.1037/0022-0663.92.1.144.

65. Cole, D. A., Cho, S., Martin, J. M., Seroczynski, A. D., Tram, J., & Hoffman, K. (2001). Effects of validity and bias on gender differences in the appraisal of children's competence: Results of MTMM analyses in a longitudinal investigation. *Structural Equation Modeling, 8*(1), 84–107. https://doi.org/10.1207/S15328007SEM0801_5.

66. Zlotnik, S., & Toglia, J. (2018). Measuring adolescent self-awareness and accuracy using a performance-based assessment and parental report. *Frontiers in Public Health*, 6. https://doi.org/10.3389/fpubh.2018.00015.

67. Cole, D. A., Cho, S., Martin, J. M., Seroczynski, A. D., Tram, J., & Hoffman, K. (2001). Effects of validity and bias on gender differences in the appraisal of children's competence: Results of MTMM analyses in a longitudinal investigation. *Structural Equation Modeling*, 8(1), 84–107. https://doi.org/10.1207/S15328007SEM0801_5.

68. Cooper, K. M., Krieg, A., & Brownell, S. E. (2018). Who perceives they are smarter? Exploring the influence of student characteristics on student academic self-concept in physiology. *Advances in Physiology Education*, 42(2), 200–208. https://doi.org/10.1152/advan.00085.2017.

69. Nietfeld, J. L., Shores, L. R., & Hoffmann, K. F. (2014). Self-regulation and gender within a game-based learning environment. *Journal of Educational Psychology*, 106(4), 961–973. https://doi.org/10.1037/a0037116.

70. Wilkerson, I. (2018, December 6). Isabel Wilkerson on Michelle Obama's "Becoming" and the Great Migration. *The New York Times*. https://www.nytimes.com/2018/12/06/books/review/michelle-obama-becoming-memoir.html.

71. Swinson, J., & Harrop, L. (2009). Teacher talk directed to boys and girls and its relationship to their behaviour. *Educational Studies*, 35(5), 515–524. https://doi.org/10.1080/03055690902883913.

Duffy, J., Warren, K., & Walsh, M. (2001). Classroom interactions: Gender of target, gender of student, and classroom subject. *Sex Roles*, 45(9-10), 579–593. https://doi.org/10.1023/A:1014892408105.

Jones, S. M., & Dindia, K. (2004). A meta-analytic perspective on sex equity in the classroom. *Review of Educational Research*, 74(4), 443–471. https://doi.org/10.3102/00346543074004443.

72. Jones, M. G., & Wheatley, J. (1990). Gender differences in teacher-student interactions in science classrooms. *Journal of Research in Science Teaching*, 27(9), 861–874. https://doi.org/10.1002/tea.3660270906.

73. Baker, C. N., Tichovolsky, M. H., Kupersmidt, J. B., Voegler-Lee, M. E., & Arnold, D. H. (2015). Teacher (mis)perceptions of preschoolers' academic skills: Predictors and associations with longitudinal outcomes. *Journal of Educational Psychology*, 107(3), 805–820. https://doi.org/10.1037/edu0000008.

74. Hinnant, J. B., O'Brien, M., & Ghazarian, S. R. (2009). The longitudinal relations of teacher expectations to achievement in the early school years. *Journal of Educational Psychology*, 101(3), 662–670. https://doi.org/10.1037/a0014306.

75. Hinnant, J. B., O'Brien, M., & Ghazarian, S. R. (2009). The longitudinal relations of teacher expectations to achievement in the early school years. *Journal of Educational Psychology*, 101(3), 662–670. https://doi.org/10.1037/a0014306.

76. Hinnant, J. B., O'Brien, M., & Ghazarian, S. R. (2009). The longitudinal relations of teacher expectations to achievement in the early school years. *Journal of Educational Psychology*, 101(3), 662–670. https://doi.org/10.1037/a0014306.

77. Jones, S., & Myhill, D. (2004). Seeing things differently: Teachers' constructions of underachievement. *Gender & Education, 16*(4), 531–546. https://doi.org/10.1080/09540250042000300411.

78. Robinson-Cimpian, J. P., Lubienski, S. T., Ganley, C. M., & Copur-Gencturk, Y. (2014). Teachers' perceptions of students' mathematics proficiency may exacerbate early gender gaps in achievement. *Developmental Psychology, 50*(4), 1262–1281. https://doi.org/10.1037/a0035073.supp.

79. Moss-Racusin, C. A., Dovidio, J. F., Brescoll, V. L., Graham, M. J., & Handelsman, J. (2012). Science faculty's subtle gender biases favor male students. *Proceedings of the National Academy of Sciences of the United States of America, 109*(41), 16474–16479. https://doi.org/10.1073/pnas.1211286109.

80. Moss-Racusin, C. A., Dovidio, J. F., Brescoll, V. L., Graham, M. J., & Handelsman, J. (2012). Science faculty's subtle gender biases favor male students. *Proceedings of the National Academy of Sciences of the United States of America, 109*(41), 16474–16479. https://doi.org/10.1073/pnas.1211286109.

81. Heilman, M. E., Wallen, A. S., Fuchs, D., & Tamkins, M. M. (2004). Penalties for success: Reactions to women who succeed at male gender-typed tasks. *Journal of Applied Psychology, 89*(3), 416–427. https://doi.org/10.1037/0021-9010.89.3.416.

82. Cartwright, N. (Writer) & Moeller, J. (Director). (2019, March 31). Girl's in the band (Season 30, Episode 19) [TV series episode]. In J. L. Brooks, J. Frink, M. Groening, A. Jean, M. Selman, & S. Simon (Executive Producers), *The Simpsons.* Gracie Films; Twentieth Century Fox Film Corporation.

83. For an extensive review of the boy crisis backlash to feminism, see: Anderson, K. J. (2015). *Modern misogyny: Anti-feminism in a post-feminist era.* Oxford University Press.

84. Jones, S., & Myhill, D. (2004). Seeing things differently: Teachers' constructions of underachievement. *Gender & Education, 16*(4), 531–546. https://doi.org/10.1080/09540250042000300411.

85. Leaper, C., Farkas, T., & Starr, C. R. (2018). Traditional masculinity, help avoidance, and intrinsic interest in relation to high school students' English and math performance. *Psychology of Men & Masculinity, 20*(4), 603–611. https://doi.org/10.1037/men0000188.

86. Vantieghem, W., & Van Houtte, V. (2015). Are girls more resilient to gender-conformity pressure? The association between gender-conformity pressure and academic self-efficacy. *Sex Roles, 73*(1–2), 1–15. https://doi.org/10.1007/s11199-015-0509-6.

87. Vantieghem, W., & Van Houtte, V. (2015). Are girls more resilient to gender-conformity pressure? The association between gender-conformity pressure and academic self-efficacy. *Sex Roles, 73*(1–2), 1–15. https://doi.org/10.1007/s11199-015-0509-6.

88. See Chapter 4 in: Anderson, K. J. (2015). *Modern misogyny: Anti-feminism in a post-feminist era.* Oxford University Press.

89. Tenenbaum, H. R., & Ruck, M. D. (2007). Are teachers' expectations different for racial minority than for European American students? A meta-analysis.

Journal of Educational Psychology, 99(2), 253–273. https://doi.org/10.1037/0022-0663.99.2.253.

90. Donvan, J. (Host). (2012, March 12). Black students more likely to be disciplined. [Audio podcast episode]. In *Talk of the Nation*. NPR.

91. Jarvis, S., & Okonofua, J. A. (2019). School deferred: When bias affects school leaders. *Social Psychological and Personality Science, 11*(4), 492–498. https://doi.org/10.1177/1948550619875150.

92. Khan, M. (2016, June 7). Black students nearly 4 times as likely to be suspended. *ABCNews*. https://abcnews.go.com/US/black-students-times-suspended/story?id=39670502.

93. For a review of this research, see Chapter 1 of: Anderson, K. J. (2010). *Benign bigotry: The psychology of subtle prejudice*. Cambridge University Press.

94. By both White and Black kids: Sagar, H. A., & Schofield, J. W. (1980). Racial and behavioral cues in black and white children's perceptions of ambiguously aggressive acts. *Journal of Personality & Social Psychology, 39*(4), 590–598. https://doi.org/10.1037/0022-3514.39.4.590.

95. For a review of racial bias in the criminal justice system, see Chapter 2 in: Anderson, K. J. (2010). *Benign bigotry: The psychology of subtle prejudice*. Cambridge University Press.

96. Crenshaw, K. W., Ocen, P., & Nanda, J. (2015). Black girls matter: Pushed out, overpoliced and underprotected. *AAPF*. http://www.aapf.org/recent/2014/12/coming-soon-blackgirlsmatter-pushed-out-overpoliced-and-underprotected.

97. Crenshaw, K. W., Ocen, P., & Nanda, J. (2015). Black girls matter: Pushed out, overpoliced and underprotected. *AAPF*. http://www.aapf.org/recent/2014/12/coming-soon-blackgirlsmatter-pushed-out-overpoliced-and-underprotected.

98. Crenshaw, K. W., Ocen, P., & Nanda, J. (2015). Black girls matter: Pushed out, overpoliced and underprotected. *AAPF*. http://www.aapf.org/recent/2014/12/coming-soon-blackgirlsmatter-pushed-out-overpoliced-and-underprotected.

99. Preston, M. J. (2016). "They're just not mature right now": Teachers' complicated perceptions of gender and anti-queer bullying. *Sex Education, 16*(1), 22–34. https://doi.org/10.1080/14681811.2015.1019665.

100. Preston, M. J. (2016). "They're just not mature right now": Teachers' complicated perceptions of gender and anti-queer bullying. *Sex Education, 16*(1), 22–34. https://doi.org/10.1080/14681811.2015.1019665.

101. Shapiro, J., Pupovac, J., & Lydersen, K. (2018, October 19). In prison, discipline comes down hardest on women. *WNIN*. http://news.wnin.org/post/prison-discipline-comes-down-hardest-women#stream/0.

102. Shapiro, J., Pupovac, J., & Lydersen, K. (2018, October 19). In prison, discipline comes down hardest on women. *WNIN*. http://news.wnin.org/post/prison-discipline-comes-down-hardest-women#stream/0.

103. Shapiro, J., Pupovac, J., & Lydersen, K. (2018, October 19). In prison, discipline comes down hardest on women. *WNIN*. http://news.wnin.org/post/prison-discipline-comes-down-hardest-women#stream/0.

104. My Brother's Keeper. (n.d.). https://obamawhitehouse.archives.gov/my-brothers-keeper https://obamawhitehouse.archives.gov/my-brothers-keeper.

105. Bryan, N. (2017). White teachers' role in sustaining the school-to-prison pipeline: Recommendations for teacher education. *Urban Review, 49*(2), 326–345. https://doi.org/10.1007/s11256-017-0403-3.

106. Bryan, N. (2017). White teachers' role in sustaining the school-to-prison pipeline: Recommendations for teacher education. *Urban Review, 49*(2), 326–345. https://doi.org/10.1007/s11256-017-0403-3.

4

Entitlement's Enablers

Peers and Popular Culture

Dr. Blasey Ford: Indelible in the hippocampus is the laughter, the laugh—the uproarious laughter between the two, and their having fun at my expense.
Senator Leahy: You've never forgotten that laughter. You've never forgotten them laughing at you.
Dr. Blasey Ford: They were laughing with each other.
Senator Leahy: And you were the object of the laughter?
Dr. Blasey Ford: I was, you know, underneath one of them while the two laughed, two friend—two friends having a really good time with one another.

—Christine Blasey Ford at the confirmation hearing of Bret
Kavanaugh for the US Supreme Court[1]

The last chapter looked at the role of influential adults—parents and teachers—and their role in facilitating children's sense of entitlement. This chapter is divided into two parts as it considers two areas of developmental influence: the peer group and mass media. The chapter begins with a look at the impact of social dominance goals (e.g., establishing power), the peer group, and the degree to which these goals affect peer interaction and disruptive classroom behavior. The extent to which boys feel pressure to adhere to traditional masculinity will affect their academic performance and their ability to accept constructive feedback for improvement. This chapter then looks at homophobic bullying, both targets of bullying and bullies themselves. We see who is entitled to dignity and what groups can be safely marginalized without the bully paying too high a price in the form of public scorn. The role of the bystander in male peer groups is a central component of this dynamic.

Next the analysis turns to how popular culture and mass media influence the valuing of dominant groups over subordinated groups. Mass media

Enraged, Rattled, and Wronged. Kristin J. Anderson, Oxford University Press. © Oxford University Press 2021.
DOI: 10.1093/oso/9780197578438.003.0005

plays a critical role in both reflecting the disparate value attached to various groups and perpetuating inequality. The different representations of gender, race, and sexuality in mass media bolster entitlement in socially preferred groups. Here we draw on empirical research using content analysis to examine gender, race, and sexuality representations in television, film, and news media. Also examined are audience studies that consider the impact of skewed representations of groups and how that fosters a sense of deservingness in dominant group members. The influence of media is considered with a review of experimental and correlational research on how media messages affect consumers.

Power of the Peer Group

He's a race-baiting, xenophobic, religious bigot.
   —US Senator Lindsey Graham December 8, 2015[2]

If you think he's a racist, that's up to you—I don't.
   —US Senator Lindsey Graham July 18, 2019[3]

One of the more enduring stereotypes about women is that they are easily influenced, whereas men are not.[4] This is a lie. Consider members of the US congress who harshly criticized Donald Trump when he was a candidate for president only to do Trump's bidding after he was elected—men like former Speaker of the House of Representatives Paul Ryan[5] and Senator Lindsey Graham—whose contradictory comments we see above. The idea that women are weak and conforming, and men are strong and independent, resonates with many people because it explains why women are managed and controlled so much. It justifies keeping women out of leadership positions such as politics, it justifies controlling their ability to use birth control and to obtain abortions, and it justifies keeping important decisions out of their hands. Girls can be vulnerable to peer influence. However, there is a special susceptibility for boys to the influence of the male peer group—a susceptibility that society ignores at its own peril.

As we saw in Chapter 2, social dominance is gendered—men have stronger dominance orientations than women.[6] Compared to girls, boys are more likely to find their peer status will be determined by competition and hierarchy. Social dominance facilitates hierarchical thinking and entitlement in boys and men who believe they are on top of the heap. The male peer group teaches boys that social dominance is a legitimate way of organizing the world and that high-status boys are entitled to good treatment, influence, and better lives. In one illustrative study, Jennifer R. Cross and Kathryn L. Fletcher followed the teen cliques at a particular school (e.g., band kids, jocks, and rural kids).[7] Girls from different groups did not differ in their social dominance orientation. In other words, having a social dominance orientation did not explain why some girls were in some groups and not others. However, boys' group membership was more often organized in terms of social dominance—meaning it mattered which kids were on top or on the bottom in those particular groups. For example, the preppy jock cluster had higher social dominance scores than the smart band kids; the rural kids had higher social dominance scores than smart band kids and the all-Around kids. Cross and Fletcher saw that the pressure to conform led boys to be assertive, competitive, and physically aggressive, and this was reflected in their higher levels of social dominance. Their study demonstrates the importance of social dominance orientations in organizing boys' peer groups. At the same time, it is worth noting that, while social dominance is more pertinent to boys' than girls' social lives, the study demonstrated that there was variation in social dominance levels across boys' cliques. That is, not all boys have the same level of social dominance attitudes and behavior. Yes, dominance is generally salient in boys' peer groups, but it is more salient in some peer groups than others. However, boys are not and do not have to be destined for dominance in their orientations toward social relationships.

Social dominance is not only relevant to group interactions. When social dominance is strong, negative consequences follow, particularly in the area of school performance. For those students invested in establishing hierarchies, toughness, getting others to do what they want, and getting people to be afraid of them, academic effort and following rules are subordinate to social dominance goals.[8] When students are focused on establishing power over their peers, they are more likely to act in ways that disrupt classes and they are less likely to put effort into their schoolwork. One study of sixth and seventh graders found that students with social dominance goals performed worse academically.[9] In contrast, intimacy goals (e.g., understanding others' feelings) are associated with effort and good grades—across genders and ethnicities.[10] Because many boys are more invested in social dominance, the negative associations between social dominance goals and academic performance is going to impact boys more than girls. Thus, concern about appearing tough undermines academic engagement.[11] As an example, adherence to both physical toughness and emotional stoicism is a negative predictor of math standardized test scores. Boys who think they should not be emotionally expressive are also likely to endorse physical toughness. This in turn, is associated with lower academic scores in middle school and lower self-esteem compared to boys who do not prioritize toughness.[12]

There seems to be so much macho performance in school, or *pressure* to perform, that even single-gender classrooms can negatively affect boys' performance. For example, single-gender classrooms in seventh grade have been found to be a negative predictor of boys' standardized test scores in reading and math in eighth grade. It may be that boys' peer groups already put some boys at a disadvantage for academic performance and that putting them in a social context where all of their peers are of the same gender might contribute to these deficits.[13] Boys' adherence to traditional gender roles prevents them from improving academically. One study (described in Chapter 3) found that to the extent that boys endorse traditional masculinity, they are not only less interested in English—a feminine-stereotyped subject—but also avoid getting help in the subject and earn lower grades. This was not the case for math—a masculine-stereotyped subject.[14] Boys who put a primacy on dominance are less likely to seek the academic help needed for long-term improvement; instead, they feel entitled to seeking quick help so they can stop working on the task.[15] For these boys, asserting control and delegating tasks may be used to establish status. Boys are more likely to do this than girls, and striving for dominance may serve as a risk factor for maladaptive help-seeking from peers. Like the findings in the last chapter, these patterns that emerge from research studies suggest that some boys feel entitled to substitute dominance and status in exchange for effort.

Gender Policing: The Tradeoff for Entitlement

We saw above that when boys experience increased pressure from peers to uphold masculine norms, their school performance suffers.[16] Study culture entails being calm, cooperative, compliant, and even tidy, which is deemed feminine and therefore undesirable. Boys are also more influenced by deviant classroom behavior than girls are.[17] *Disruptive behavior* here refers to things like skipping class, taking something from someone, and hitting someone. Boys with an initially low level of deviant behavior are more influenced by their deviant classmates than are teens who already show disruptive behavior. Once disruptive group behavior reaches a certain point, a contagion effect sets in whereby other kids in a class begin to act disruptively. Alternatively, when a class contains only a few deviant peers, you do not see the contagion effect.[18] Because deviant behavior is more normatively acceptable for boys compared to girls, peer influences on deviant behavior is stronger for boys than for girls.

Just as with deviant behavior, homophobic acts are contagious as well. The power of the peer group influences boys beyond social dominance goals and includes gender policing primarily through misogynistic and homophobic bullying. Boys' own reports[19] and their actual behavior[20] indicate they feel more pressure to conform to peers than do girls. At stake for boys is the relentless and all-encompassing threat of the feminine. For many boys, multiple decisions in a day are motivated by avoiding in any way appearing feminine or girl-like. Because the homophobia directed toward boys and men is rooted in misogyny and antifemininity, homophobic bullying is the chief tactic in boys' gender policing of one another. Longitudinal research of teens finds that being called homophobic names is associated with later calling *others* homophobic names.[21] Some boys and men conclude that a way to stave off accusations of femininity or homosexuality is to redirect those allegations toward others. Boys in particular use homophobic name-calling to assert their dominance over others and to gain status.[22] The greater the masculine attitudes of the peer group, the greater the homophobic name-calling. Overall, boys and young men who bully, who have been called homophobic names themselves, and who have friends with traditionally masculine attitudes, will be the most likely to call others homophobic slurs.[23]

How does gender policing relate to entitlement? Homophobic bullying keeps boys and men in line and away from veering into what they consider forbidden and despicable femininity. What keeps men entitled is their power *as* men, resulting from one's status as a member of a preferred group. The price for entitlement is the all-out avoidance of femininity and all-in conformity to male norms. Boys and men may come to see conforming to rigid gender rules as a relatively small price to pay for privilege and entitlement associated with their gender. Men, White people, heterosexuals, and those who are wealthy only get away with acting entitled because enough of us acquiesce to their implicit sense of superiority. Men have a vested interest in keeping men from veering into the feminine and staying within rigid and narrow rules of masculinity. For if a man can veer away from the masculine and into the feminine, then any man or all men could. If so, men's high status no longer appears natural, inevitable, and automatic. If men's high status can be questioned, masculinity loses its magic.

Richard Mohr argues that homophobic stereotypes function to reinforce traditional gender roles in order to maintain men's high status in society. Mohr contends, if "one is free to choose one's social roles independently of gender, many guiding social divisions both domestic and commercial might be threatened. The socially gender-linked distinctions would blur between breadwinner and homemaker, protector and protected, boss and secretary . . ." Accusations such as "fag" and "dyke" are used to "keep women in their place and to prevent men from breaking ranks and ceding away theirs."[24] Gay-baiting and bullying can target boys and men whether or not they are actually gay. Boys and men learn early in their social lives that, in order to be respected as men, they must steer clear of femininity and gayness, and they also learn early that an effective way to patrol the boundaries of gender are to use misogynistic and homophobic slurs with their male peers.

Precarious Manhood and the Entitlement Tradeoff

Thus far in this chapter we see that boys police other boys' gender-related behavior. Joseph Vandello and Jennifer Bosson offer the term *precarious manhood* to describe how the nature and makeup of manhood is so tenuous and hard to achieve that boys and men go out of their ways to perform it—for the most part for other boys and men—sometimes to their own and others' detriment.[25] The notion of precarious manhood helps explain why men have hyperbolic emotional reactions if someone wounds their pride, and this fact has some serious cultural consequences beyond individual men's feelings getting hurt. We can expect some boys and men to become unhinged if they are called gay or girly.[26] Women generally do not have a similarly emotional (and physically violent) response if they are linked to lesbianism or masculinity. One major difference between conceptions of womanhood and manhood in the United States is that manhood is a status that is precarious. Womanhood is not. The most trivial experiences can threaten masculinity. Not so for femininity.

There are three aspects of manhood that reflect its precariousness.[27] First, manhood is an elusive, achieved status, one that has to be earned. In other words, one doesn't just become a man at a certain age—say when he turns

18. In contrast, womanhood is a status based on biology—the onset of menstruation or turning age 18. This is not to say that manhood is social and womanhood is biological. Both manhood and womanhood are socially constructed, just in different ways. A girl tends to be seen as a woman when she becomes an adult, and there really aren't circumstances that could revert her back to being a girl. In contrast, a man's masculinity and manhood can be routinely questioned regarding whether he is sufficiently masculine. Second, once manhood is achieved, its status is tenuous and impermanent—it can be lost or taken away if a man does not behave appropriately manly. Manhood includes an *antifemininity mandate*—if you act like a woman (or a gay man) you will lose your manhood. Third, manhood has to be demonstrated over and over and it requires public evidence. The behaviors that are most effective in demonstrating manhood are those that can be confirmed by others and are difficult to fake (e.g., feats of strength, treating women in certain ways). After all, if *any* behaviors could suffice, then manhood would lose its value, and it would become difficult to distinguish "real" men from those merely pretending to be men.[28]

So how do we know all this about masculinity's precariousness? That is, how have Vandello and Bosson measured this construct? It turns out that precarious manhood is pretty easy to induce in men. One way to get men nervous about their manhood is to give them a "personality test" and then provide them false feedback—feedback the researchers make up that has nothing to do with the men's actual responses. Tell half the men that their personality results were similar to the typical man (nonthreatening condition) and the other half that they responded to the items in a way typical for women (threatening condition). Researchers can do the same with women participants. They tell them they responded like men (threatening) or like women (not threatening). However, this threat prime doesn't really work on women because they aren't much bothered by being associated with men. When women are associated with being like men, they are linked to a high-status group—the preferred gender category. When men are associated with women, they lose status because women are the subordinated gender group and boys and men know this well. Men who receive this gender-threatening prompt exhibit more physically aggressive thoughts compared to the men who received gendered-affirming feedback.[29]

One clever experiment conducted by Vandello and Bosson asked an ethnically diverse sample of men to complete a braiding task. Men were randomly assigned to one of two conditions. In the threat condition, the men were asked to braid the long hair on a mannequin and tie the braid with a pink ribbon. In the nonthreat condition men were asked to perform the same task but with rope and no pink ribbon. After the task, men could choose to engage in a gender-neutral puzzle task or a physical punching task. More than twice as many men chose the punching task if they completed the hair-braiding task than if they completed the rope task.[30] Vandello and Bosson suggest that choosing the punching task was a way to restore men's compromised masculinity that resulted from having to do a typically feminine task of braiding hair. The men who braided rope were not triggered, their masculinity was not compromised, and therefore they did not feel the need to act out physically.

Ironically, men's concerns are somewhat overblown. Men hold distorted and exaggerated beliefs about the levels of masculinity that people expect and desire from them. For example, men tend to overestimate the aggressiveness of their male peers' response to a provocation—in other words, men tend to assume other men are more aggressive than they actually are. Men also overestimate how negatively others will view them if they respond to an offense *non*aggressively.[31] Heterosexual men incorrectly assume that women prefer an aggressive to a nonaggressive response to provocation, but women themselves report being more attracted to nonaggressive men.[32] Other research similarly finds that men exaggerate the extent to which they would be judged as less masculine for certain behaviors. For example, in a study of involuntarily unemployed adults, men expected harsher denigration of their gender status than women did. Men also displayed more inaccuracy than women did with regard to their gender status in other people's eyes. Men's concerns about their audiences' perceptions of them pertain primarily to male observers.[33] In other words, men tend to care more about what other men think of them than what women think of them.

There are consequences of the investment in maintaining traditional aspects of manhood for individual men. Men learn to be concerned about performing masculinity, which often entails aggression. Again, men tend to believe that aggression is more typical than it actually is, and that women find aggressive men appealing when, in fact, women more often view aggression as weakness, not sexy or charming.[34] These latter consequences go beyond the individual man's life and spill over to society where, to some degree, we all deal with precarious manhood. One may wonder why men bother with all of this. The answer: performing obligatory masculinity is a tradeoff, and the price is worth it when entitlement is the result. In order to maintain their status as men—relative to women and the feminine—men put forth great effort repeatedly to achieve manhood and distance themselves from the lower echelon of femininity. Many men make this conscious or unconscious calculation and have determined the benefits, such as feeling entitled to benefits of being a high-status group, outweigh the limitations.

Boys as Bystanders

Chapter 2 looked at the limits of the individualist perspective to understanding phenomena that are systemic. For example, sexism is not simply a person's antipathy toward women, but rather is an historic and ongoing system of patriarchy embedded in institutions such as education, health care, and marriage. Intimate partner violence is often treated as an individual issue caused by men's personality flaws (and the belief that women with low self-esteem allow themselves to be abused by men). In his book, *The Macho Paradox*,[35] Jackson Katz argues against the few-bad-apples notion of perpetrators of gender violence. According to Katz, most men who abuse women are not sociopaths. They are average men who see sexist treatment as normal—how men are supposed to treat women. They have learned to feel entitled to treat women in misogynist ways. Intimate partner violence epitomizes men's entitlement in that perpetrators feel justified treating women in ways they would never treat strangers. In some male peer groups, the mistreatment of girls and women is not condemned and it might even help men gain status within that group. Some men perform masculinity for the benefit of other men, and their routine involves elevating themselves by denigrating women.[36] The mistreatment of women to bond men was reflected in the quotation at the beginning of this chapter. In Dr. Christine Blasey Ford's description the sexual assault by Brett Kavanaugh and a friend serves to bond the two young men—"two good friends having a really good time with one another." Blasey Ford was merely an instrument in this process, a conduit to their homosocial bonding.

If the mistreatment of women is seen as normal, and a tool for men to achieve status in the eyes of other men, reframing it as *abnormal* will change men's behavior. That is, if expectations of how men are supposed to behave changed, that is, if the standard for treating women changed, then men's behavior toward women would change. Moreover, in preventing men's violence, Katz finds it is ineffective to target men as potential perpetrators because most men do not identify this way. They don't see what they do as a problem. Katz's approach then is to intervene with men as *bystanders*, not as perpetrators. A bystander is someone who is not directly involved as a perpetrator or victim but is indirectly involved—someone who witnesses violence but does nothing to stop it. Katz wants men's abuse of women to be stigmatized. The goal here is to change norms so men who engage in such behavior would lose approval and status among peers. The fact that men care a great deal about what other men think of them[37] presents the opportunity to earn other men's respect and approval but not for misogynist behavior.[38] The challenge—albeit formidable—is to undermine the policing mechanisms of male culture that gives value to misogyny. Men's speaking out against misogyny in male peer groups is so counter normative that those who do speak out against sexist behavior are viewed as wimps and even gay. Katz argues it's easy to be one of the guys. To conform is easy. To speak out and risk ostracism is difficult. Experimental studies find that indeed few men intervene against sexism when the peer norm is sexism, rather than when the peer norm is more ambiguous.[39] Think about this. Misogyny is so routine in our culture and in men's peer groups in particular, that a man's masculinity, even his sexuality, is questioned if he resists sexist treatment of women. Sadly, there are plenty of women who have these same beliefs, which further legitimizes the abuse cycle.

In addition to men's violence against women, homophobic bullying also serves to strengthen this damaging and toxic kind of masculinity. Those individuals, women and men, who are heterosexual and who endorse traditional masculine gender roles (e.g., that boys should play with trucks, not dolls, and men should be emotionally stoic) tend to think that one should not intervene when presented with a homophobic bullying scenario.[40] In contrast, queer individuals and those who reject traditional masculinity support intervention in the scenario. In other words, heterosexuals with traditional gender attitudes are more likely to think that homophobic bullying is tolerable, maybe even appropriate, whereas queer individuals and those who reject rigid gender roles view bullying as something to call out and reject. But there is a price to pay for calling out homophobia. Boys are more likely than girls to report that they would not stay friends with a peer who disclosed they are lesbian or gay.[41]

Those who report intervening in homophobic bullying and defending queer peers score higher on measures of leadership, courage, altruism, justice sensitivity, and have more queer friends than those who fail to act.[42] Cultivating these qualities could lead students to intervene in homophobic behavior. Girls and women are less homophobic than boys and men,[43] so (1) boys may support homophobic behavior more than girls and (2) boys may fear retaliation if they defend a queer kid. Homophobic bullying affects more than specific targets of the abuse. A negative school climate—when the majority of students view their peers as prejudiced—is problematic for many adolescents' academic performance. When schools are characterized by high levels of perceived prejudice, adolescents' grades suffer regardless of their own individual perceptions or treatment.[44]

Online Abuse and Peer Group Support

Internet trolling is gendered, as well, and is buoyed by online peer support. Online abuse can include bigoted reader comments, publishing targets' private information (known as doxing), revenge porn, threats of violence, and Internet stalking, among other abuse. The *Guardian* analyzed 70 million article comments over a 10-year period and found that although the majority of *Guardian* writers are White men, women experience most of the abuse, regardless of the article content. Of the ten most-targeted writers for abuse, eight were women (four White and four non-White) and two were Black. Of the ten least-abused writers, all were men (race unspecified). Online abuse is indeed gendered and raced.[45] Misogynist comments directed toward women are also more likely to be sexual and sexually violent than abusive comments directed at men.[46]

Internet abuse directed at women, people of color, queer people, and other marginalized groups epitomizes dominant-group entitlement. Those who target and troll feel entitled to online spaces, and they view marginalized group members' claim on these spaces as overstepping boundaries, as illegitimate, and as "uppity." Dominant group members feel entitled to move freely around the Internet without being confronted with opinions from marginalized group members making them uncomfortable or questioning their entitlement. Perpetrators find supportive online communities that normalize and condone abusive online behavior. Revenge porn is one of these extreme forms of online abuse. It is the sharing of sexual images of a person without their consent with the purposeful attempt to ruin the life of the victim, often in revenge for breaking up the relationship. The images might also include the victim's name, address, or other personal information. Male peer support allows men to feel normal and justified when committing violence against current and former intimate partners. Men's proprietariness is also associated with male peer support and the tendency to think of women as sexual and reproductive property men own and can exchange. Off and online peer support motivates and reinforces men who lash out against the women they can no longer control.[47]

Online abuse is different from actual rape or sexual assault. However, the same norms and power structures underpin these acts. Online harassment functions to discipline women for speaking in public.[48] Men's threats of sexualized violence directed at women who dare to have opinions are frightening to the women who are targets. And they have good reason to be frightened, as many women whose personal information has been released have had electronic threats turn into real threats. Real-world consequences ensue, and many women have had to relocate to avoid men who want to make real the threats they made or read about online. Online abuse against women by men in some circles is so routine that in her analysis of online abuse, Emma Alice Jane finds a uniformity to the comments. There is a tedious repetition; comments are generic as if the perpetrators are following a gendered script—threats of rape and murder, calling the woman a slut, ugly, and fat.[49] Jane suggests this type of gendered violence has little to do with the particular women and what they have written or done, but rather this script is about reinforcing men's prominent position in the public sphere. Just as street harassment of women by men conveys men's dominion over public spaces, online harassment of women by men signifies men's dominion over the Internet—another public space.

Entitlement Reflected in Mass Media

Movies are the most powerful empathy machine in all the arts.
—Film Critic, Roger Ebert[50]

We just explored the role of the peer group in ballasting one's sense of entitlement. This section takes a look at mass media's role in the development of entitlement. The average child under age 12 years spends 11 hours per week consuming streaming video.[51] Mass media no doubt influence how children see the world, their role in it, and their developing sense of entitlement. Therefore, it is worth first noting who is represented in mass media, that is, whose stories are told and who matters enough to be represented in television, film, and advertisements. Second, the nature of roles associated with group membership tells us how we should think about various groups. Media messages lead children and adults to infer that White people are the normal, ideal people who should be regarded with care and humanity; that men are those who are legitimately in power and accomplish important things; and that cisgender people and heterosexuals have the normal and ideal gender and romantic lives. Finally, how media messages affect actual viewers gets us beyond merely assuming media influences people in vague ways. We can see some concrete effects of media exposure and its relevance to entitlement.

Media Content: Framing Who Matters

I'm here at the Academy Awards, otherwise known as the White People's Choice Awards.
                    —Chris Rock, 2016 host of the Academy Awards[52]

The White, cisgender, heterosexual boy or man is centered in media. He gets to see himself in rich and complicated roles, making an impact, having power, and having a life that matters and whose story is worth telling. Media validates to members of dominant groups that they are entitled to see themselves represented in mass media and popular culture. People from marginalized communities have little reason to feel entitled to the same representation.

Who Is Entitled to Fair Treatment and Who Should We Be Afraid Of?
Representation in television news stories is a very telling indication of whose lives are valuable, whose deaths are worth reporting, and who deserves empathy. For example, media coverage of anti-queer bullying centers certain victims and erases others. Here too White men are overrepresented as victims. The typical victim portrayal of anti-queer bullying is a college-age White man. In fact, middle school children are at greater risk of victimization, and people of color are victimized at similar rates to White people. [53] This bias in media reporting perpetuates the false idea that most queer people are White and that men of color and women are not at risk for victimization, or their victimization isn't significant enough to be newsworthy. The fact that younger kids—like middle schoolers—are not part of news representations

of anti-queer bullying normalizes this kind of bullying in schools as simply what kids do—boys being boys.

News stories also tell us who we should be afraid of and who does not deserve our empathy. For example, White men are overrepresented as victims of crime and underrepresented as criminal perpetrators, compared to real-life crime rates. The opposite is true of African American men who are overrepresented as criminal perpetrators and underrepresented as victims of crime, compared to actual crime rates.[54] Latinx people are also overrepresented as perpetrators compared to their real-life behavior, and they are underrepresented as victims compared to their actual victimization in real life.[55] African American crime suspects are much more likely than Whites to be portrayed in police custody and in mug shots. Moreover, African American suspects often appear in more threatening and menacing ways than White suspects. In contrast, White suspects are more likely to be depicted in a dignified way.[56] For example, recall from Chapter 3 when convicted rapist Brock Turner, a White man, was often shown in the media in his Stanford yearbook photograph. These biases in representations guide the viewer to believe that White men's lives matter, as those are the individuals who are entitled to dignity and humanity. White men learn that they are entitled to fair, even preferential treatment, given they are underrepresented as criminals.

Muslims are greatly overrepresented as terrorists in news stories.[57] This last pattern is particularly noteworthy because the biggest threat of terrorism in the United States is from White Christian-oriented (or non-Muslim) men—crimes in the form of mass shootings and right-wing terrorism. For example, White right-wing extremists have been responsible for 73% of extremist-related domestic-terror murders between 2008 and 2018, compared to Islamic extremists who were responsible for only 23%. And in 2018 alone, right-wing extremists were responsible for every extremist murder in the United States.[58] Even under the White supremacist administration of Donald Trump, the US Department of Homeland Security in 2020 reported that White supremacists presented the greatest terror threat to the United States.[59]

Instead of reflecting these facts, the news teaches viewers that Muslims are the ones to fear, which likely explains the rise in anti-Muslim hate crimes over the last two decades.[60] The viewer learns, inaccurately, that they need not worry about White men as they are not presented as threats. These depictions lead the viewer to believe that White people are entitled to empathy and care;

in contrast, Brown and Black people must be threatening, dangerous, criminal, and deserving of punishment, not empathy.

Crime-based "reality" shows like *Cops* or *Live PD* overrepresent crime compared to what is going on in the world. Reality programming does not reflect reality. What do viewers learn from these shows? Viewers see a world that is much more dangerous than it actually is. *Cops* shows four times the amount of violent crime, three times the amount of drug arrests, and ten times the amount of prostitution that occurs in real-life policing. On *Cops*, 92% of the traffic stops end in arrest, but only 2% of real-life traffic stops do. These programs only depict *successful* stops, searches, seizures, and arrests— meaning the officers on the shows find something or someone worthy of arresting pretty much any time they stop someone.[61] This offers the viewer the false idea that all stops police make in real-life are lawful, appropriate, and expose criminal activity. After all, these are "reality" shows, showing actual police officers carrying out actual law enforcement activities.[62] The lesson for the viewer is: police stopping drivers or pedestrians for minor traffic infractions, anomalies of behavior, possessing out-of-state license plates, or acting "squirrely," is appropriate because it invariably leads to the arrest of criminals.[63] When you combine the typical story line in crime-based reality shows with the real-life fact that people of color are detained by police in staggeringly higher numbers than are Whites,[64] you have a set up that justifies racial profiling of people of color. The viewer of these shows comes to believe that police accurately pull over the correct people because everyone they detain on *Cops* ends up having contraband, an outstanding warrant, or are high or drunk. The viewer concludes stopping people of color is a good use of police time because on TV when people are stopped, they are guilty.

Cops, and other shows like *Live PD*, offer a pro-policing narrative, and fan clubs even exist for officers who appear in episodes.[65] When you pair the ethnic patterns in news programming with data from crime-based so-called reality shows, one gets the impression that the world is a dangerous place and that White people are its main victims. But these shows do more than this. These shows actually normalize rough treatment by mostly White police officers against "guilty" suspects. Because these guilty criminals have resisted arrest, the audience agrees they deserved the rough treatment. Because, again, the suspects on the shows are guilty and if they resist, they are resisting as criminals, and therefore deserve rough treatment.[66] What might viewers take from these scenes? Viewers may come to believe that cops in real-life are entitled to violate the constitutional rights of suspects or department policy because suspects are assumed to be guilty.[67]

And the victim position in episodes may surprise you. Stephanie Whitehead analyzed domestic violence calls on *Cops*.[68] Whitehead finds that White men cops are actually portrayed as the victims in those episodes, and the women victims essentially become the perpetrators in the portrayals. The audience watches as the women scream and curse and argue with the officers. The women's belligerence contrasts with the officer who appears calm as the voice of reason. The woman domestic violence complainant is out of control, and the cop who is trying to calm her down becomes her victim. He is the passive recipient of the woman's violence and is more deserving of the viewer's sympathy and compassion than she is. In the final segment of each episode, the officer whose story has been told in the episode recaps what happened and frames for the audience how to understand what happened. They offer their interpretation of what happened, and the audience, who is meant to empathize with them throughout, is likely to take as legitimate the officer's assessment of the situation.[69] This construction of officer-as-sympathetic-victim in domestic violence calls creates a stage for the viewer to blame the actual victim. The woman victim is so awful, she's probably at fault for what happened to her anyway.

The effect of shows like *Cops* and *Live PD* have on its viewers is significant, especially for certain types of viewers. Mary Beth Oliver studied the influence of crime-based reality shows on White viewers' attitudes.[70] She found that men tend to enjoy this genre more than women (and men have more favorable ratings of actual police than women do); those with authoritarian personalities are more likely to enjoy these shows than nonauthoritarians; and authoritarians are more likely than nonauthoritarians to view police officers favorably in these shows and have more negative ratings of criminal suspects. When viewers were exposed to either White or Black suspects, they found that authoritarianism was unrelated to enjoyment of the footage featuring White suspects, but authoritarians enjoyed the footage more when it featured African American suspects.[71] In other words, White viewers with authoritarian attitudes are satisfied when they see African American people detained and arrested and subjected to the criminal justice system. White men see themselves reflected in the lives of police officers and learn to sympathize with those officers and to believe that officers are doing noble, necessary work.

To summarize, crime-based "reality" shows do the following: (1) they show the world as more dangerous than it actually is; (2) they justify broad and sweeping stops of citizens without probable cause because most TV stops end in arrest; (3) the viewer is likely to support the overpolicing of people of color as they are more likely to be shown in news stories as criminals; (4) they depict police action through the eyes of the police and thus encourage empathy in only one direction; (5) rough treatment of citizens by officers appears justified; and (6) in some cases, the officers are actually victims of citizen violence; and, finally, (7) these shows are particularly of interest to White men with authoritarian worldviews—among the more entitled groups of people.

Who Is Entitled to Positive Representation?

This is a huge deal because as people in the movie business know the absolute hardest thing in the whole world is to persuade a straight male audience to identify with a woman protagonist to feel themselves embodied by her. This more than any other factor explains why we get the movies we get and the paucity of the roles where women drive the film. It's much easier for the female audience because we were all grown up, brought up identifying with male characters from Shakespeare to Salinger.

—Actor Meryl Streep[72]

Whiteness dominates other media domains, including scripted television. White people see themselves in all genres in a wide variety of positive and negative roles. Latinx individuals are significantly underrepresented compared to their existence in the United States. For example they represent only 9% of regular characters compared to their 18% representation in the population.[73] Native Americans are almost entirely absent from television shows.[74] People with disabilities are grossly underrepresented, as well, at 3%.[75] In contrast, queer characters are more representative of the population on television, as they make up 10% of the regular characters on broadcast primetime television, and more than half are women, and queer people of color are accurately represented.[76]

The numbers matter, but there's more at issue than simple representation. It is also important to track the reliance on stereotypes and stock characters. Latinx characters are portrayed as hypersexual relative to White (Anglos) and African Americans.[77] African American women are more likely to be shown in sexually objectified ways than women of other ethnicities.[78] Gender nonconformity functions to support the larger narrative of gender as a binary. Gender nonconformity is portrayed as untrustworthy and clownish and not as a legitimate identity. In Spanish-speaking telenovelas—the most common Spanish language television played in the United States—light-skinned actors are more likely to play high-status roles, whereas dark-skinned characters play low-status roles. Consistent with other genres, when gender nonconforming people are represented in telenovelas, they tend to be portrayed for laughs.[79]

Video games also make up a significant part of the media landscape today. Analysis of video game advertisements in print magazines finds ads center on the White male hero relative to women and people of color.[80] Whites account for 82% of all characters in these ads, and White men make up 60% of the sample. The White female body is the object of desire (with the occasional exception of Asian women). White men are represented as more physically attractive than Black men, and Black men are hyper-muscular, consistent with the Black criminal trope—the unattractive and hyper-masculine criminal. Asian male characters tend to fill ninja or villain roles, figures who are highly violent and use swords instead of guns. White men are portrayed as less violent and less likely to carry a weapon. White men are more often the hero.[81]

Popular culture tells us it is good to be a man. For every woman or girl seen in television or film, you can find two men or boys. Women and girls comprise only 34% of speaking characters.[82] In top-grossing US films, men still outnumber women 2 to 1.[83] Again, representation is not just about numbers, it is also about roles. Men see themselves in a variety of roles, doing things—good and bad—and they are the ones who matter. As an example, let's take age as it intersects with gender. When you consider the age of actors and characters, the representations of women are even bleaker. In both prime-time television[84] and popular films,[85] women are most frequently seen in the age range of 20 to 30, whereas men are more likely to be in their 30s and 40s. When you consider the 50s and 60s, women virtually disappear.[86] Popular culture has little use for older women. The fact that women in their 50s and 60s nearly disappear in representations is particularly interesting because the largest percentage of women in the US population is in the 51+ group.[87] Ironically, the largest age demographic of women in real life is the least likely to be seen in celluloid life. In addition to the mismatch between representation in media and representation in real life, there is another reason why the erasure of older women in television and film is significant. Typically, older adults on TV and in film have more power, status, and leadership, but this is true for men, not women. For example, in TV and film, men in their 40s and 50s are more likely to play leaders than younger men, and women in the same age range. Men in their 50s have greater occupational power than women in their 50s.[88] So as they get older, men gain prestige and power; women, they disappear. Women disappear in sheer numbers and in terms of their status, power, and significance as characters.

Men are depicted with more authority than women across many domains, including holding more occupational power in advertisements.[89] While primary characters in commercials in the United States do not differ by gender in terms of numbers, women are nevertheless depicted as younger than men. Television voiceovers are an important feature of commercials as a narrator conveys authority, gravity, and wisdom. Women's voices make up only 27% of commercial voiceovers compared to men's 73%.[90] Like most of the other media genres, television commercials convey the message that men are proactive, they are experts with authority, whereas women are trivial and often relegated to the domestic setting.

Fictional crime dramas have been a staple of television for decades. White men are the dominant gender and race group at 45% of all characters, followed by White women, who far surpass African American women and men.[91] The typical crime victim in these shows is a White woman or girl. Compared to Black women, Black men, and White men, White women and girls stand the greatest chance of being victims of rape, murder, or some other kind of violence. And the typical perpetrator in these shows is a stranger to the victim.[92] This pattern is significant because, in real life, the most frequent victim of violence is an African American man. And when murder or sexual assault is committed in real life, it is typically committed, not by strangers, but by family members, friends, or acquaintances. So why do these shows tell a different story? What do they reveal and conceal about perpetrators and victims? They suggest viewers are most comfortable seeing White women as victims of violence. Why? Perhaps White women are more dramatically valuable in their victimhood than are women (and men) of color. Perhaps a dead White woman splayed out on *Law & Order: Special Victims Unit* provokes our outrage and empathy more than other types of victims. Perhaps, but these portrayals also objectify White women—they are voiceless objects even if they are objects of pity. The White woman–victim trope is misleading, not only because it does not match up to real life. These portrayals could mislead people into believing that strangers pose the main risk to their safety, whereas family members are not a threat. This is not true for girls and women. Girls and women are more likely to be murdered by people they know—usually romantic partners or former partners.[93]

The normalization of White, heterosexual men in popular culture is revealed in linguistic minority-marking through terms such as "chick flick," "Black film," and "gay film." Chick flicks are films featuring women characters with storylines supposedly of interest to women but not men. "Regular," "normal," or "universally appealing" movies are dominated by men characters. Films that recycle plots with White heterosexual cisgender men are not marked because they are thought to hold universal appeal. White, heterosexual, cisgender men are entitled to a full range of representations. Anyone should want to watch a Tom Cruise film, but only a small segment of the population should be interested in a film fronted by Regina King. Because television and film until very recently have shown almost exclusively cisgender heterosexual content, queer individuals have historically had two options: they could avoid popular culture altogether, as it did not relate to their lives and relationships, or they could view this material about cisgender and heterosexual lives and do a translation—substitute some of the characters with their own gender and sexual identity. Straight lives and straight relationships are foisted upon the queer viewer if that viewer wants to follow popular culture. In contrast, dominant group members rarely have to switch things up. Rarely are they inconvenienced. Their stories are the ones that get told. Everyone is supposed to empathize with the preferred group. Dominant groups get to label films about their lives as simply "films," and label films about queer people as gay films—signifying that those films are not for them and will not have universal appeal. They feel no obligation to include gay films in their viewing repertoire, but when queer people critique the lack of representation in mainstream film, they are dismissed as complainers or worse—as pushing a queer agenda. This is the epitome of entitlement for those in the norm.

It's Good to Be a Boy

Television, advertisements, gaming, film, and magazines are not the only media that perpetuate the normalization and idealization of the dominant group and then their corresponding entitlement. Consider something as seemingly innocuous as a birth announcement. Recall from Chapter 3 that well into the twenty-first century, parents in North America still prefer sons to daughters. The relative thrill of having a baby boy is reflected in birth announcements. For example, in a study that examined 2500 birth announcements in Canadian newspapers, parents of newborn boys expressed more pride than parents of newborn girls, although parents of girls expressed greater happiness.[94] Pride is what psychologists call a social emotion; it is tied to rank and status, how you compare to others. Popular culture dutifully perpetuates this status difference in birth congratulation cards.[95] In addition to the color pink for girls and blue for boys, visual images indicative of physical activity, such as action toys and active babies, are more prominent on boy than girl cards.[96] Girls are instead passive: sitting, lying down, or sleeping. Even as newborns, girls are meant to be cooperative and docile. Verbal messages of expressiveness, including sweetness and "little," appear on more girl than boy cards.[97] In contrast to the Canadian study finding that parents expressed more happiness (but less pride) in the birth of a daughter, this study found that happiness is more likely to be conveyed with cards about the birth of boys.[98]

Birth announcement cards are consistent with stereotypes about girls and boys: that boys are active, athletic, and coordinated, and girls are soft, little, and passive. However, the attributes depicted in these cards and announcements do not reflect truths about how girls and boys *are*. Rather, they reflect a fantasy about how girls and boys *should* be. For instance, on average, newborn boys outweigh newborn girls by a whopping one tenth of a kilogram. Boy babies have slightly larger head sizes than girls; however, newborn girls outscore boys on the Apgar scale, which measures muscle activity, pulse, and breathing. At 8 months girls outscore boys on motor skills.[99] Differences between newborn girls and boys are negligible.

The popular culture representations of infants reflect the idea that girls and then women will be sweet, small, and passive—hardly a stage set for developing a sense of entitlement. In contrast, boys are expected to be active and bold, and to take up the space they will learn to feel entitled to. These gender stereotypes of infants have their corresponding adult version. In a study of 442 Mother's Day and Father's Day Hallmark cards, father cards reflect active themes such as focusing on work and achievement and outdoor scenes (e.g., fishing), whereas mother cards focus on nurturing and indoor scenes (e.g., laundry)—a surprise to no one.[100] Additionally, there were more animals and sports equipment on dad cards and more parent-child pairs on mom cards. The color schemes for Mother's and Father's Day cards reflect birth congratulation cards with softer pastel colors on mom cards and bold colors on dad cards. Like the messages about babies, these cultural artifacts are important sources of societal expectations and both reflect and shape expectations about gender. Gender-based greeting cards is but one media data point that reveals what people should expect of girls and boys and correspondingly what girls and boys will expect themselves. Boys learn they should be active and adventurous and will have hobbies outside of the home, and girls learn they should be sweet and passive and should take care of the home.

Media Effects: Internalizing Messages About Importance

As we have discussed, the way groups are portrayed in mass media and popular culture tell us about who is valued and who is not. These messages go out to both privileged and marginalized groups. Members of preferred groups can take for granted the confirmation of their existence because they see themselves in all domains of media, and their portrayals will be more or less positive, affirming their status as normal and typical. Members of marginalized groups learn a different lesson. Their existence is made tenuous in that they may not appear in the media—their lives don't merit stories or representation. If they are represented, they may be criminalized, hypersexualized, or trivialized. Accordingly, the result is that marginalized group members have no expectation of a sympathetic or well-drawn reflection.

Experimental and correlational studies exist that track the impact of media representations on people's attitudes about various groups. People are influenced by what they see. Even brief exposure to media messages can have, at a minimum, short-term effects on people's attitudes and stereotypes about marginalized groups. First, let's begin with attributions people make based on social category. When White research participants are exposed to a news story that varies to include either a Black, a White, or a race-unknown criminal suspect, White suspects are assumed to be less guilty than the other two groups—even when their conduct is identical.[101] So Whites are given a benefit of the doubt that people of color are not. White people can expect fair or even privileged treatment. African Americans cannot. In fact, when White people see Black criminal suspects in the news, they react by making internal attributions about the negative behavior of a later unrelated person, regardless of race.[102] In other words, seeing a Black person in highly negative and stereotyped depictions (e.g., as criminals) makes participants later assume the negative behavior of anyone is due to a personality flaw versus a situational or temporary benefit-of-the-doubt explanation. This pattern suggests that because African Americans are associated with criminality;

their stereotypical depictions prime viewers to think about crime more generally.

The pattern also emerges when viewers see negative, stereotypical African American media personalities. Participants report greater stereotypical beliefs about African Americans, more internal attributions, increased hostile feelings toward African Americans, and an overall lack of support for affirmative action compared to those who see counterstereotypical positive African American media characters.[103]

In a test of the effects of media on people's attitudes, Karen E. Dill and Melinda C. R. Burgess exposed White college students to two different representations of Black men: either a "thug" character from the video game *Grand Theft Auto* or a professional.[104] Dill and Burgess then gathered White respondents' attitudes about unrelated Black and White men running for political office. They found that priming media examples of Black men influences how people view unrelated members of the racial group portrayed in the images. If respondents saw a Black male professional, they were more likely to vote for an unrelated Black man, whereas exposure to the Black male "thug" character led respondents to report being less willing to vote for a Black candidate. In addition, respondents' attitudes toward African Americans in general changed based on the type of Black man they were exposed to: when they saw the "thug" character, they later reported lower pro-Black attitudes compared to those who were exposed to a Black professional.

The reverse is also true because exposure to news stories about counterstereotypical African American media personalities as compared to stereotypical ones can reduce stereotypical perceptions by White Americans about African Americans in general. In one study, when participants read news stories about counterstereotypical African American media celebrities rather than stereotypical ones, respondents later reported fewer stereotypical perceptions of African Americans in general and reduced subtle symbolic racist beliefs. This in turn increased support for affirmative action policies. At least in the short term, a few atypical media exemplars are able to shape perceptions about the entire group. These findings suggest there is effectiveness in offering vivid, atypical, and interesting counterstereotypical exemplars in news stories. Furthermore, these favorable attitudes translate into an increased willingness to support affirmative action policies (mostly White college students).[105] We can see then how potent the media can be in tapping into people's schemas about race and reinforcing their racist views or, conversely, offering alternative ideas about people of color.

People's ideas about gender are also affected by the sexism baked into the media. For example, the more media (e.g., TV, films, sports, men's magazines) young men consume, the more likely they subscribe to traditional and rigid ideas about masculinity. This includes that men are stoic, always sexually interested and sexually aggressive, and should avoid femininity.[106] The more media consumed, the greater the belief that men *should* behave in these ways. Furthermore, the type of media men enjoy correlates with their attitudes toward the treatment of women. As a whole, men have stronger rape myth beliefs than women,[107] and the more men prefer films with sexual violence, the more they are inclined to subscribe to rape myths. One study examined people's reaction to a film with a realistic and brutal gang rape scene based on an actual incident (*The Accused*). Perhaps due to sympathy toward the film's victim and the consequences to the perpetrators portrayed, women who viewed the film were less likely to subscribe to rape myths after viewing the scene compared to women who watched a control film. However, for men who watched the rape, they were just as likely to subscribe to rape myths as men who watched the control film.[108] In other words, men in the study were not impacted by the film, whereas women were. Men's higher support of rape myths may account for this difference in impact of the film. If you think only bad women get raped, that women could avoid rape if they really wanted to, and that men are entitled to sexual access to women's bodies, then you are not going to be outraged about rape.[109] Film content can affect women's attitudes about gender as well. When women are exposed to a sexualized-victim female character, they are less likely to subscribe to egalitarian beliefs than women who were not exposed to that content.[110] Damsel-in-distress characters influence female audience members to be more traditional in their gender attitudes.

Even channels such as Nickelodeon and Disney that are specifically marketed toward 9 to 12 year-olds have a detrimental effect. The influence these channels have on tween boy viewers is disconcerting. One study found that 11-year-old boys who view Nickelodeon, Disney Channel, and music television are more likely to view women as sex objects if they also experience high levels of gender-stereotyped messages from parents. Interestingly, while marketed as age appropriate, tween TV seems to have similar effects on adolescent boys as music television, which offers highly sexualized and objectifying images of women. For boys, repeated exposure to stereotypical portrayals of women and men may increase the adoption and endorsement of the view that men are sex-driven and women are sex objects and, in turn, they are more likely to objectify women's bodies.[111]

Finally, mass media in the form of reading materials in schools affect children's learning and comprehension. One study examined the influence of gender-stereotypical textbooks on students' comprehension of a science lesson. Much has been made in recent decades of how women and girls are shut out of science. Jessica J. Good and her colleagues asked ninth and tenth graders to read an excerpt from a chemistry lesson, and there were three versions of accompanying images: images that contained only women, only men, or both women and men. The students' comprehension of the lesson was then tested. Girls scored higher on comprehension when the lesson included more pictures of women than men.[112] Similarly, boys had higher comprehension when the lesson contained more images of men than women. There were no gender differences in comprehension when the lesson contained mixed-gender images. The study is significant given the fact that science textbooks tend to be dominated by boys and men,[113] and people are more likely to associate men with science than women with science.[114] If those texts were updated to include both women and men, both girls and boys would benefit from gender representation, taking a step toward closing the gender divide in science education.

Another study found how fragile masculinity manifests in boys not wanting to get outside of their gender comfort zone. Unlike science, technology, engineering, and mathematics (STEM) fields, boys' reading skills suffer relative to that of girls. A question for educators and policy makers is how do we get boys interested in reading? One study found out what *not* to do. This study assessed sixth and seventh grade students on whether or not girls and boys can read books that feature characteristics of the other gender. Girls were as willing to read the boy book as the boys were. However, the boys were much less willing than the girls to read the girl book. The authors also conducted a "hallway test." They asked the students to imagine a boy carrying a specific girl book down the hallway and a girl carrying a specific boy book. According to most students, the boy book was safe for girls to carry down the hallway. However, it was *not* okay for boys to be seen carrying a girl book. For girls with a boy book it would be unnoticed or at most elicit mild curiosity. For a boy reading a girl book, he would likely be subject to teasing and ridicule. His masculinity may be called into question, and his sexuality a matter of public debate.[115] This study is consistent with earlier discussions in this chapter about the toxicity of femininity for boys, and the narrowness with which boys can traverse roles. There is a lot at stake for masculinity, and, again, boys learn that the rigid confines of gender rules must be the price to pay for relative power, privilege, and entitlement.

Conclusion

This chapter explored peer groups and the mass media as enablers of entitlement. The peer group puts into practice attitudes and behaviors that facilitate entitlement. Compared to girls', boys' peer groups are more likely to be organized hierarchically with an emphasis on social dominance. Boys themselves admit to being susceptible to the pressure of peers, and even adult men report being concerned about their manhood status in the eyes of other men.[116] The pressure boys face to appear tough surely takes a toll on boys' and men's emotional lives. In addition, it affects their school performance and is disruptive to those in classes with boys who put a primacy on masculine performance.

Boys and men learn they can gain status by denigrating marginalized others—feminine kids in middle school, for example, or women writers online or women on the street.[117] Domestic violence researcher Rachel Louise Snyder writes that men worry about impressing other men on the street. Mistreating a woman is one way.[118] Homophobic and misogynist mistreatment, wherever it is, functions to maintain heterosexual cisgender men's status and entitlement. In the discussion on power in Chapter 1, you will recall the notion of power by association: this refers to the occurrence of gaining a sense of or actual power through one's association with another's actual power. We can think of the male peer group in these terms. Complying with homophobic, misogynistic, and racist norms of marginalizing minorities bolsters one's own status and sense of entitlement. Those who endorse traditional masculine ideology—boys should play with trucks rather than dolls or men should be detached in emotionally charged situations—tolerate homophobic bullying and believe that there is no need or desire to intervene. In contrast, sexual minorities and those who reject traditional masculine ideology are more likely to endorse intervention.[119] Homophobic slurs are tools not only to regulate sexuality but also to enforce traditional masculinity and gender roles.

A negative school climate—when the majority of students view their peers as prejudiced—negatively impacts adolescents' academic performance. When schools were characterized by high levels of perceived prejudice, adolescents' grades suffered regardless of their own individual perceptions. This is not about a specific kid's own sense of victimization but rather the entire atmosphere at the school. Additionally, though, in terms of individuals, adolescents' feelings of belonging and connectedness to their school suffered more when their own perceptions of peer prejudice exceeded those of their schoolmates.[120]

There's an old saying, *If you can't see it, you can't be it*, which means it's hard to become something—an astronaut or a nurturing caregiver—if you do not see people like you in those roles. Mass media could offer wild possibilities of what one can be, but these possibilities are constrained by the narrow representations we see in media and popular culture. Among other messages, mass media tell us whose lives matter and who we should be afraid of. We learn that White people, men, cisgender people, and heterosexuals are fully fleshed out humans. News coverage teaches viewers that they should be more afraid of Black and Brown people than they should be, and less afraid of White men than they should. Crime-based reality shows make people think the world is a more dangerous place than it actually is. We have some insight into who these shows resonate with: authoritarians for one. These shows reinforce their view of the world as mean, hierarchical, and punishing. White men with authoritarian worldviews are especially plugged into these shows—reinforcing their own authoritarian viewpoint.

It's good to be a White, cisgender, heterosexual man in film and scripted television. It is their lives that matter. Women are grossly underrepresented, especially in film, and people of color are underrepresented and play narrow roles. It's good to be a boy or man in mass media as evidenced from everything from storylines and representation in film, to voiceovers in commercials, to birth announcements and greeting cards. African American and Latinx women are presented in hypersexualized and objectified ways, compared to White women.

The role that media play in the development of entitlement is more than mere representation. Racist, sexist, and homophobic media content affects viewers' attitudes and behavior. For example, seeing African Americans presented as criminals affects White viewers differently from content that presents White people as criminals. Typical media give White criminals the benefit of the doubt by assuming they are less guilty than African Americans who are depicted in the exact same way. When viewers see negative, stereotypical depictions of African Americans in media, they later report greater stereotypical beliefs about Black people, have more hostile feelings toward Black people, and are less likely to support programs such as affirmative action when compared to those who saw counterstereotypical information about African Americans. Whites are entitled to leniency in a way that people of color are not. Longitudinal studies on media effects tend to examine influence of viewing over days or months, not years. We know about short-term effects. Imagine the cumulative effects of a lifetime of media consumption on viewers.

Film critic Roger Ebert called films empathy machines, but films ask little of dominant group members when it comes to putting themselves in the shoes of marginalized people. White heterosexual men get to see a popular culture repertoire that reflects their lives, and when a piece of media happens to not center the dominant group, it gets tagged as a "Black film" or a "chick flick." Media encourages this sense of entitlement in preferred groups because it doesn't require these groups to stretch—to consume media that may not center them. It is hardly surprising then that boys would be mortified to carry a book that centers girls and women in their school hallways. We must ask dominant group members to stretch in a way that subordinated groups always have.

Finally, mass media can be used for positive change. Interviews with queer youth find that their media use may buffer some of the effects of marginalization, such as isolation and victimization. Popular culture can provide an emotional outlet through escapism or by creating meaning and queer youth report that media use contributed to their resilience by fostering community.[121] Participants exposed to an educational television sitcom with diverse, yet relatable Arab Muslim characters had lower scores on implicit and explicit measures of prejudice than participants exposed to a control sitcom featuring an all-White cast. The prejudice reduction effect persisted four weeks after exposure. In this experiment, increased identification with target group members was associated with greater prejudice reduction.[122]

The makeup of peer groups, the values of peer groups, how status is achieved and lost, and the amount of influence the peer group has on individuals are not inevitable unless left unchallenged. The patterns we see in popular culture can change and have changed. None of this is biologically determined. In order to make change, we should understand the power of the peer group and the power of popular culture in creating and maintaining norms that impact how we see ourselves, what we think we deserve, and how we treat others. Boys' and men's peer groups should not be dismissed as "boys will be boys." When their conduct is abusive, it should not be minimized as "locker room talk." And when popular culture plays such a powerful role in our lives, we must understand its cumulative effects. Any activity we engage in for hours every day will influence us, but we are not helpless.

Notes

1. The Washington Post. https://www.washingtonpost.com/news/national/wp/2018/09/27/kavanaugh-hearing-transcript/.
2. CNN. (2015, December 8). Graham: Trump is a "race-baiting xenophobic" bigot [Video]. *CNN*. https://www.cnn.com/videos/politics/2015/12/08/lindsey-graham-donald-trump-xenophobic-bigot-interview-newday.cnn.
3. Kwong, J. (2019, July 18). Lindsey Graham says Donald Trump's not racist, but called him a "race-baiting bigot" in 2015. *Newsweek*. https://www.newsweek.com/lindsey-graham-trump-not-racist-tweets-1450060.
4. Broverman, I. K., Vogel, S. R., Broverman, D. M., Clarkson, F. E., & Rosenkrantz, P. S. (1972). Sex-role stereotypes: A current appraisal. *Journal of Social Issues, 28*(2), 59–78. https://doi.org/10.1111/j.1540-4560.1972.tb00018.x.
5. See this: CBS News. (2016, October 10). Ryan won't help Trump [Video]. *CBSN*. https://www.cbsnews.com/video/paul-ryan-i-will-not-defend-trump/ and then this: Polman, D. (2018, December 12). Paul Ryan's compromised legacy. *The Atlantic*. https://www.theatlantic.com/politics/archive/2018/12/paul-ryans-legacy-compromised-his-trump-support/577942.
6. Rosenthal, L., Levy, S. R., & Earnshaw, V. A. (2012). Social dominance orientation relates to believing men should dominate sexually, sexual self-efficacy, and taking free female condoms among undergraduate women and men. *Sex Roles: A Journal of Research, 67*(11–12), 659–669. https://doi.org/10.1007/s11199-012-0207-6.
7. Cross, J. R., & Fletcher, K. L. (2011). Associations of parental and peer characteristics with adolescents' social dominance orientation. *Journal of Youth and Adolescence, 40*, 694–706. https://doi.org/10.1007/s10964-010-9585-7.
8. Kiefer, S. M., & Ryan, A. M. (2008). Striving for social dominance over peers: The implications for academic adjustment during early adolescence. *Journal of Educational Psychology, 100*(2), 417–428. https://doi.org/10.1037/0022-0663.100.2.417.
9. Kiefer, S. M., & Ryan, A. M. (2008). Striving for social dominance over peers: The implications for academic adjustment during early adolescence. *Journal of Educational Psychology, 100*(2), 417–428. https://doi.org/10.1037/0022-0663.100.2.417.
10. Kiefer, S. M., & Ryan, A. M. (2008). Striving for social dominance over peers: The implications for academic adjustment during early adolescence. *Journal of Educational Psychology, 100*(2), 417–428. https://doi.org/10.1037/0022-0663.100.2.417.
11. Santos, C. E., Galligan, K., Pahlke, E., & Fabes, R. A. (2013). Gender-typed behaviors, achievement, and adjustment among racially and ethnically diverse boys during early adolescence. *American Journal of Orthopsychiatry, 83*(2–3), 252–264. https://doi.org/10.1111/ajop.12036.
12. Santos, C. E., Galligan, K., Pahlke, E., & Fabes, R. A. (2013). Gender-typed behaviors, achievement, and adjustment among racially and ethnically diverse boys during early adolescence. *American Journal of Orthopsychiatry, 83*(2–3), 252–264. https://doi.org/10.1111/ajop.12036.

13. Santos, C. E., Galligan, K., Pahlke, E., & Fabes, R. A. (2013). Gender-typed behaviors, achievement, and adjustment among racially and ethnically diverse boys during early adolescence. *American Journal of Orthopsychiatry, 83*(2–3), 252–264. https://doi.org/ 10.1111/ajop.12036.

14. Leaper, C., Farkas, T., & Starr, C. R. (2018). Traditional masculinity, help avoidance, and intrinsic interest in relation to high school students' English and math performance. *Psychology of Men & Masculinity, 20*(4), 603–611. https://doi.org/10.1037/ men0000188.

15. Kiefer, S. M., & Shim, S. S. (2016). Academic help seeking from peers during adolescence: The role of social goals. *Journal of Applied Developmental Psychology, 42,* 80–88. https://doi.org/10.1016/j.appdev.2015.12.002.

16. Vantieghem, W., & Van Houtte, V. (2015). Are girls more resilient to gender-conformity pressure? The association between gender-conformity pressure and academic self-efficacy. *Sex Roles, 73,* 1–15. https://doi.org/10.1007/s11199-015-0509-6.

17. Busching, R., & Krahé, B. (2018). The contagious effect of deviant behavior in adolescence: A longitudinal multilevel study. *Social Psychological and Personality Science, 9,* 815–824. https://doi.org/10.1177/1948550617725151.

18. Busching, R., & Krahé, B. (2018). The contagious effect of deviant behavior in adolescence: A longitudinal multilevel study. *Social Psychological and Personality Science, 9,* 815–824. https://doi.org/10.1177/1948550617725151.

19. Vantieghem, W., & Van Houtte, V. (2015). Are girls more resilient to gender-conformity pressure? The association between gender-conformity pressure and academic self-efficacy. *Sex Roles, 73,* 1–15. https://doi.org/10.1007/s11199-015-0509-6.

20. Busching, R., & Krahé, B. (2018). The contagious effect of deviant behavior in adolescence: A longitudinal multilevel study. *Social Psychological and Personality Science, 9,* 815–824. https://doi.org/10.1177/1948550617725151.

21. Birkett, M., & Espelage, D. L. (2015). Homophobic name-calling, peer-groups, and masculinity: The socialization of homophobic behavior in adolescents. *Social Development, 24,* 184–205. https://doi.org/ 10.1111/sode.12085.

22. Laing, T. (2017). Black masculinities expressed through, and constrained by, brotherhood. *Journal of Men's Studies, 25,* 168–197. https://doi.org/10.1177/ 1060826516661186.

23. Birkett, M., & Espelage, D. L. (2015). Homophobic name-calling, peer-groups, and masculinity: The socialization of homophobic behavior in adolescents. *Social Development, 24,* 184–205. https://doi.org/10.1111/sode.12085.

24. Page 587 in: Mohr, R. D. (2014/1988). Anti-gay stereotypes. In P. S. Rothenberg, & K. S. Mayhew (Eds.), *Race, class, and gender in the United States* (pp. 585–591). Worth Publishers.

25. Vandello, J. A., & Bosson, J. K. (2013). Hard won and easily lost: A review and synthesis of theory and research on precarious manhood. *Psychology of Men & Masculinity, 14*(2), 101–113. https://doi.org/10.1037/a0029826.

26. Saucier, D. A., Till, D. F., Miller, S. S., O'Dea, C. J., & Andres, E. (2015). Slurs against masculinity: Masculine honor beliefs and men's reactions to slurs. *Language Sciences, 52,* 108–120. http://dx.doi.org/10.1016/j.langsci.2014.09.006.

27. Vandello, J. A., & Bosson, J. K. (2013). Hard won and easily lost: A review and synthesis of theory and research on precarious manhood. *Psychology of Men & Masculinity*, *14*(2), 101–113. https://doi.org/10.1037/a0029826.

28. Vandello, J. A., & Bosson, J. K. (2013). Hard won and easily lost: A review and synthesis of theory and research on precarious manhood. *Psychology of Men & Masculinity*, *14*(2), 101–113. https://doi.org/10.1037/a0029826.

29. Vandello, J. A., & Bosson, J. K. (2013). Hard won and easily lost: A review and synthesis of theory and research on precarious manhood. *Psychology of Men & Masculinity*, *14*(2), 101–113. https://doi.org/10.1037/a0029826.

30. Vandello, J. A., & Bosson, J. K. (2013). Hard won and easily lost: A review and synthesis of theory and research on precarious manhood. *Psychology of Men & Masculinity*, *14*(2), 101–113. https://doi.org/10.1037/a0029826.

31. Vandello, J. A., & Bosson, J. K. (2013). Hard won and easily lost: A review and synthesis of theory and research on precarious manhood. *Psychology of Men & Masculinity*, *14*(2), 101–113. https://doi.org/10.1037/a0029826.

32. Vandello, J. A., & Bosson, J. K. (2013). Hard won and easily lost: A review and synthesis of theory and research on precarious manhood. *Psychology of Men & Masculinity*, *14*(2), 101–113. https://doi.org/10.1037/a0029826.

33. Vandello, J. A., & Bosson, J. K. (2013). Hard won and easily lost: A review and synthesis of theory and research on precarious manhood. *Psychology of Men & Masculinity*, *14*(2), 101–113. https://doi.org/10.1037/a0029826.

34. Vandello, J. A., & Bosson, J. K. (2013). Hard won and easily lost: A review and synthesis of theory and research on precarious manhood. *Psychology of Men & Masculinity*, *14*(2), 101–113. https://doi.org/10.1037/a0029826.

35. Katz, J. (2019). *The macho paradox: Why some men hurt women and how all men can help*. Sourcebooks.

36. Snyder, R. L. (2019). *No visible bruises: What we don't know about domestic violence can kill us*. Bloomsbury.

37. Vandello, J. A., & Bosson, J. K. (2013). Hard won and easily lost: A review and synthesis of theory and research on precarious manhood. *Psychology of Men & Masculinity*, *14*(2), 101–113. https://doi.org/10.1037/a0029826.

38. Katz, J. (2019). *The macho paradox: Why some men hurt women and how all men can help*. Sourcebooks.

39. Leone, R. M., Parrott, D. J., Swartout, K. M. (2017). When is it "manly to intervene? Examining the effects of a misogynistic peer norm on bystander intervention for sexual aggression. *Psychology of Violence*, *7*, 286–295. https://doi.org/10.1037/vio0000055.

40. Rosenberg, A., Gates, A., Richmond, K., Sinno, S. (2017). It's not a joke: Masculinity ideology and homophobic language. *Psychology of Men & Masculinity*, *18*, 293–300. https://doi.org/10.1037/men0000063.

41. Poteat, V. P., Espelage, D. L., & Koenig, B. W. (2009). Willingness to remain friends and attend school with lesbian and gay peers: Relational expressions of prejudice among heterosexual youth. *Journal of Youth and Adolescence*, *38*(7), 952–962. https://doi.org/10.1007/s10964-009-9416-x.

42. Poteat, V. P., & Vecho, O. (2016). Who intervenes against homophobic behavior? Attributes that distinguish active bystanders. *Journal of School Psychology, 54*, 17–28. https://doi.org/10.1016/j.jsp.2015.10.002.

43. Herek, G. M. (2000). The psychology of sexual prejudice. *Current Directions in Psychological Science, 9*(1), 19–22. https://doi.org/10.1111/1467-8721.00051.

44. Benner, A. D., Crosnoe, R., & Eccles, J. S. (2015). Schools, peers, and prejudice in adolescence. *Journal of Research on Adolescence, 25*(1), 173–188. https://doi.org/10.1111/jora.12106.

45. Gardiner, B., Mansfield, M., Anderson, I., Holder, J., Louter, D., & Ulmanu, M. (2016, April 12). The dark side of Guardian comments. *The Guardian.* https://www.theguardian.com/technology/2016/apr/12/the-dark-side-of-guardian-comments.

46. Fileborn, B. (2018, April 17). How misogyny, narcissism and a desperate need for power make men abuse women online. *The Conversation.* http://theconversation.com/how-misogyny-narcissism-and-a-desperate-need-for-power-make-men-abuse-women-online-95054.

47. DeKeseredy, W. S., & Schwartz, M. D. (2016). Thinking sociologically about image-based sexual abuse: The contribution of male peer support theory. *Sexualization, Media, and Society, 2*(4). https://doi.org/10.1177/2374623816684692.

48. Cole, K. K. (2015). "It's like she's eager to be verbally abused": Twitter, trolls, and (en)gendering disciplinary rhetoric. *Feminist Media Studies, 15*(2), 356–358. https://doi.org/10.1080/14680777.2015.1008750.

49. Jane, E. A. (2014). "Back to the kitchen, cunt": Speaking the unspeakable about online misogyny. *Continuum: Journal of Media & Cultural Studies, 28*(4), 558–570. https://doi.org/10.1080/10304312.2014.924479.

50. Ebert, R. (2005, June 24). Ebert's walk of fame remarks. *Roger Ebert.* https://www.rogerebert.com/rogers-journal/eberts-walk-of-fame-remarks.

51. Watson, A. (2019, June 3). Weekly hours spent streaming to a TV among kids in the U.S. 2016-2018. *Statista.* https://www.statista.com/statistics/949963/hours-spent-streaming-tv-children-us/.

52. Rock, C. (2016, February 28). Chris Rock's opening Oscar monologue: A transcript. *The New York Times.* https://www.nytimes.com/2016/02/29/movies/chris-rock-monologue.html.

53. Paceley, M. S., & Flynn, K. (2012). Media representations of bullying toward queer youth: Gender, race, and age discrepancies. *Journal of LGBT Youth, 9*(4), 340–356. https://doi.org/10.1080/19361653.2012.714187.

54. Oliver, M. B. (2003). African American men as "criminal and dangerous": Implications of media portrayals of crime on the "criminalization" of African American men. *Journal of African American Studies, 7*(2), 3–18. https://doi.org/10.1007/s12111-003-1006-5.

55. Dixon, T. L. (2017). Good guys are still always in white? Positive change and continued misrepresentation of race and crime on local television news. *Communication Research, 44*(6), 775–792. https://doi.org/10.1177/0093650215579223.

56. Chiricos, T., & Eschholz, S. (2002). The racial and ethnic typification of crime and the criminal typification of race and ethnicity in local television news. *Journal*

of Research in Crime and Delinquency, 39(4), 400–420. https://doi.org/10.1177/002242702237286.

57. Dixon, T. L., & Williams, C. L. (2015). The changing misrepresentation of race and crime on network and cable news. *Journal of Communication, 65*(1), 24–39. https://doi.org/10.1111/jcom.12133.

58. Anti-Defamation League. (2019, January 23*). Right-wing extremism linked to every 2018 extremist murder in the U.S., ADL finds.* https://www.adl.org/news/press-releases/right-wing-extremism-linked-to-every-2018-extremist-murder-in-the-us-adl-finds.

59. Swan, B. W. (2020, September 4). DHS draft document: White supremacists are greatest terror threat. *Politico.* https://www.politico.com/news/2020/09/04/White-supremacists-terror-threat-dhs-409236.

60. Levin, B., & Grisham, K. (2016). *Special status report. Hate crime in the United States.* Center for the study of hate and extremism. https://big.assets.huffingtonpost.com/SPECIALSTATUSREPORTv5.pdf.

61. Prosise, T. O., & Johnson, A. (2004). Law enforcement and crime on Cops and World's Wildest Police Videos: Anecdotal form and the justification of racial profiling. *Western Journal of Communication, 68*(1), 72–91. https://doi.org/10.1080/10570310409374789.

62. Prosise, T. O., & Johnson, A. (2004). Law enforcement and crime on Cops and World's Wildest Police Videos: Anecdotal form and the justification of racial profiling. *Western Journal of Communication, 68*(1), 72–91. https://doi.org/10.1080/10570310409374789.

63. Prosise, T. O., & Johnson, A. (2004). Law enforcement and crime on Cops and World's Wildest Police Videos: Anecdotal form and the justification of racial profiling. *Western Journal of Communication, 68*(1), 72–91. https://doi.org/10.1080/10570310409374789.

64. NYCLU. (2019, March). Stop-and-frisk in the de Blasio Era. https://www.nyclu.org/sites/default/files/field_documents/20190314_nyclu_stopfrisk_singles.pdf.

65. Garfield, B. (Host). (2019, October 25). What "Running from Cops" learned from "Cops" [Audio podcast episode]. In *When they come for you.* WNYC Studios. https://www.wnycstudios.org/podcasts/otm/segments/what-running-cops-learned-cops.

66. Prosise, T. O., & Johnson, A. (2004). Law enforcement and crime on Cops and World's Wildest Police Videos: Anecdotal form and the justification of racial profiling. *Western Journal of Communication, 68*(1), 72–91. https://doi.org/10.1080/10570310409374789.

67. For a discussion of the tendency to assume criminal suspects are guilty even when they are not, see Chapter 2 in: Anderson, K. J. (2010). *Benign bigotry: The psychology of subtle prejudice.* Cambridge University Press.

68. Whitehead, S. N. (2014). Cops and the performance of white masculine decline. *Race, Gender & Class, 21,* 174–188. https://www.jstor.org/stable/43496991.

69. Whitehead, S. N. (2014). Cops and the performance of white masculine decline. *Race, Gender & Class, 21*(3/4), 174. https://www.jstor.org/stable/43496991.

70. Oliver, M. B. (1996). Influences of authoritarianism and portrayals of race on Caucasian viewers' responses to reality-based crime dramas. *Communication Reports, 9,* 141–150.

71. Oliver, M. B. (1996). Influences of authoritarianism and portrayals of race on Caucasian viewers' responses to reality-based crime dramas. *Communication Reports, 9*, 141–150.

72. Graduationwisdom.com. https://www.graduationwisdom.com/speeches/0069-streep.htm.

73. Townsend, M. (2020). Where we are on TV: 2019–2020. https://www.glaad.org/sites/default/files/GLAAD%20WHERE%20WE%20ARE%20ON%20TV%202019%202020.pdf.

74. Tukachinsky, R., Mastro, D., & Yarchi, M. (2015). Documenting portrayals of race/ethnicity on primetime television of a 20-year span and their association with national-level racial/ethnic attitudes. *Journal of Social Issues, 71*(1), 17–38. https://doi.org/10.1111/josi.12094.

75. Townsend, M. (2020). Where we are on TV: 2019–2020. https://www.glaad.org/sites/default/files/GLAAD%20WHERE%20WE%20ARE%20ON%20TV%202019%202020.pdf.

76. Townsend, M. (2020). Where we are on TV: 2019–2020. https://www.glaad.org/sites/default/files/GLAAD%20WHERE%20WE%20ARE%20ON%20TV%202019%202020.pdf.

77. Tukachinsky, R., Mastro, D., & Yarchi, M. (2015). Documenting portrayals of race/ethnicity on primetime television of a 20-year span and their association with national-level racial/ethnic attitudes. *Journal of Social Issues, 71*(1), 17–38. https://doi.org/10.1111/josi.12094.

78. Tukachinsky, R., Mastro, D., & Yarchi, M. (2015). Documenting portrayals of race/ethnicity on primetime television of a 20-year span and their association with national-level racial/ethnic attitudes. *Journal of Social Issues, 71*(1), 17–38. https://doi.org/10.1111/josi.12094.

79. Rivadeneyra, R. (2011). Gender and race portrayals on Spanish-language television. *Sex Roles, 65*(3–4), 208. https://doi.org/10.1007/s11199-011-0010-9.

80. Behm-Morawitz, E. (2017). Examining the intersection of race and gender in video game advertising. *Journal of Marketing Communications, 23*(3), 220–239. https://doi.org/10.1080/13527266.2014.914562.

81. Behm-Morawitz, E. (2017). Examining the intersection of race and gender in video game advertising. *Journal of Marketing Communications, 23*(3), 220–239. https://doi.org/10.1080/13527266.2014.914562.

82. Smith, S. L., Choueiti, M., Pieper, K. (2016). Inclusion or invisibility? Comprehensive Annenberg report on diversity and entertainment. USC Annenberg School for Communication and Journalism.

83. Neville, C., & Anastasio, P. (2018). Fewer, younger, but increasingly powerful: How portrayals of women, age, and power have changed from 2002 to 2016 in the 50 top-grossing U.S. films. *Sex Roles, 80*(7–8), 503. https://doi.org/10.1007/s11199-018-0945-1.

84. Lauzen, M. M., & Dozier, D. M. (2005). Recognition and respect revisited: Portrayals of age and gender in prime-time television. *Mass Communication & Society, 8*(3), 241–256. https://doi.org/10.1207/s15327825mcs0803_4.

85. Lauzen, M. M., & Dozier, D. M. (2005). Maintaining the double standard: Portrayals of age and gender in popular films. *Sex Roles, 52*(7–8), 437. https://doi.org/10.1007/s11199-005-3710-1.

86. Neville, C., & Anastasio, P. (2018). Fewer, younger, but increasingly powerful: How portrayals of women, age, and power have changed from 2002 to 2016 in the 50 top-grossing U.S. films. *Sex Roles: A Journal of Research, 80*(7–8), 503. https://doi.org/10.1007/s11199-018-0945-1.

87. Greenberg, B. S., & Worrell, T. R. (2007). New faces on television: A 12-season replication. *Howard Journal of Communications, 18*(4), 277–290. https://doi.org/10.1080/10646170701653651.

88. Lauzen, M. M., & Dozier, D. M. (2005). Maintaining the double standard: Portrayals of age and gender in popular films. *Sex Roles, 52*(7–8), 437. https://doi.org/10.1007/s11199-005-3710-1.

Lauzen, M. M., & Dozier, D. M. (2005). Recognition and respect revisited: Portrayals of age and gender in prime-time television. *Mass Communication & Society, 8*(3), 241–256. https://doi.org/10.1207/s15327825mcs0803_4.

89. Neville, C., & Anastasio, P. (2018). Fewer, younger, but increasingly powerful: How portrayals of women, age, and power have changed from 2002 to 2016 in the 50 top-grossing U.S. films. *Sex Roles, 80*(7–8), 503. https://doi.org/10.1007/s11199-018-0945-1.

90. Paek, H.-J., Nelson, M. R., & Vilela, A. M. (2011). Examination of gender-role portrayals in television advertising across seven countries. *Sex Roles, 64*(3–4), 192–207. https://doi.org/10.1007/s11199-010-9850-y.

91. Parrott, S., & Parrott, C. T. (2015). US television's "mean world" for White women: The portrayal of gender and race on fictional crime dramas. *Sex Roles, 73*(1–2), 70–82. https://doi.org/10.1007/s11199-015-0505-x.

92. Parrott, S., & Parrott, C. T. (2015). US television's "mean world" for White women: The portrayal of gender and race on fictional crime dramas. *Sex Roles, 73*(1–2), 70–82. https://doi.org/10.1007/s11199-015-0505-x.

93. Petrosky, E., Blair, J. M., Betz, C. J., Fowler, K. A., Jack, S. P. D., & Lyons, B. H. (2017, July 21). Racial and ethnic differences in homicides of adult women and the role of intimate partner violence–United States, 2003-2014. Centers for Disease Control and Prevention. https://www.cdc.gov/mmwr/volumes/66/wr/mm6628a1.htm?s_cid=mm6628a1_w#T1_down.

94. Gonzalez, A. Q., & Koestner, R. (2005). Parental preference for sex of newborn as reflected in positive affect in birth announcements. *Sex Roles, 52*(5–6), 407–411. https://doi.org/10.1007/s11199-005-2683-4.

95. Bridges, J. (1993). Pink or blue: Gender-stereotypic perceptions of infants as conveyed by birth congratulations cards. *Psychology of Women Quarterly, 17*(2), 193–205. https://doi.org/10.1111/j.1471-6402.1993.tb00444.x.

Willer, L. R. (2001). Warning: Welcome to your world baby, gender message enclosed. An analysis of gender messages in birth congratulation cards. *Women and Language, 1*, 16.

96. Bridges, J. (1993). Pink or blue: Gender-stereotypic perceptions of infants as conveyed by birth congratulations cards. *Psychology of Women Quarterly, 17*(2), 193–205. https://doi.org/10.1111/j.1471-6402.1993.tb00444.x.

97. Bridges, J. (1993). Pink or blue: Gender-stereotypic perceptions of infants as conveyed by birth congratulations cards. *Psychology of Women Quarterly, 17*(2), 193–205. https://doi.org/10.1111/j.1471-6402.1993.tb00444.x.
   Willer, L. R. (2001). Warning: Welcome to your world baby, gender message enclosed. An analysis of gender messages in birth congratulation cards. *Women and Language, 1,* 16.

98. Bridges, J. (1993). Pink or blue: Gender-stereotypic perceptions of infants as conveyed by birth congratulations cards. *Psychology of Women Quarterly, 17*(2), 193–205. https://doi.org/10.1111/j.1471-6402.1993.tb00444.x.
   Willer, L. R. (2001). Warning: Welcome to your world baby, gender message enclosed. An analysis of gender messages in birth congratulation cards. *Women and Language, 1,* 16.

99. Fausto-Sterling, A. (2015). How else can we study sex differences in early infancy? *Developmental Psychobiology, 58*(1), 5–16. https://doi.org/10.1002/dev.21345.

100. Auster, C. J., & Auster-Gussman, L. A. (2016). Contemporary mother's day and father's day greeting cards: A reflection of traditional ideologies of motherhood and fatherhood? *Journal of Family Issues, 37*(9), 1294–1326. https://doi.org/10.1177/0192513X14528711.

101. Mastro, D., Lapinski, M. K., Kopacz, M. A., & Behm-Morawitz, E. (2009). The influence of exposure to depictions of race and crime in TV news on viewer's social judgments. *Journal of Broadcasting & Electronic Media, 53*(4), 615–635. https://doi.org/10.1080/08838150903310534.

102. Hurley, R. J., Jensen, J., Weaver, A., & Dixon, T. (2015). Viewer ethnicity matters: Black crime in tv news and its impact on decisions regarding public policy. *Journal of Social Issues, 71*(1), 155–170. https://doi.org/10.1111/josi.12102.

103. Ramasubramanian, S. (2011). The impact of stereotypical versus counterstereotypical media exemplars on racial attitudes, causal attributions, and support for affirmative action. *Communication Research, 38*(4), 497–516. https://doi.org/10.1177/0093650210384854.

104. Dill, K. E., & Burgess, M. C. R. (2013). Influence of black masculinity game exemplars on social judgments. *Simulation & Gaming, 44*(4), 562–585. https://doi.org/10.1177/1046878112449958.

105. Ramasubramanian, S. (2011). The impact of stereotypical versus counterstereotypical media exemplars on racial attitudes, causal attributions, and support for affirmative action. *Communication Research, 38*(4), 497–516. https://doi.org/10.1177/0093650210384854.

106. Giaccardi, S., Ward, L. M., Seabrook, R. C., Manago, A., & Lippman, J. (2016). Media and modern manhood: Testing associations between media consumption and

young men's acceptance of traditional gender ideologies *Sex Roles*, *75*(3–4), 151. https://doi.org/10.1007/s11199-016-0588-z.

107. Emmers-Sommer, T. M., Pauley, P., Hanzal, A., & Triplett, L. (2006). Love, suspense, sex, and violence: Men's and women's film predilections, exposure to sexually violent media, and their relationship to rape myth acceptance. *Sex Roles*, *55*(5–6), 311–320. https://doi.org/10.1007/s11199-006-9085-0.

108. Emmers-Sommer, T. M., Pauley, P., Hanzal, A., & Triplett, L. (2006). Love, suspense, sex, and violence: Men's and women's film predilections, exposure to sexually violent media, and their relationship to rape myth acceptance. *Sex Roles*, *55*(5–6), 311–320. https://doi.org/10.1007/s11199-006-9085-0.

109. For a discussion on representations of rape (and rape myths) in popular culture, see: hooks, b. (1996). *Reel to real: Race, class and sex at the movies.* Routledge. .

110. Pennell, H., & Behm-Morawitz, E. (2015). The empowering (super) heroine? The effects of sexualized female characters in superhero films on women. *Sex Roles*, *72*(5–6), 211–220. https://doi.org/10.1007/s11199-015-0455-3.

111. Rousseau, A., Rodgers, R. F., & Eggermont, S. (2019). A short-term longitudinal exploration of the impact of TV exposure on objectifying attitudes toward women in early adolescent boys. *Sex Roles*, *80*(3–4), 186–199. https://doi.org/10.1007/s11199-018-0925-5.

112. Good, J. J., Woodzicka, J. A., & Wingfield, L. C. (2010). The effects of gender stereotypic and counter-stereotypic textbook images on science performance. *Journal of Social Psychology*, *150*(2), 132–147. https://doi.org/10.1080/00224540903366552.

113. See for instance: Potter, E. F., & Rosser, S. V. (1992). Factors in life science textbooks that may deter girls' interest in science. *Journal of Research in Science Teaching*, *29*(7), 669–686. https://doi.org/10.1002/tea.3660290705.

114. Carli, L. L., Alawa, L., Lee, Y., Zhao, B., & Kim, E. (2016). Stereotypes about gender and science: Women not equal scientists. *Psychology of Women Quarterly*, *40*(2), 244–260. https://doi.org/10.1177/0361684315622645.

115. Munson-Warnken, M. (2017). The high cost of "girl books" for young adolescent boys. *Reading Teacher*, *70*(5), 583–593. https://doi.org/10.1002/trtr.1562.

116. Vandello, J. A., & Bosson, J. K. (2013). Hard won and easily lost: A review and synthesis of theory and research on precarious manhood. *Psychology of Men & Masculinity*, *14*(2), 101–113. https://doi.org/10.1037/a0029826.

117. Snyder, R. L. (2019). *No visible bruises: What we don't know about domestic violence can kill us.* Bloomsbury.

118. Snyder, R. L. (2019). *No visible bruises: What we don't know about domestic violence can kill us.* Bloomsbury.

119. Rosenberg, A., Gates, A., Richmond, K., Sinno, S. (2017). It's not a joke: Masculinity ideology and homophobic language. *Psychology of Men & Masculinity*, *18*(4), 293–300. https://doi.org/10.1037/men0000063.

120. Benner, A. D., Crosnoe, R., & Eccles, J. S. (2015). Schools, peers, and prejudice in adolescence. *Journal of Research on Adolescence, 25*(1), 173–188. https://doi.org/10.1111/jora.12106.

121. Craig, S. L., McInroy, L., McCready, L. T., & Alaggia, R. (2015). Media: A catalyst for resilience in lesbian, gay, bisexual, transgender, and queer youth. *Journal of LGBT Youth, 12*(3), 254–275. https://doi.org/10.1080/19361653.2015.1040193.

122. Murrar, S., & Brauer, M. (2018). Entertainment-education effectively reduces prejudice. *Group Processes & Intergroup Relations, 21*(7), 1053–1077. https://doi.org/10.1177/1368430216682350.

5

Entitlement Makes People Ignorant, Egocentric, and Mean

It's a great time to be alive if you're dumb and mean.
— Comedian Andy Richter[1]

In the latter half of the twentieth century, the United States saw in politics a growing movement toward simplistic and shallow analysis and away from expertise. This trend has been referred to as a rise in anti-intellectualism. Educated and thoughtful people have been mocked and ridiculed and are disparagingly referred to as "elites." In contrast, the ignorant and incurious are popular enough to be elected president of the United States of America. In the United States, the Republican Party owns anti-intellectualism.[2] Anti-intellectualism has been a winning strategy for Republicans who have denied the science of evolution, the human element in climate change, and public health research on virus transmission. Abstinence-only education is a method of pregnancy prevention that tells young people to simply refrain from sex. This policy is not supported by any major medical association, as it increases teen pregnancy and does not protect against sexually trans-mitted infections.[3] And yet, it is a substantive piece of the Republican Party agenda, and state legislatures have poured millions of dollars into these failed programs.[4] The phony "birther" controversy epitomizes the anti-intellectual movement that helped Donald Trump gain national attention, setting the stage for his win in 2016.

Conservatives over the last 30 years have ridiculed liberals with advanced degrees and have instead favored anti-intellectual giants such as Ronald Reagan, George W. Bush, and, of course, Donald Trump. Bookishness is for weaklings (and Democrats) and the strain of hypermasculinity that makes ignorance manly has so infiltrated the modern Republican Party it could be part of the Republican Party platform.[5] In Chapter 3 we saw a school-age version of this last point when we found that, for boys, appearing tough and threatening is incompatible with academic engagement.[6] Reagan, Bush, and

Enraged, Rattled, and Wronged. Kristin J. Anderson, Oxford University Press. © Oxford University Press 2021.
DOI: 10.1093/oso/9780197578438.003.0006

Trump were disproportionately popular with voters who were White men. These three men could be contrasted with Democratic men of the same time period who were seen as smart, experienced, and articulate, and yet they were characterized as nerds and wimps: Jimmy Carter, John Kerry, Michael Dukakis, and Barack Obama.

As president, Donald Trump took the denigration of experience and expertise to new depths by appointing to cabinet positions individuals who have no experience in the field to which they were appointed: the person who ran the Department of Education had little experience with public education; a surgeon with no experience in public housing headed housing and urban development for the federal government; a top diplomat did not believe in diplomacy; and an antienvironmentalist crusader was assigned to lead the Environmental Protection Agency. Whatever metric Trump used to choose these people, experience and expertise was nowhere on the list. And of course, Donald Trump was elected with no experience in politics, government, or public service.[7] Some have argued that the Republican embrace of anti-intellectualism is disingenuous, a put on.[8] It's a con to get the votes of uneducated, White working-class voters. Whether Reagan, Bush, and even Donald Trump were actually ignorant is beside the point. Anti-intellectualism—as an ideology, a performance, or a political tactic—works for Republican politicians because Republican voters vote for it.

So this is the political and cultural era in which we find ourselves. This chapter discusses how power and privilege increase entitlement allowing people to think and behave ignorantly, egocentrically, inconsiderately, and reactively. Power is often seen through influence by coercion and threats, and power can certainly take these forms. But power and privilege entitle the person to behave in other unfortunate ways because entitled individuals are allowed to engage in shoddy information processing. Compared to those who are marginalized, dominant group members tend to think in shortcuts, behaving inconsiderately, egocentrically, and unempathically. Entitlement's role in dehumanizing the Other and ignoring other people's suffering is also explored in this chapter. Entitled people tend to think their perspective is more important than others' and that their own thoughts and lives are more valuable. They are also hypersensitive to being challenged and dismissed. Therefore, the latter part of this chapter considers US honor culture and blind patriotism. These two concepts help explain how White men hold onto their power and privilege and yet how desperate and panic-stricken they become when their manhood is challenged.

The Convenient Cluelessness of Entitlement

*You cannot lynch me and keep me in ghettos without becoming some-
thing monstrous yourselves. And furthermore you give me a terrifying
advantage. You never had to look at me. I had to look at you. I know
more about you than you know about me.*

—Writer James Baldwin[9]

Tony Schwartz, the ghostwriter who penned Donald Trump's bestseller *The
Art of the Deal*, has described Trump as having little attention span and "a
stunning level of superficial knowledge and plain ignorance."[10] Schwartz
said, "I seriously doubt that Trump has ever read a book straight through in
his adult life."[11] Power entitles people to be uninformed.[12] As we know from
Chapter 1, compared to those without power, power holders experience fewer
constraints on their behavior and fewer challenges to their thinking. Thus,
they do not need to scrutinize their decisions and behavior because they are
less likely to be held to account. In contrast, those without power are required
to consider consequences of their actions and ponder their judgments because they have to; often their employment and their safety make them vig-
ilant in a way that power holders do not need to be. Power holders are freer
to stereotype. Power holders can be careful and deliberate in their thinking
when motivated, but they are quite comfortable relying on stereotypes
when evaluating people—especially if those they are evaluating have little
power. Research studies on attention find that power holders pay attention to
stereotype-consistent information—they encode and store information that
matches their stereotypes—and ignore information that contradicts their
stereotypes. In contrast, those without power are more likely to attend evenly
to all information. And from the power holder's perspective, why not stereotype? Stereotyping others doesn't really cost power holders anything. Their
power entitles them to stereotype with few consequences. They feel comfortable about how they view the world. They feel prouder and have higher self-
esteem than powerless people. They tend to pay attention to positive things
about themselves and ignore negative information. Power holders are more
likely to be guided by their whims than powerless people who tend to deliberate more. Those who lack power are more likely to override stereotyped
thinking.[13] They are more careful because they have to be.

When we think of social and cultural power outside the laboratory, that is,
when we put things in terms of already-existing dominant and subordinated

groups, we can see how dominant group members know relatively little about subordinate groups, but subordinate groups are compelled to be well-informed about dominant groups. The quotation from James Baldwin at the beginning of this section reflects this power dynamic. For instance, an administrative assistant knows a lot about her boss—when the boss is in a good mood, what they order for lunch, how they talk to their spouse on the phone. A boss knows little about their administrative assistant. They know little about her preferences and wishes, and her personal life—the boss doesn't need to. And this arrangement might be preferable for the boss as this lack of personalization allows them to view employees as expendable and exchangeable. This dynamic undergirds W.E.B. DuBois's notion of "double consciousness," by which African Americans are "gifted with second-sight in this American world."[14] It also informs Gloria Anzaldúa's concept of *la facultad*: "the capacity to see in surface phenomena the meaning of deeper realities, to see the deep structure below the surface. . . . Those who do not feel psychologically safe or physically safe in the world are more apt to develop this sense. Those who are pounced on the most have it the strongest—the females, the homosexuals of all races, the darkskinned, the outcast, the persecuted, the marginalized, the foreign."[15] The flip side of this capacity, this perceptiveness, is the ignorance afforded to the powerful and the entitled.

Power entitles dominant group members to be ignorant of the powerless but not vice versa. Aside from one's livelihood not depending on what powerless people are like, another reason powerholders know little about the powerless is their lack of representation in media. A good number and variety of images of the dominant group are available through television, film, magazines, books, and news sites. In schools, dominant group members' history, progress, and influence tend to be showcased. A meme shared on social media a few years back said simply, "White privilege is your history being part of the core curriculum and mine being taught as an elective."[16] Everyone is required to know about the preferred group's history—the history of marginalized groups is not required. In contrast to the amount of information in media about dominant groups, there are relatively few depictions of subordinated groups as main characters, and the depictions tend to be negative,[17] the roles unimportant, resulting in the dominant group members having somewhat cartoonish views of subordinated groups.

There are other ways power entitles a person to be ignorant. For example, power can alter one's sense of time. Power holders are more likely to underestimate the time it takes to accomplish a task compared to those without power. Powerful people are not actually more likely to complete a task quickly; it's just that their predictions are more likely to be off.[18] This fact might seem trivial, but imagine how this might work in an organization. Supervisors and managers are less likely to have accurate information about how long it will take to complete a project than subordinates, and yet subordinates are evaluated on how long it takes to accomplish a task. Power and entitlement could even explain the gender difference in divorce filings. Among heterosexual couples, women initiate about 70% of all divorces.[19] There are also reports in the popular press that many men are blindsided by divorce—they just do not see it coming.[20] There could be all kinds of reasons for this gender difference. Perhaps men are generally more satisfied in a marriage than women are. Perhaps women's complaints to their husbands are too subtle for husbands to recognize. Or perhaps the relative power of men to women outside the marriage, if not within it, teaches some men that they do not have to pay attention to the signs of a declining relationship. After all, as we found in Chapter 3, gender socialization teaches girls and women that attending to relationships is their domain.[21] It would make sense then that some men do not see the early cracks in a declining relationship the way women are taught to.

Sexual Misconduct and the (Myth of the) Male Bumbler

As seen in Chapters 1 and 3, power and privilege allow dominant group members to be overconfident in their abilities in various domains, thinking they are smarter than they actually are. Paradoxically, they may be misguided and even less accurate in their actual observations, and this is because they are not compelled to be. They feel entitled to not pay attention to those with less status, to not be concerned with marginalized people. One issue that brings these patterns to light with such high stakes is men's sexual harassment and sexual assault of women. The #MeToo movement that rose to global attention in 2017 was a reckoning for some powerful men who had gotten away with groping, assaulting, and raping women for years and sometimes decades. Several high-profile men were rightly forced to account (although almost none of them faced criminal penalties). Enter the convenient bumbler. Emma Gray[22] writes about men "misremembering" violating women. Gray argues, when men feel entitled to women's bodies, their bad behavior feels normal, even routine, to them. When you are used to taking advantage of people, taking advantage of someone is not noteworthy. In fact, it doesn't even feel like taking advantage. So why would an entitled man remember something exploitative he did years before? A brutal irony of sexual assault and harassment is that the traumas that frequently determine the trajectory of survivors' lives are often unremarkable to the men who have inflicted them. This may be why some men seem shocked when they are asked to answer for their actions. When perpetrators respond to claims against them with "nothing happened," they may, in many cases, be lying. But an alternative explanation offered by Emma Gray is that when some men say, "nothing happened," it's not just a denial—it's that they truly believe the incident was not a big deal and so trivial that they do not remember it.[23]

Inga Muscio describes her fear-driven upbringing by a mother who, she learns only in adulthood, had been raped at the age of 9 years old, profoundly shaping her and her daughters' lives. Muscio writes that "the two men who raped our mother have no idea either of us exist on the planet to have been raised under the shadow of their action."[24] The perpetrator has learned that he is entitled, even expected, to treat women in these ways. What crushes a woman's self-esteem, her ability to trust, her relationships, her sexual life, her sleep, and her ability to move freely through the world may mean nothing to the person who caused it all.

In an article entitled "The Myth of the Male Bumbler,"[25] Lili Loofbourow writes that the male bumbler is astonished to discover that men have power relative to women, that he has ever had power over anyone, let alone that he was perceived as using it. *What power* he says. *Who, me?* Loofbourow says there's a reason for this sudden claim of cluelessness: The bumbler's ignorance exonerates him. And ignorance and incompetence are less damaging than malice. "The bumbler takes one of our culture's most muscular myths—that men are clueless—and weaponizes it into an alibi," writes Loofbourow. "Our culture makes this script available. We need to shed the exculpatory scripts that have mysteriously enabled all these incompetent bumblers to become rich, successful, and admired even as they maintain that they're moral infants." It is the epitome of entitlement that a person's cruel and exploitative behavior can be culturally framed in this way while his victim constructs her life around the damage he has done.

Alongside the male bumbler are many articles in the popular press written for men about how to read women's "confusing" signals. It's almost as if these women—these mysterious creatures—use such secret language to convey their desires that it requires a Rosetta Stone or a team of writers from *Men's*

Health magazine to decode their signals. One article begins with the ludi-crous, "In most cases, when a woman gives you mixed signals, she is simply testing to see how confident you really are."[26] Take note of the gendered nature of "signals"—a term rarely attributed to men's communication. That women are believed to deploy "mixed signals" suggests an indirectness, a subtlety that contrasts with men's straightforward and direct communication.

Are women really as confusing as some men claim? Are men really con-founded by women's words? Is it necessary for a woman to say a hard No be-fore a man understands she's not interested in giving him her phone number? In day-to-day interactions, when adults do not want to accept an invitation, do they simply say, No? Advice offered to women to just say No is simplistic and it ignores the sophisticated and complex manner in which both women and men typically conduct refusals in everyday life. It is unusual to just say an unequivocal No in any context. It is precisely women's knowledge of the cul-turally normative ways of doing refusals that makes it challenging for them to simply say No to an unwanted invitation.

Do men understand these same social rules? Research from Rachael O'Byrne and her colleagues says yes.[27] O'Byrne conducted focus groups with heterosexual undergraduate men in Australia to see how they compre-hend and perform refusals. Think about how refusals work in social life. Say a coworker invites you to a dinner party you do not want to attend. Do you simply say, "Nope!"? Or even "No thanks"? No. You don't, because one goal of a refusal is to make it hearable to the recipient while avoiding negative consequences for either the person refusing or the person receiving it. The men in O'Byrne's study were first asked how they would respond if invited to a pub by a friend when they do not want to go. Like adults who live in the world, they come up with all kinds of nuanced responses—they make an excuse, and, for example, they say they *can't* go rather than they *won't* go. People rarely just flat out say No, and those who do don't have much of a so-cial life. These same men are then asked how they would refuse sex. Again, simply saying No is not in their repertoire. They say they are not ready, or that they didn't have this in mind. They would use nonverbal cues too. Instead of pouring a drink and sitting on the sofa, they would turn on the TV. Then the men in the study are asked how they would know a woman isn't inter-ested in sex. She would say it's getting late. She'd ask about calling a ride, and again, body language—she looks at her watch.[28] These are all good strate-gies for politely refusing. And yet, when these same men were presented with an acquaintance rape scenario, several men became confused and made statements such as, "Well, when does no mean no and yes means yes?" and "The perpetrator could actually really be the victim when a woman is throwing themselves on you but later says, 'Well, I said no.'"[29]

Based on these data, men understand and use the same information anybody else would and yet some become curiously confused in this context. So why do some men commit acquaintance rape? Certainly, for most men, it does not result from an innocent misunderstanding of women's ambiguous refusals (and of course many women give *un*ambiguous refusals that are ignored). More likely, it comes from the witting intention of men to engage in coercive sex while, at the same time, not seeing themselves as rapists because they have been taught that they are entitled to sex from women. Imagining themselves confused is their way out of being accountable.

People, women, as well as men, tend to underestimate how difficult it is to reject someone they are not romantically or sexually interested in.[30] Those who have experienced being a target of unwanted advances—again both women and men—are more likely to rate the prospect of rejecting someone they are not interested in as more difficult than those who have not been in that situation. Women report being more likely to have been in that situation than men, so they may have a better appreciation of that difficulty. Requesters seemed to be egocentrically focused on their own fears of rejection and seem oblivious to their target's concerns. This egocentric bias may be exacerbated when the pursuer is in a position of power over a sexual/romantic target.[31] Power generates what Rebecca Solnit describes as a cushion of obliviousness around it.[32] Solnit writes that there is an old truism that knowledge is power, but the converse is also true—that power is often ignorance. The powerful surround themselves in obliviousness in order to avoid the pain of others. For example, knowing the strategies women use to be safe around men is, for men, optional.

Unwitting or willful ignorance can occur in any dominant group, not only among men. For example, White people can be ignorant about racial discrimination in convenient and self-serving ways. If you track opinions about racial equality over decades, you find that White people demonstrate a curious knowledge gap. White individuals are quite accurate at acknowledging *past* racial inequality—say the inequality of the 1970s. However, when their judgment of present-day inequality is measured against actual present-day inequality, their accuracy at correctly evaluating present inequality is dismal.[33] Why the discrepancy between evaluating past and present inequality? Perhaps present-day White people do not have anything to lose in acknowledging past inequality—they can safely imagine they are not responsible for it. However, admitting that inequality exists in the present, when they are beneficiaries of it, suggests that if they care about fairness, they would need to take some action to ameliorate it. Or they may feel guilty about it. Or they may be forced to realize that what they believe they have earned fairly may not be deserved. A noteworthy additional finding from the same study is that high-income Whites are especially inaccurate at evaluating the degree of present-day inequality (low-income African Americans tend to be the most accurate).[34] In other words, White individuals who are the most economically comfortable (and powerful) are the least likely to have accurate knowledge about inequality. Wealth entitles White people to be especially ignorant to racism.

The Egocentrism of Entitlement

Power and privilege entitle people to see the world from their own perspective with few repercussions. Entitled people assume others share their perspective, that their point of view is the only view that makes sense, and that others welcome their opinions. Some men feel entitled to tell women they should smile. Why is that? Why would anyone think that a person walking down a public street minding her own business, trying to get somewhere, would be interested in accommodating a stranger in this way? Men who tell women to smile seem to be conveying their need for women around them (even women they encounter only for a moment) to be unthreatening, to put them at ease, and to make the men feel comfortable and acknowledged. Why do men tell women, but not other men, to smile? Why is it women do not tell men to smile? There may be multiple explanations for this gendered phenomenon. One possibility is that some men have learned that women exist to take care of their needs, to boost them up, to make them feel good, regardless of how the woman doing this emotional labor is actually feeling herself.

Recall that power holders tend to have higher self-esteem, feel prouder, and are more confident in their own judgments, than those without power. They are less likely than powerless people to conform to others' opinions and can be immune from others' advice.[35] They can also be egocentric. One way to examine self-centeredness is to see whether a person can take another's perspective. One study found that when people were asked to draw an "E" on their forehead, those primed for power were more likely to draw it self-oriented, as one is reading it oneself, as opposed to other-oriented, as if another person is reading it.[36] A simple power prime affects whether a person follows an instruction centered on themselves as opposed to the viewer. High-power participants focus too heavily on their own vantage point and are less likely to adjust to others' perspectives.[37]

Think about what you find inspiring. Is it someone's story of courage in the face of terrible odds? Do you think of Nelson Mandela? Greta Thunberg? Who inspires you? If you're a power holder, you are more likely to be inspired by *yourself* than by someone else. That's what was found in a series of studies conducted by Gerben Van Kleef and his colleagues. They found that those who have a high personal sense of power (agreeing to statements such as, "I can get others to do what I want," and "I think I have a great deal of power"), are more likely to derive inspiration from themselves ("I can get really inspired by talking about the things I experience") rather than others ("I find it inspiring to listen to other people's stories").[38] This pattern holds true even in face-to-face conversations when both partners were instructed to talk about an inspiring event. The patterns continued whether participants in studies were primed to feel powerful (*vs.* those primed to feel less powerful) or were asked to think of themselves as powerful (*vs.* those who don't think of themselves as powerful).

Studying the self-centeredness of privileged people can lead to some fun methodological designs and interesting findings. Paul Piff and his colleagues conducted a field study to see whether upper-class individuals (measured by the type of car they drive)[39] behave more selfishly (and illegally) than lower-class individuals.[40] Piff had observers stand near four-way traffic intersections, code the status of the vehicle (e.g., late model Mercedes vs. older Honda Civic), and code whether or not the driver waited their turn before crossing the intersection. Interestingly, luxury car drivers were more likely to cut off others than lower-class drivers—even after controlling for the time of day, the driver's perceived gender and age, and amount of traffic. Piff and his colleagues also found that upper-class drivers were more likely than lower-class individuals to drive through a crosswalk that a pedestrian entered (violating the law). Upper-class people—at least those who drive more expensive cars—seem to feel entitled to drive as though their time is more valuable and perhaps assume that others will accommodate them rather than vice versa. Lower-class drivers seem to not make those assumptions.

If you're rich, others are less likely to be seen as potentially rewarding, threatening, or otherwise worth attending to. Supporting this point with data, one study indicated that social classes differ in the amount of attention their members direct toward other human beings. Researchers supplied participants with wearable technology used to film the visual fields of pedestrians on city streets. Higher-class participants looked less at other people than did lower-class participants.[41] Social networks are a form of insurance as in, if you look out for me, I'll look out for you. However, with economic security, social networks are not a matter of life and death.

Like drivers entitled to violate the law, entitled people tend to think rules do not apply to them. They are actually less likely to follow directions than less-entitled people. When put in scenarios in which they would be given money for following directions and lose money for not, entitled people are less likely to follow directions than nonentitled people—even when following directions is only a minor inconvenience.[42] Entitled people react with anger when they have to follow rules. They would rather incur a personal cost than agree with something they think undermines their autonomy. They do not like to be controlled or managed—probably because they have been able to avoid being controlled and managed. And entitled people tend to assume they can avoid punishment, compared to those who feel less entitled.[43]

Piff conducted another study, this time an experiment on selfishness that provides more insight into the entitlement that accompanies those who are well off relative to others.[44] In this particular study, rather than examine the behavior of upper- and lower-class individuals based on the cars they drive, Piff and his colleagues manipulated class feelings by activating higher- and lower-class mindsets. Participants were asked to compare themselves to people with the most (or least) money, the most (or least) education, and the most (or least) respected jobs, resulting in two groups of people—those who feel better off than others and those who feel worse off than others. This exercise primed for feelings of high social class or low social class. Participants were asked to complete several surveys, and at the end of the study, the researcher made available a jar of candies, ostensibly for children in a nearby room, but informed the participants that they could take some if they wanted. The number of candies they took served as a measure of selfishness. People who were primed to feel better off than others took more candy than those who were primed to feel worse off. A simple temporary prime produced different amounts of candy people felt entitled to. Imagine the entitlement of those who have been better off than others their entire lives. How much candy would they take? Many politicians favor what has been described as "trickle-down economics"—make sure the richest people have the most and that wealth will trickle down through their increased investment to the rest of us. This study suggests that in contrast to heaping more money onto the already-wealthy benefiting society, the well-off just feel entitled to take more.

Another manifestation of entitled egocentrism is the degree to which one engages in self-promotion. In academia, article citations—the number of times a scholar refers to another scholar's work—is a marker of authority on a topic and influence in a field. If an article gets cited by others hundreds of times, it's a good indicator that the author is making a mark on their field. In making tenure and promotion decisions, universities will sometimes use number of citations in decisions about a professor's importance and influence on the field. This study was described in Chapter 2, but it's worth summarizing here. Molly M. King[45] and her colleagues set out to find how often so-called self-citation occurs. *Self-citation* refers to the number of times authors cite their own previous work in an article or book they write. King and her colleagues examined gender patterns in self-citation from a massive database of academic work: 1.5 million research papers in JSTOR, a digital library of academic books and papers. King and her colleagues found a huge difference in self-citation patterns between women and men. Men cite their own papers 56% more than women do. And in recent decades, men have stepped up their self-citation game relative to women: "In the last two decades of our data, men self-cite 70% more than women." This self-citation gap held true across every major academic field the authors studied, including biology, sociology, philosophy, and law. King and her colleagues offer a number of hypotheses for why men may be more likely to cite themselves. For starters, as we now know, men generally have a higher opinion of their own abilities than women do. Additionally, men typically face fewer social penalties for self-promotion. Ambitious women face what has been described as a *dominance penalty* in the form of being disliked relative to ambitious men.[46] A similar reaction comes to people of color, in the form of a *hubris penalty*, when they appear (too) confident even when that behavior is similar to White men.[47]

Whitesplaining and Mansplaining

Chapter 2 contains a quotation from cartoon in *New Yorker* magazine. In the cartoon, a woman and man are sitting at a table each with a drink. The man talks while the woman sits silent. The quote below the image says, "Let me interrupt your expertise with my confidence."[48] The cartoon illustrates how, for some people, confidence is a proxy for their expertise—when it should not be. The study on academic men's proclivity toward citing themselves in their own work exposes a paradox with the bumbling male described earlier in this chapter. Some men claim ignorance when they might get in trouble, but some also claim knowledge when they don't have it. Donald Trump claimed to be an expert on terrorism ("I know more about ISIS than the generals do."),[49] renewable energy ("I know more about renewables than any human being on Earth."),[50] technology ("I know tech better than anyone."),[51] and on and on. People from dominant groups tend to feel comfortable weighing in on an issue they know nothing about. Entitlement provides few repercussions from inaccuracy and failure to honestly self-reflect. An international study of 15-year-olds found that young men, compared to women, are more likely to claim knowledge on a topic they don't actually have.[52] When asked about their expertise on a variety of topics, *some of which were made up*, not only did men report having more knowledge on the topic than did women, but so did rich people compared to working-class and poor individuals.

Wherever there is a dominant group, there is a corresponding subordinated group to which the dominant group feels entitled to instruct. Thus, we have the phenomena *whitesplaining* and *mansplaining*. In her cataloguing of instances, Maisha Z. Johnson describes whitesplaining as a White person who talks about racial issues to a person of color with the paternalistic assumption that a person of color doesn't know enough to accurately articulate their own experience.[53] Whitesplainers have been conditioned to believe that they are somehow more qualified to speak about a marginalized group than a person who belongs to that group. There's an implicit assumption built into the whitesplainer that people of color do not have real experiences or legitimate perspectives, but dominant group members do. The whitesplainer most likely doesn't believe they are motivated by racist superiority when they do it; they probably believe they are gifting the person of color with crucial information from an authoritative perspective.

As we saw in Chapter 3, White people and men are conditioned to believe that what they say is legitimate and correct because their opinions are reinforced by teachers, parents, and the larger culture. A White man may be quite comfortable sharing his opinion about, say, how a Black woman should think about racism. And if she rolls her eyes or objects, he may not even notice because he cannot conceive that he could be ignorant on the subject and that the recipient of his wisdom wouldn't be grateful. Whitesplaining includes White people dismissing people of color as angry and overreactive. When a person of color talks about their experience with racism, the whitesplainer may hijack the conversation in order to declare that they are not racist. In fact, when a people of color talk about racism, their points may not be about accusing the person they are talking to of racism. But some White individuals egocentrically assume they are being accused of racism. Recall the limitations of an individualist perspective from Chapter 2. Some White people feel confident in their assessment of what is racist and what is not. They somehow feel themselves to be good arbiters of what is classifiable as racism, while having no direct personal experience with it. Some whitesplainers claim that talking about racism is unseemly and even suggest it is divisive to our country. Sounding the alarm about racial bias in policing, immigration, education, housing, or health care gets coded by some in the news and in social media as divisive. Accordingly, discussions *about* racism are the problem, not actual racism. Because dominant groups do not have a lifetime of firsthand experience with being a member of a subordinated group, it's best for them to approach these social justice issues with humility; they probably should do more listening than talking. However, this may be difficult for someone who is not used to proceeding with modesty and caution.

In a funny but cringe-worthy article about men's entitlement, writer Rebecca Solnit tells the story of a man she meets at a party who educates her on a topic he feels very knowledgeable about.[54] After disregarding her attempts to interject, he chatters on and on about a brilliant book he has just read. He had to be told several times that it was *her* book he was telling her about with authority before it finally sunk in. Sometime after Solnit's article, the term *mansplaining* was born. Solnit argues that women are not seen as reliable witnesses to their own lives, that the truth is not their property. Accordingly, mansplaining has come to define the act of a man who confidently if not condescendingly lectures a woman on the basics of a topic about which he knows very little, under the mistaken assumption that she knows even less. Most women who have expertise on a subject have experienced the ill-informed, condescending, and long-winded phenomena of mansplaining. Whitesplaining and mansplaining epitomize the clueless egocentrism of entitlement. Explainers are blind to the idea that they may have something to learn from another person, especially one from a marginalized group.

An ancillary phenomenon is when dominant group members claim they want to engage in a "rational debate" but actually want to dismiss another's experience. A cousin to this is when a dominant group member plays devil's advocate. They want to debate someone's actual traumas as if they are abstract far away things that don't actually affect anyone. Comedian Hari Kondabolu sums up the devil's advocate strategy this way: "Why do people have to play devil's advocate, right? It's basically a phrase you can hide behind to say whatever contrarian bullshit you wanna say while pretending you're being objective when you're usually just being an asshole."[55] One can debate the use of the Oxford comma, but someone's personal *experience* really is not up for debate.

Feeling Entitled to the Center: The Center-Stage Problem

Another manifestation of the egocentrism of entitlement is the center-stealing analogy. *Center stealing* refers to the reaction a dominant group member has when they are exposed to subordinate group experiences and reflexively desire to recenter concerns back to themselves. Here's an example: upon hearing from an African American about the trauma of being searched and roughed up by police, a White listener might say, "I was profiled as a drug dealer when I used to drive a van." Now, on the one hand, analogizing might facilitate coalition building between groups because one way we empathize with others is to find similarities between our own and others' situations. On the other hand, as Trina Grillo and Stephanie Wildman argue, analogizing can perpetuate White supremacy when White people believe that their situation is the same as people of color who have been subjected to institutional and systemic racial oppression.[56] The person who analogizes forgets the difference between experiencing the routine indignities and violence perpetuated by White supremacy and the occasional negative experience of a dominant group member. Analogizing can shift the focus to oneself—stealing back the center—without grappling with the other person's reality. For example, a White woman with little experience in thinking about racism but who knows about another form of oppression, sexism, may assume she comprehends the experiences of people of color and thus assumes she has standing to speak on their behalf or with authority. Grillo and Wildman argue that White supremacy creates in White people the expectation that issues of concern to them will be central in every discourse.

Analogizing can range from a genuine attempt to build bridges of understanding (even if limited and misguided) or it can be a selfish and cynical attempt at high-jacking another's experience and centering the discussion on dominant group members. And of course, analogizing doesn't occur only regarding race. Upon hearing a queer person's trauma of a homophobic parent's exclusion of them, a straight listener might say, "I can relate. I dated this guy that my parents hated, and they started excluding us from family events." Many years ago, I attended a presentation on female genital cutting (described by some as female genital mutilation or female circumcision). When the speaker finished, she opened up the discussion for questions. The first person to speak was a man who did not ask a question about the topic but instead asked the speaker to address what he viewed as the barbarism of *male* circumcision. Now, this practice may be worthy of debate, but the topic of the evening was the rarely discussed but widely practiced brutality of female genital cutting. I assume this man would not attend a presentation on cancer and ask that the discussion turn to heart disease. Grillo and Wildman note that when a dominant group member sees the attention put on a subordinate group, they feel compelled to steal back the center. Attention taken away from the dominant group member, even for a moment, feels like discrimination when you are used to the center. Analogies serve to perpetuate this expectation of centrality, what Grillo and Wildman refer to as the center-stage problem. Dominant group members are accustomed to being on center-stage. They have been treated that way by society; it feels natural, comfortable, and in the order of things. Thus, members of preferred groups assume that their perceptions are the pertinent perceptions, that their problems are the problems that need to be addressed. And in discourse they should be the speaker rather than the listener, and the subject of all inquiry. Once an analogy is taken to heart, it seems to the center stealer that they are not stealing the center, but rather are continuing the discussion on the same topic, one they know well. In sum, when the marginalized speak up however briefly, they are viewed as usurpers by dominant group members who are motivated to take back the center.

One analogy that results in stealing back the center is the entitled cry of "White Lives Matter" as a response to Black Lives Matter protests. The Movement for Black Lives was created in 2012 after a series of fatal shootings of unarmed African Americans by police officers and White vigilantes. The slogan *Black Lives Matter* was meant to remind the public that African American lives were historically and are presently dehumanized, degraded, and dismissed by institutions that do not regard African Americans as worthy of the same regard and dignity as White lives. The slogan Black Lives Matter means Black people's lives matter too. Similarly, June is Pride Month in the United States. Inevitably, some heterosexual people complain about why there is not a "Straight Pride" parade. This annual center-stealing strategy resulted in the popular meme that stated, "Gay pride was not born of a need to celebrate being gay, but our right to exist without persecution. So instead of wondering why there isn't a straight pride movement, be thankful you don't need one."[57]

Power Entitles People to Dehumanize the Other

Power does more than render the powerful clueless and self-centered. Power entitles people to dismiss and dehumanize others. In experiments, participants assigned to a power role are more likely to cheat at a game than those in the low-power role. And, hypocritically, those same powerful people are more likely than the powerless to condemn others' cheating, even as they cheat more.[58] Power can also make people insensitive to others' suffering.[59] One study looked at how power influences emotional reactions to the suffering of another person. Power was assessed by people's agreement with statements such as "I can get people to listen to what I say," and "I can get others to do what I want."[60] Participants were paired with same-gender strangers and were asked to talk about a distressing event each had had. Each person served as listener and speaker. Sure enough, there was a difference in responses to distress between low- and high-power participants. Lower-power individuals displayed more compassion and distress in response to the other person's pain. High-power participants were less affected by their partner's distress. Their compassion and distress were unaffected by their partner's distress even when they heard more intense stories from the low-power speakers. In addition, powerful people were less motivated to respond to others' distress than were lower-power participants.

Power entitles people to distance themselves from others who are lower in status. One way to do that is to dehumanize the other—to perceive them as less than human and attribute emotions and intellect more akin to animals or even to machines, than to humans. A simple power manipulation can reveal the way power affects someone with low or high status. One study randomly assigned people to either the role of a manager (high power) or an assistant (low power).[61] Assistants were instructed to review resumes of job applicants and provide information that was submitted to the manager who then made decisions about hiring. Later, participants (managers and assistants) rated each other on traits that would capture dehumanization. Those assigned to the manager role were less likely to attribute uniquely human traits to their assistants. Specifically, managers assumed assistants were less refined, mature, cultured, educated, and morally enlightened, compared to how assistants rated managers. Again, this is a study in which people were randomly assigned to the powerful and powerless position. Imagine the attributions made by a person in real life who has experienced power for decades toward a person with little power. Power holders are entitled to their full humanity, and those without power are not.

Compared to people with less power, the powerful are more likely to dehumanize foreigners they do not know. Joris Lammers and Diederik Stapel categorized participants by power based on their responses to questions about one's personal sense of power (e.g., the extent to which they have power and influence over others).[62] Participants then read about a fictional country and its inhabitants. They were then asked various questions about the people and the country. Powerful participants were more likely to dehumanize the people of the fictional country, compared to those who were not powerful. For instance, they saw the fictional country as more primitive, less decent, and lacking self-control, than those who are not powerful. Similar findings were obtained when the researchers conducted the same study using a different power manipulation: they manipulated the experience of power by asking half of the participants to write about an experience when they had control over others, and the other half of the participants wrote about a time when they were controlled by someone else.[63]

The studies described above have the following in common. With the exception of one of Lammers and Stapel's studies, power was randomly assigned to participants in these studies. Power groups were not assigned based on participants arriving to the study with years of behaving powerful or powerless. No, they were arbitrarily assigned a role and then moments later their behavior had diverged based on their assigned status. The results from these studies suggest that power does something to those who have it: it encourages them to disregard the humanity of those viewed as lesser, it makes them respond with less empathy, and they view the Other not as a fully fleshed-out human worthy of attention and regard.

Honor as Entitlement

An honor killing is defined in many ways, but to me it's an ego killing. It's to restore men's honor.

—Khalida Brohi, author of *I Should Have Honor*[64]

We have explored the paradox of entitlement revealed in both claims of ignorance (e.g., the male bumbler) or actual ignorance with claims of expertise (e.g., the explainer). We also considered how dominant group members feel entitled to behave uncaringly and dismissively. Yet another perk of privilege is feeling entitled to honor, to care about maintaining it, and to defend it. There are many cultures and subcultures around the world that anthropologists label *cultures of honor*. Cultures of honor may take different forms in different regions but they tend to share the idea that a conflict or dispute can damage a person's pride or a family's reputation and that damage to reputation requires retaliation or remedy. In honor cultures even small disputes (at least from an outsider's perspective) require the restoration of reputation and social status.

One such region is the Southern United States, and one such group is White Southern men. Richard E. Nisbett and his colleagues conducted several research studies examining the culture of honor in the US South.[65] Culture of honor, which, in this context, refers to the acceptance of aggression and violence when a man has been dishonored, when his pride is threatened. They found that compared to men in the North, Southern White men are more likely to commit "honor-related" violent crimes—violent responses to arguments or disputes that threaten one's pride or reputation. Nisbett locates this regional distinction in the different economic conditions for Southerners and Northerners in the early years of the United States. Northerners were more likely to manage crops and factories, whereas Southerners (and those living in western states) tended to manage cattle and other herd animals that could be stolen out from under them. So it was more necessary for Southerners to demonstrate their toughness so they would not easily be taken advantage of. For many years, the state of Texas has run an antilitter campaign with the slogan, "Don't Mess with Texas," a slogan that invokes honor culture. It is hard to imagine a successful "Don't Mess with Wisconsin" anti-litter campaign.

Empirical support for the regional difference in honor-related aggression among White men can be seen in one clever set of field experiments. Nisbett and his colleagues put college men in a situation in which another man bumped into them and then called them "asshole."[66] The researchers then tracked the men's responses. Northern men were more likely to shrug off the insult and even seemed amused by it, whereas Southern men were fixin' for a fight. After the insult, Southern men's cortisol and testosterone increased, they reported feeling their masculinity had been challenged, and they were more likely to respond aggressively against the person who insulted them compared to Northern men.

Living in the South is associated with other behavior that could contribute to violence. For instance, Southerners are more likely than Northerners to carry guns, and these regional differences in carrying firearms are driven primarily by White people versus people of color.[67] Nisbett's work on the Southern culture of honor examined only men, but the research on firearm possession reveals that White women may be part of Southern honor culture as well. For whereas Southern White men are more than twice as likely than Northern White men to carry guns; Southern White women are six times more likely than Northern White women to carry guns.[68] The reason for this dramatic regional difference among women is unknown—Southern women could also embrace honor culture, or they may carry more guns to protect themselves from all the Southern men who carry guns.

There are important implications of the plethora of firearms in the South. The availability of guns increases the likelihood of suicide. Deaths by suicide differ by region and race. For example, White men are more likely than Black men to take their own lives; and Southernness is linked to higher suicide rates among White men, but not African American men. Similarly, White women have higher suicide rates than Black women; and Southernness was associated with higher suicide rates for White but not Black women.[69] There are regional differences in school shootings as well. High school students in culture of honor states are more likely than students in non–culture of honor states to bring weapons to school. For example, in a study of 106 school shootings, 75% occurred in honor states, and, consistent with the gendered nature of school shootings, 97% of the shooters were boys; most were White (67%); and most (60%) of the shootings occurred in rural settings.[70] And consistent with expectations for honor culture, the most common motive for the shootings was some kind of reputation threat—such as romantic rejection and homophobic taunting. More recently, larger studies of school shootings find that White youth in rural settings who have been bullied are the most likely perpetrators of these crimes.[71]

The Southern culture of honor seems to be a phenomenon, but is honor culture confined to the US South? Do men, regardless of their geographic locale, embrace honor culture? Donald Saucier and his colleagues have explored individual differences in honor beliefs and find that some men hold honor beliefs while others do not.[72] Saucier and his colleagues looked at attitudes that correlate with what he calls *masculine honor beliefs*. Masculine honor beliefs are captured by statements about *masculine courage* ("A man should not be afraid to fight"), *pride in manhood* ("A man should be embarrassed if someone calls him a wimp"), *socialization* ("You would want your son to stand up to bullies"), *virtue* ("Physical violence is the most honorable way to defend yourself"), *protection* ("A man should protect his wife"), *provocation* ("If a man's mother is insulted, his manhood is insulted"), and *family and community bonds* ("It is important for a man to be loyal to his family"). And thus, Saucier categorizes men in terms of their adherence to these beliefs. Saucier finds that masculine honor beliefs correlate with aggression and anger, but, surprisingly, not with self-esteem or political conservatism. Masculine honor beliefs are also correlated with both benevolent and hostile sexism—the two types of sexism we discussed in Chapter 2. That is, men with these beliefs are more likely to prefer traditional to nontraditional women, and to view the condescending and patronizing behavior of benevolent sexism as an appropriate way to regard women. Not surprisingly, men more than women believe that men should adhere to honor beliefs.[73] In other words, men are more invested than women in men adhering to these rules. Unfortunately, Saucier's research has examined this work among White participants so we do not know the extent to which these attitudes resonate with men (and women) of color.

Like Nisbett's work on culture of honor noting regional differences, Saucier's work on masculine honor beliefs (regardless of geographic region) predicts aggressive responses in men whose masculinity has been questioned, threatened, or undermined. What is the most efficient way to get under a man's honor-related skin? Call him a woman or a homosexual. When asked if they had ever gotten in a fight after being called a name, men report that homophobic and feminine slurs are the most powerful in instigating aggressive responses.[74] That men find homophobic and feminine slurs most threatening demonstrates how minimally valued women and queer people are. It seems clear that men feel entitled to be regarded as distinct and more valued than gay men or women—two subordinated groups. For heterosexual men to be associated with either suggests debasement and weakness. Women and gay men are so repugnant that—for many men—a violent reaction feels justified to such an allegation. If men are as lowly as homosexuals and women, then they really are not men at all. It is not surprising then, that people with masculine honor beliefs are more likely to think it is appropriate for a man to physically assault a woman who has rejected him and to call a woman names like *slut* if she rejects his advances.[75] That honor beliefs make

it acceptable to engage in violence against women—at least certain women—
reveals that "honor" might be a bankrupt concept that is really just about
some men's egos and misplaced concepts of "ownership" of women, as the
quotation at the beginning of this section argues.

Consistent with honor culture (as well as the centuries-old damsel-in-
distress trope), the sexual assault of a woman is viewed by many as an attack
on the honor of the men associated with her, such as her husband or family
members. In an honor context, reactions to sexual assault have little to do
with the violation of another person's bodily sovereignty. What sexual assault
does to the victim is secondary when honor is salient. Therefore, do not mis-
take the outrage at a sexual assault as reverence for the woman victim. Those
with masculine honor beliefs are also likely to have negative perceptions of
rape victims and to engage in victim blaming. They endorse such myths as a
woman could avoid being raped if she really wanted to, or only promiscuous
women get raped.[76]

In the United States, honor states have higher rates of rape and intimate
partner murder by men than non-honor states, even when socioeconomic
status, rurality, and religiosity are controlled for. When men derive their
worth from adherence to the honor code, they may come to view women as
both rewards for and affirmations of their honor. Honor has the dual duty
of condoning violence by men against women while simultaneously man-
dating men to protect women.[77] Similarly, a study of women and men college students in Spain found that those respondents with higher honor scores
were more likely to blame the rape victim in an acquaintance rape than in a
stranger rape. This finding implies that when a woman is a raped by an acquaintance, she allowed the rape to occur because she is immoral and, thus,
she does not deserve the empathy and regard that a victim of stranger rape
deserves. Respondents, both women and men, believe sexual purity matters
for female honor but view it as irrelevant to male honor.[78]

I have spent a considerable amount of space on masculine honor. Why?
How does masculine honor relate to entitlement? Honor is a privilege. The
ability to respond with violence, or even the ability to respond at all when
one's ego is injured, epitomizes that privilege. Because only those with relative power can behave this way. There is no cultural or political support for a
marginalized person to commit violence because they feel disrespected. If a
lesbian is hassled by a stranger on a bus does she have the cultural capital to
respond with violence at the slight directed at her? Can a woman respond to
an insult with violence? She would find little support in her culture for such

a hyperbolic reaction. Honor-related violence is a luxury for some and not others. Honor-related aggression is selective as well. A man who gets kicked around by his boss is not likely to direct his frustration toward his boss, but he can "demand respect" from his family. The man might feel marginalized due to his social class or his race if he is a person of color, but he is still able to cash in his male privilege. Only certain groups feel entitled to harm someone because their ego has been hurt.

Masculine Honor and Blind Patriotism

Individuals who embrace masculine honor values are concerned with defending their reputations against interpersonal threats, and research suggests this defensiveness extends to nation-level threats—foreign entities or people inside the United States that endeavor to harm it. Nation-level provocation produces defensiveness in part because one's country is an important component of some people's self-concept. *Blind patriotism* is a term that captures a noncritical allegiance to one's country and the sentiment of "whatever my country ordains is right" and "I support US policies for the very reason that they are the policies of my country."[79] Individuals who are blindly patriotic tend to be hypersensitive to perceived threats against their country, to favor military action, and to oppose illegal immigration. Blind patriotism also correlates with masculine honor ideologies. Those with masculine honor ideologies are personally affronted by groups perceived to be national threats.[80] Similarly, masculine honor beliefs are correlated with severe and simplistic attitudes about allegiance to the United States. For example, those high in masculine honor believe that "teaching appreciation for different world cultures is a practice that should be avoided so that students aren't discouraged from being committed first and foremost to the US" and "students who refuse to say the US Pledge of Allegiance should be disciplined so they understand the importance of national loyalty."[81] By avoiding critical engagement with their country, honor endorsers attempt to ensure that their specific view of a traditional world is not lost to uncertain tomorrows. If you witnessed Donald Trump's rhetoric during the 2016 presidential election, you could see that the slogan "Make America Great Again" and his rhetoric about immigrants, refugees, and Muslims drew on honor and a simplistic view of groups perceived to undermine the country. Ironically, those who uncritically accept their government, and refuse to question its leaders, undermine the democratic process and make possible political corruption, ultimately weakening the nation they hold in such high regard.[82]

Conclusion

Power emboldens people to be careless without repercussions, at least compared to those without power. Power holders do not feel compelled to view things from another person's perspective and they do not feel obliged to know much about people with less power. For marginalized people, their very lives depend on them understanding the idiosyncrasies of power holders and they understand these dynamics much better than powerful people. Power entitles people to conveniently and self-servingly assume they know both *more* than they actually know when it comes to telling women and people of color how to think about sexism and racism, and *less* than they actually know when they are called to account for sexual violence. There are real-world implications of these dynamics. Some men claim to know very little about women when they want to avoid responsibility for mistreating them. At the same time, men politicians make decisions about women's reproductive rights, overruling a woman's right to control her own body. I write this in a moment of unprecedented assault on women's reproductive freedom carried out almost exclusively by politicians who are men. Combine these patronizing and controlling policies about issues that should be women's to decide, with the antiscience, antiexpertise political moment of late and we have a recipe for turning away from progress and toward a primitive era that will take decades to reverse.

The blood spilled by honor culture splatters across many victims, including those who happen to be in math class when a young White man decides to commit his own form of ego killing with an AR-15. Or a man who beats his wife because that is more acceptable than him beating his boss. Or a man who starts a fight in a bar when another patron calls him a homophobic slur. The lack of gun regulations in the United States can certainly be attributed in part to honor (or ego) culture. Honor culture and blind patriotism also discourage openness and empathy toward those who are different. They contribute to inhumane policies and treatment toward those on the margins. Those who are narrowed by entitlement and rendered ethnocentric and suspicious by blind patriotism find the idea of compromise for a larger good anathema to who they are. The entitled do not see the possibility of giving up something for a larger good because they have learned they do not need to.

In her book *No Visible Bruises*, Rachel L. Snyder writes that preventing domestic violence is not just about asking men not to be violent. "Violence is such a core aspect of their identity because of socialization, for these men, you're asking them to not be men."[83] Of course, not every man succumbs to these pressures. There are plenty of men who have no use for constantly proving their manliness with aggression. Or some men demonstrate their manliness in other ways such as being successful in their careers. But it is crucial to note that there are men all over that do not play by these highly restrictive and damaging gender roles. Alternative models of masculinity are possible. But know that those men who refuse to adhere to rigid traditional masculinity are indeed gender renegades who have had to figure out how to be men; they are certainly aware of the pressure, and they have negotiated a healthy identity without succumbing to pressure. If you know a man like this, or a woman who transgresses the rules of traditional femininity, shake their hand because they make all of our lives easier by offering up an alternative model of gender as they help loosen the vice grip of gender rules.

For now, we deal with those who dig into these roles, who squeeze out all the benefits from their dominant-group status and then rage against those they perceive as threatening their natural place in the world. What happens when entitled people feel threatened and marginalized themselves, and the messes they create, are the concerns of the next chapter. The next chapter addresses the societal repercussions when dominant group members become enraged, rattled, and wronged.

Notes

1. Richter, A. [@AndyRichter]. (2016, December 5). It's a great time to be alive if you're dumb and mean [Tweet]. Twitter. https://twitter.com/AndyRichter/status/805955473606209537.
2. Boot, M. (2016, July 31). How the "stupid party" created Donald Trump. *The New York Times*. https://www.nytimes.com/2016/08/01/opinion/how-the-stupid-party-created-donald-trump.html.
3. University of Georgia. (2011, November 29). Abstinence-only education does not lead to abstinent behavior, researchers find. *ScienceDaily*. https://www.sciencedaily.com/releases/2011/11/111129185925.htm.

4. Burns, J. (2017, August 23). Research confirms that abstinence-only education hurts kids. *Forbes*. https://www.forbes.com/sites/janetwburns/2017/08/23/research-confirms-the-obvious-that-abstinence-only-education-hurts-kids/#12a074ad6615.

5. Katz, J. (2016). *Man enough? Donald Trump, Hillary Clinton, and the politics of presidential masculinity*. Interlink Books.

6. Santos, C. E., Galligan, K., Pahlke, E., & Fabes, R. A. (2013). Gender-typed behaviors, achievement, and adjustment among racially and ethnically diverse boys during early adolescence. *American Journal of Orthopsychiatry, 83*(2–3), 252–264. https://doi.org/10.1111/ajop.12036.

7. Regarding Donald Trump's deficiencies as president, there are many data points. For instance, his own biographer reported that he doubted Trump ever read a book. Trump's Secretary of State referred to him as a "fucking moron," and his Chief of Staff described him as an "Idiot."

8. Boot, M. (2016, July 31). How the "stupid party" created Donald Trump. *The New York Times*. https://www.nytimes.com/2016/08/01/opinion/how-the-stupid-party-created-donald-trump.html.

9. Page 103 in: Baldwin, J. (2017). *I am not your Negro: A major motion picture directed by Raoul Peck*. Vintage International.

10. Mayer, J. (2016, July 18). Donald Trump's ghostwriter tells all. *The New Yorker*. https://www.newyorker.com/magazine/2016/07/25/donald-trumps-ghostwriter-tells-all.

11. Mayer, J. (2016, July 18). Donald Trump's ghostwriter tells all. *The New Yorker*. https://www.newyorker.com/magazine/2016/07/25/donald-trumps-ghostwriter-tells-all.

12. This immediate discussion draws on an extensive review of the social cognition of power by Ana Guinote: Guinote, A. (2015). Social cognition of power. APA Handbook of personality and social psychology, volume 1: Attitudes and social cognition (pp. 547–569). American Psychological Association. https://doi.org/10.1037/14341-017.

13. Again, this discussion draws on an extensive review of the social cognition of power by Ana Guinote: Guinote, A. (2015). Social cognition of power. *APA Handbook of personality and social psychology, volume 1: Attitudes and social cognition* (pp. 547–569). American Psychological Association. https://doi.org/10.1037/14341-017.

14. Page 7 in: Du Bois, W. E. B. (2005/1903). *The souls of black folk*. Simon & Schuster.

15. Page 38 in: Anzaldúa, G. (1987). *Borderlands/la frontera: The new Mestiza*. Aunt Lute Books.

16. My apologies for not knowing the source of this meme.

17. For a review of media patterns, see Chapters 1 and 4 in: Anderson, K. J. (2010). *Benign bigotry: The psychology of subtle prejudice*. Cambridge University Press. Also see Chapters 1, 2, and 4 in: Anderson, K. J. (2015). *Modern misogyny: Anti-feminism in a post-feminist era*. University Press .

18. Weick, M., & Guinote, A. (2010). How long will it take? Power biases time predictions. *Journal of Experimental Social Psychology, 46*(4), 595–604. https://doi.org/10.1016/j.jesp.2010.03.005.

19. LaBier, D. (2015, August 28). Women initiate divorce much more than men, here's why. *Psychology Today*. https://www.psychologytoday.com/us/blog/the-new-resilience/201508/women-initiate-divorce-much-more-men-heres-why.

20. Toler, L. (2011, May 25). Why so many men never see their divorce coming. *HuffPost*. https://www.huffpost.com/entry/why-so-many-men-never-see_b_815502.
    Divorcedmoms.com. https://divorcedmoms.com/sudden-divorce-syndrome-3-reasons-men-are-blindsided-by-divorce/.

21. Mahalik, J. R., Morray, E. B., Coonerty-Femiano, A., Ludlow, L. H., Slattery, S. M., & Smiler, A. (2005). Development of the conformity to feminine norms inventory. *Sex Roles, 52*(7–8), 417–435. https://doi.org/10.1007/s11199-005-3709-7.

22. Gray, E. (2017, November 22). When men "misremember" violating women. *HuffPost*. https://www.huffingtonpost.com/entry/when-men-misremember-violating-women_us_5a15926fe4b025f8e932d903.

23. Medium.com. https://medium.com/s/jessica-valenti/kavanaugh-is-the-face-of-american-male-rage-eded62c5eda9.

24. Page 154 in: Muscio, I. (1998). *Cunt: A declaration of independence*. Seal Press.

25. Loofbourow, L. (2017, November 15). The myth of the male bumbler. *The Week*. http://theweek.com/articles/737056/myth-male-bumbler.

26. Bacon, D. (n.d.). Why do women give mixed signals? *The Modern Man*. https://www.themodernman.com/dating/why-do-women-give-mixed-signals.html.

27. O'Byrne, R., Rapley, M., & Hansen, S. (2006). "You couldn't say 'No', could you?": Young men's understandings of sexual refusal. *Feminism & Psychology, 16*(2), 133–154. https://doi-org/10.1177/0959-353506062970.

28. O'Byrne, R., Rapley, M., & Hansen, S. (2006). "You couldn't say 'No', could you?": Young men's understandings of sexual refusal. *Feminism & Psychology, 16*(2), 133–154. https://doi-org/10.1177/0959-353506062970.

29. Hansen, S., O'Byrne, R., & Rapley, M. (2010). Young heterosexual men's use of the miscommunication model in explaining acquaintance rape. *Sexuality Research & Social Policy: A Journal of the NSRC, 7*(1), 45–49. https://doi.org/10.1007/s13178-010-0003-4.

30. Bohns, V. K., & DeVincent, L. A. (2018). Rejecting unwanted romantic advances is more difficult than suitors realize. *Social Psychological and Personality Science, 10*(8), 1102–1110. https://doi-org/10.1177/1948550618769880.

31. Bohns, V. K., & DeVincent, L. A. (2018). Rejecting unwanted romantic advances is more difficult than suitors realize. *Social Psychological and Personality Science, 10*(8), 1102–1110. https://doi-org/10.1177/1948550618769880.

32. Solnit, R. (2018, March). Nobody knows. *Harper's Magazine*. https://harpers.org/archive/2018/03/nobody-knows-3/2/.

33. Kraus, M. W., Rucker, J. M., & Richeson, J. A. (2017). Americans misperceive racial economic equality. *PNAS Proceedings of the National Academy of Sciences of the United States of America, 114*(39), 10324–10331. https://doi-org/10.1073/pnas.1707719114.

34. Kraus, M. W., Rucker, J. M., & Richeson, J. A. (2017). Americans misperceive racial economic equality. *PNAS Proceedings of the National Academy of Sciences of
the United States of America*, *114*(39), 10324–10331. https://doi-org/10.1073/
pnas.1707719114.

35. Again, see the extensive review from: Guinote: Guinote, A. (2015). Social cognition
of power. *APA Handbook of personality and social psychology, volume 1: Attitudes and
social cognition* (pp. 547–569). American Psychological Association. https://doi-org/
10.1037/14341-017.

36. Galinsky, A. D., Magee, J. C., Inesi, M. E., & Gruenfeld, D. H. (2006). Power and
perspectives not taken. *Psychological Science*, *17*(12), 1068–1074. https://doi-org/
10.1111/j.1467-9280.2006.01824.x.

37. Galinsky, A. D., Magee, J. C., Inesi, M. E., & Gruenfeld, D. H. (2006). Power and
perspectives not taken. *Psychological Science*, *17*(12), 1068–1074. https://doi-org/
10.1111/j.1467-9280.2006.01824.x.

38. Van Kleef, G. A., Oveis, C., Homan, A. C., van der Löwe, I., & Keltner, D. (2015).
Power gets you high: The powerful are more inspired by themselves than by others.
Social Psychological and Personality Science, *6*(4), 472–480. https://doi-org/10.1177/
1948550614566857.

39. Turns out, vehicles are reliable indicators of a person's social rank and wealth: Frank,
R. J. (1999). *Luxury fever: Why money fails to satisfy in an era of excess*. Free Press.

40. Piff, P. K., Stancato, D. M., Côté, S., Mendoza-Denton, R., & Keltner, D. (2012). Higher
social class predicts increased unethical behavior. *PNAS Proceedings of the National
Academy of Sciences of the United States of America*, *109*(11), 4086–4091. https://doi-
org/10.1073/pnas.1118373109.

41. Dietze, P., & Knowles, E. D. (2016). Social class and the motivational relevance of
other human beings: Evidence from visual attention. *Psychological Science*, *27*(11),
1517–1527. https://doi.org/10.1177/0956797616667721.

42. Zitek, E. M., & Jordan, A. H. (2019). Psychological entitlement predicts failure to
follow instructions. *Social Psychological and Personality Science*, *10*(2), 172–180.
https://doi.org/10.1177/1948550617729885.

43. Zitek, E. M., & Jordan, A. H. (2019). Psychological entitlement predicts failure to
follow instructions. *Social Psychological and Personality Science*, *10*(2), 172–180.
https://doi.org/10.1177/1948550617729885.

44. Piff, P. K., Stancato, D. M., Côté, S., Mendoza-Denton, R., & Keltner, D. (2012). Higher
social class predicts increased unethical behavior. *PNAS Proceedings of the National
Academy of Sciences of the United States of America*, *109*(11), 4086–4091. https://doi-
org/10.1073/pnas.1118373109.

45. Summarized in: Ingraham, C. (2016, August 1). New study finds that men are often
their own favorite experts on any given subject. *The Washington Post*. https://www.
washingtonpost.com/news/wonk/wp/2016/08/01/new-study-finds-that-men-are-
often-their-own-favorite-experts-on-any-given-subject/?postshare=4581470057910
393&tid=ss_tw.

46. For a review of these patterns, see Chapter 5 in: Anderson, K. J. (2015). *Modern misogyny: Anti-feminism in a post-feminist era*. Oxford University Press.

47. Hall, E. V., & Livingston, R. W. (2012). The hubris penalty: Biased responses to "cele-bration" displays of Black football players. *Journal of Experimental Social Psychology*, 48(4), 899–904. https://doi.org/10.1016/j.jesp.2012.02.004.

48. Katzenstein, J. A. (2018). *Let me interrupt your expertise with my confidence* [Cartoon]. Condé Nast. https://condenaststore.com/featured/let-me-interrupt-your-expertise-with-my-confidence-jason-adam-katzenstein.html.

49. Britzky, H. (2019, January 5). Everything Trump says he knows "more about than anybody." *Axios*. https://www.axios.com/everything-trump-says-he-knows-more-about-than-anybody-b278b592-cff0-47dc-a75f-5767f42bcf1e.html.

50. Britzky, H. (2019, January 5). Everything Trump says he knows "more about than anybody." *Axios*. https://www.axios.com/everything-trump-says-he-knows-more-about-than-anybody-b278b592-cff0-47dc-a75f-5767f42bcf1e.html.

51. Benen, S. (2019, January 11). Trump claims "professional" expertise when it comes to technology. *MSNBC*. http://www.msnbc.com/rachel-maddow-show/trump-claims-professional-expertise-when-it-comes-technology.

52. Ingraham, C. (2019, May 29). Rich guys are most likely to have no idea what they're talking about, study suggests. *Star Tribune*. http://www.startribune.com/rich-guys-are-most-likely-to-have-no-idea-what-they-re-talking-about-study-suggests/509127092/.

53. Johnson, M. Z. (2016, February 7). 6 ways well-intentioned people whitesplain racism (and why they need to stop). *Everyday Feminism*. http://everydayfeminism.com/2016/02/how-people-whitesplain-racism/.

54. Solnit, R. (2014, August 28). The archipelago of arrogance. *TomDispatch*. http://www.tomdispatch.com/blog/175887/best_of_tomdispatch%3A_rebecca_solnit%2C_the_archipelago_of_arrogance/.

55. About minute 43. Kondabolu, H. (2018). *Warn your relatives*. Netflix. http://netflix.com.

56. Grillo, T., & Wildman, S. M. (1991). Obscuring the importance of race: The implication of making comparisons between racism and sexism (or other -isms). *Duke Law Journal*, 1991(2), 397–412. https://doi-org/10.2307/1372732.

57. Source unknown.

58. Lammers, J., Stapel, D. A., & Galinsky, A. D. (2010). Power increases hypoc-risy: Moralizing in reasoning, immorality in behavior. *Psychological Science*, 21(5), 737–744. https://doi-org/10.1177/0956797610368810.

59. Sturm, R. E., & Antonakis, J. (2015). Interpersonal power: A review, critique, and research agenda. *Journal of Management*, 41(1), 136–163. https://doi-org/10.1177/0149206314555769.

60. van Kleef, G. A., Oveis, C., van der Löwe, I., LuoKogan, A., Goetz, J., & Keltner, D. (2008). Power, distress, and compassion: Turning a blind eye to the suffering of others. *Psychological Science*, 19(12), 1315–1322. https://doi-org/10.1111/j.1467-9280.2008.02241.x.

61. Gwinn, J. D., Judd, C. M., & Park, B. (2013). Less power = less human? Effects of power differentials on dehumanization. *Journal of Experimental Social Psychology*, 49(3), 464–470. https://doi-org/10.1016/j.jesp.2013.01.005.

62. Lammers, J., & Stapel, D. A. (2011). Power increases dehumanization. *Group Processes & Intergroup Relations, 14*, 113–126. https://doi-org/10.1177/1368430210370042.

63. Lammers, J., & Stapel, D. A. (2011). Power increases dehumanization. *Group Processes & Intergroup Relations, 14*, 113–126. https://doi-org/10.1177/1368430210370042.

64. Gross, T. (2018, September 4). Her father gave her the courage to speak out against "honor killings." *NPR.* https://www.npr.org/programs/fresh-air/2018/09/04/644506865.

65. Nisbett, R. E. (1993). Violence and U.S. regional culture. *American Psychologist, 48*(4), 441–449.

66. Cohen, D., Nisbett, R. E., Bowdle, B. F., & Schwarz, N. (1996). Insult, aggression, and the southern culture of honor: An "experimental ethnography." *Journal of Personality and Social Psychology, 70*(5), 945–960.

67. Crowder, M. K., & Kemmelmeier, M. (2017). New insights on cultural patterns of suicide in the United States: The role of honor culture. *Cross-Cultural Research, 51*(5), 521–548. https://doi-org/10.1177/1069397117712192.

68. Crowder, M. K., & Kemmelmeier, M. (2017). New insights on cultural patterns of suicide in the United States: The role of honor culture. *Cross-Cultural Research, 51*(5), 521–548. https://doi-org/10.1177/1069397117712192.

69. Crowder, M. K., & Kemmelmeier, M. (2017). New insights on cultural patterns of suicide in the United States: The role of honor culture. *Cross-Cultural Research, 51*(5), 521–548. https://doi-org/10.1177/1069397117712192.

70. Brown, R. P., Osterman, L. L., & Barnes, D. D. (2009). School violence and the culture of honor. *Psychological Science, 20*, 1400–1405. https://doi-org/10.1111/j.1467-9280.2009.02456.x.

71. Agnich, L. E. (2015). A comparative analysis of attempted and completed school-based mass murder attacks. *American Journal of Criminal Justice, 40*, 1–22. https://doi-org/10.1007/s12103-014-9239-5.

72. Saucier, D. A., Till, D. F., Miller, S. S., O'Dea, C. J., & Andres, E. (2015). Slurs against masculinity: Masculine honor beliefs and men's reactions to slurs. *Language Sciences, 52*, 108–120. https://doi.org/10.1016/j.langsci.2014.09.006.

73. Stratmoen, E., Greer, M. M., Martens, A. L., & Saucier, D. A. (2018). What, I'm not good enough for you? Individual differences in masculine honor beliefs and the endorsement of aggressive responses to romantic rejection. *Personality and Individual Differences, 123*, 151–162. https://doi-org/ http://dx.doi.org/10.1016/j.paid.2017.10.018.

74. Saucier, D. A., Strain, M. L., Hockett, J. M., & McManus, J. L. (2015). Stereotypic beliefs about masculine honor are associated with perceptions of rape and women who have been raped. *Social Psychology, 46*, 228–241. https://doi-org/10.1027/1864-9335/a000240.

75. Stratmoen, E., Greer, M. M., Martens, A. L., & Saucier, D. A. (2018). What, I'm not good enough for you? Individual differences in masculine honor beliefs and the endorsement of aggressive responses to romantic rejection. *Personality and Individual Differences, 123*, 151–162. http://dx.doi.org/10.1016/j.paid.2017.10.018.

76. Saucier, D. A., Strain, M. L., Hockett, J. M., & McManus, J. L. (2015). Stereotypic beliefs about masculine honor are associated with perceptions of rape and women who have been raped. *Social Psychology, 46,* 228–241. https://doi-org/10.1027/1864-9335/a000240.

77. Brown, R. P., Baughman, K., & Carvallo, M. (2018). Culture, masculine honor, and violence toward women. *Personality & Social Psychology Bulletin, 44*(4), 538–549. https://doi-org/10.1177/0146167217744195.

78. Canto, J. M., Perles, F., & San Martín, J. (2017). Culture of honour and the blaming of women in cases of rape/La cultura del honor y la inculpación de la mujer en casos de violación. *Revista De Psicologia Social, 32*(1), 80–107. https://doi-org/10.1080/02134748.2016.1250488.

79. Barnes, C. D., Pomerantz, A., & Yashko, L. (2016). Children cover your eyes: Honor and the role of blind patriotism in teaching national allegiance to posterity. *Political Psychology, 37,* 817–834. https://doi-org/10.1111/pops.12291.

80. Barnes, C. D., Pomerantz, A., & Yashko, L. (2016). Children cover your eyes: Honor and the role of blind patriotism in teaching national allegiance to posterity. *Political Psychology, 37,* 817–834. https://doi-org/10.1111/pops.12291.

81. Barnes, C. D., Pomerantz, A., & Yashko, L. (2016). Children cover your eyes: Honor and the role of blind patriotism in teaching national allegiance to posterity. *Political Psychology, 37,* 817–834. https://doi-org/10.1111/pops.12291.

82. Barnes, C. D., Pomerantz, A., & Yashko, L. (2016). Children cover your eyes: Honor and the role of blind patriotism in teaching national allegiance to posterity. *Political Psychology, 37,* 817–834. https://doi-org/10.1111/pops.12291.

83. Page 116 in: Snyder, R. L. (2019). *No visible bruises: What we don't know about domestic violence can kill us.* Bloomsbury.

6

Enraged, Rattled, and Wronged

*If I grew up in a country in which my religious holidays were the na-
tional holidays, it would feel like marginalization to have my children
grow up in a more egalitarian country in which their religious holidays
and traditions are just one of many. If I grew up in a society in which
every character in the movies I see and television programs I watched
looked like me, it would feel like marginalization to see the occasional
protagonist who does not. I would start to feel my culture is no longer
"for me." If I grew up seeing men as heroes and women as passive objects who worship them, it would feel like oppression to be robbed of my
felt birthright by having to regard women as equals in the workplace or
on the battlefield. Rectifying unjust inequalities will always bring pain
to those who benefited from such injustices. This pain will inevitably be
experienced by some as oppression.*

—Jason Stanley in *How Fascism Works*[1]

One of the targets of the global movement to fight climate change in 2019
was the plastic straw. Offered as a standard accoutrement in restaurants, the
single-use plastic straw was targeted by activists for its unnecessary produc-
tion and waste. Plastics harm the environment because they linger long after
their use and do not disintegrate the way paper products do.[2] Restaurants
began using paper straws or no straws, and, in some cases, customers were
encouraged to bring their own reusable metal straws. There was a swift
backlash by those who believe they should not have to adapt to changing
circumstances. This backlash was spearheaded by none other than the president of the United States. In response to the efforts against the use of plastic
straws, donaldjtrump.com began selling red plastic straws. The Trump straws
were touted as "laser engraved" with the all-caps "TRUMP" in, of course,
gold lettering. The description next to the $15 ten pack said, "Liberal paper
straws don't work. STAND WITH PRESIDENT TRUMP and buy your pack
of recyclable straws today."[3] Acts as simple as recycling trigger resistance
from those not accustomed to being asked to change. There's an additional

Enraged, Rattled, and Wronged. Kristin J. Anderson, Oxford University Press. © Oxford University Press 2021.
DOI: 10.1093/oso/9780197578438.003.0007

potential barrier to recycling—at least for men. A study found that when men recycle or use reusable shopping bags, perceivers question their sexual orientation.[4] The implication here is that some men might avoid recycling for fear that showing concern for the environment might make them appear gay. The ravages of the climate crisis could not be as painful as a random stranger thinking you might be gay if you put your beer can in a recycling bin. Another example of hyperbolic backlash occurred when vegans protested a meat-centered Toronto restaurant that was serving the cruelly prepared foie gras. The chef responded to the protestors by carving up a deer leg in the front window of the restaurant.[5]

Consider the antiscience position of the Republican Party noted in the last chapter. Then consider its adherents like those described above. Combine these two reflexes and you have a perfect storm of ignorance and misdirected notions of freedom that lead to the worst response to the COVID-19 global pandemic. Well into the pandemic, the Pew Research Center polled Americans about the negative impact of COVID-19 on their lives and the different responses of Democrats and Republicans were revealing.[6] The most-cited negative impact of the virus for Democrats was concern for their families. The number one negative effect for Republicans? Having to wear a mask. Take a moment to process that fact. Republicans were more bothered by the prospect of having to wear a mask than they were by the prospect of a family member or themselves becoming ill. They were more concerned about having to wear a mask than concerns about employment. When Democrats did cite masks in their response, they were likely to express frustration with people not wearing them and refusing to follow safety precautions. These people were likely Republicans because Republicans accounted for 92% of those expressing skepticism and opposition to masks.

Dominant group members are not used to being bossed around. They tend to be unfamiliar with having to adapt to changing circumstances, and their resistance to change comes in many forms with a range of consequences to themselves and others. Dominant group members are highly sensitive to criticism but also sensitive to being ignored. Those used to being the norm, the center, the ideal, the legitimate, feel entitled to take up space, to have their worldview validated, and to not modify their behavior. At the same time, they can feel ignored and decentered—for instance by LGBTQ+ Pride Month or a Black Lives Matter sign. The entitled can feel enraged, rattled, and wronged in the face of even the gentlest request for minority rights and the most modest creep of social progress.

In previous chapters, we explored how entitlement develops in individuals. We considered how power entitles people to be careless, egocentric, and unempathic. This chapter dives into the darkness that emerges in an environment when entitled people feel decentered, erased, criticized, or pushed to the margins. Privilege makes one so used to being at the center of what's important and normal, that those with it come to expect preferential treatment as "the way things work." To the person experiencing it, this understanding does not even need reminders, conscious recognition, or explicit demonstration. It is the status quo, but when it is disturbed, the entitled experience confusion, anger, and a desire to lash out. This chapter delves into these manifestations of entitled resentment.

When entitlement is questioned and confronted, the entitled scratch and snarl and spit and cry and act out. Their panic makes them clamp down cognitively, shrinking away from difference or perceived difference. The Other is seen as ruining the country, not playing by the rules, unjustly rewarded, and flouting their newly elevated position in society. Entitlement and its threat of loss is so powerful that to cling to their status and power, the entitled will pull down everything around them. They will burn the house down—including their own house. They will accept the ideology and governing of authoritarians if their leader confirms their status as superior yet under siege. If it means they can feel centered and valued, they will destroy democracy. Let's lay some groundwork in order to understand the recent and current cultural discord that has resulted from entitled resentment and the grievance politics it produces.

Producing an Entitled Race: The History of Divide and Rule

Sociologist Herbert Blumer views racism as a set of beliefs about group position. In a 1958 essay, Blumer argues that to understand racism we should look at it in terms of the relationship between groups as opposed to feelings housed within the individual.[7] According to Blumer, there are four beliefs present in the racism of the dominant group: (1) the dominant group feels a sense of superiority; (2) the dominant group believes the subordinated group is intrinsically different and alien; (3) the dominant group feels a proprietary claim to certain areas of privilege and advantage; and (4) there is fear and suspicion that the subordinate group harbors designs to usurp benefits of the dominant race. Although Blumer only discussed racial prejudice in his essay, his structure is useful for dominant-group conceptions of other target groups such as women and queer people. These four beliefs are about the positional arrangement of groups and the allocation of resources. Blumer notes that the sense of group position supplies dominant groups with their framework of perception, their standard of judgment, their patterns of sensitivity, and their emotional reactions. Group position is the lens through which everything is filtered. His third and fourth points are particularly relevant to this discussion. Looking at #3, one can see that dominant groups feel entitled to exclusive rights in important areas of life—living in certain areas, a right to certain jobs, a claim to certain positions of control and decision-making, and membership in particular groups such as schools and clubs. Socially-preferred groups feel welcomed in most places. Similarly, and more recently, Isabel Wilkerson, the author of the book *Caste*, writes:

> If there is anything that distinguishes caste in America, it is, first, the policing of roles and behavior expected of people based on what they look like, and second, the monitoring of boundaries—the disregard for the boundaries of subordinated castes or the passionate construction of them by those in the dominating caste, to keep the hierarchy in place.[8]

Like the White women who call the police on African Americans living their lives, dominant group members monitor the boundaries that keep them in their preferred position.

Regarding #4, there is the belief that the subordinated group threatens the position of the dominant group by questioning their natural superiority, and not staying in their place. The type of entitlement captured in Blumer's structure makes clear that most of this is about *subjective* relations between groups. It is about the dominant group's sense of where the two groups belong, not necessarily where they are. (Of course, dominant group members *do* have more resources and power than subordinate group members.)

One popular question in recent years is how a less-educated working-class White person comes to share a sense of the same group position to that of wealthy and influential White person. Despite their low education and class status, many working-class Whites see even accomplished people of color as inferior to them. What does their Whiteness gain them if they are toiling in a minimum wage job where they can't afford healthcare, and barely make rent? The answer can be traced back to before the founding of the United

States and to the racial bribe offered to lower-class Whites by the elites.[9] In the early years of the colonies, before there was a United States, African and European indentured servants made relationships as neighbors and as intimate partners. This arose organically as they shared a common position relative to the European elites who exploited their labor. They also sometimes revolted—escaping their indentures together and getting punished together. Indentured servants, regardless of their origin or skin tone, had much in common with each other through being exploited and marginalized by rich people. In order to prevent further uprisings by the many more marginalized Africans and Europeans compared to the few elites, and in order to maintain a cheap labor force, colonial legislatures began building a racial strategy to split off poor Europeans from Africans and Native Americans. African indenture became lifelong enslavement, whereas White indenture ended after a period of time. Laws were passed preventing Africans and Native Americans from voting. To prevent Europeans from intimate relationships with Africans and Native Americans, interracial marriage became illegal. A European woman could be whipped for marrying a Black man, for instance. Poor Europeans were not treated much better than Africans and Native Americans but they were assigned symbolic status—such as only Europeans could be overseers of enslaved Africans. Europeans were recruited for slave patrols, further delineating the difference between Africans and Europeans and the superiority of Europeans. Only Europeans could possess guns or learn to read. Only (the wealthiest) European men could own land.

The Psychological Wage of Whiteness

> *Those accustomed to being the measure of all that is human can come to depend on the reassurance that while they may have troubles in their lives, at least they are not at the bottom. As long as the designated bottom dwellers remain in their designated place, their own identities and futures seem secure.*
>
> —Author Isabel Wilkerson[10]

Rather than raise their wages, poor Europeans, now called Whites, were paid what W.E.B. Du Bois called a racial bribe—a *public and psychological* wage of Whiteness.[11] Whites' elevated status relative to Blacks did not necessarily put more food on their table, but at least they were superior to someone.

Non-elite Whites came to develop feelings of superiority over people of color and found refuge in the fact that even if they were poor, at least they weren't Black. Throughout American history there is a pattern of lower-class Whites cutting themselves off from their economic allies—lower-class people of all colors. Whites came to see themselves as having more in common with the richest Whites even as those elites continued to keep their wages low and their lives on the margins. As president, Richard Nixon utilized the divide-and-rule strategy of the racial bribe to benefit his election. So did Ronald Reagan. So did Donald Trump.

Recall from Chapter 1 that, on average, men more than women are susceptible to the illusory power transference—the tendency to adopt others' power as one's own due to one's association with that powerful other person.[12] Men's greater sensitivity toward feeling powerful leads them to psychologically latch onto the powerful with whom they cooperate, in order to feel powerful themselves. This holds true no matter how weak and ephemeral the association with those others might be. In research studies, the tendency to psychologically identify with another who has power occurred even though the partner's power was randomly assigned and extremely short-lived. In the experiment, there was no way for the men to leverage their previous partners' power. In contrast, women tend not to perceive themselves to be more powerful in such situations because they seem to recognize the power level of their partners in no way corresponds to their own power.

If I Feel Wronged, I Don't Need to Be Right

The entitled feel wronged by social progress. They feel victimized by "diversity." They feel decentered by women's and ethnic minorities' advancements whether actual or perceived. And by queer rights. As Arlie Hochschild puts it, they feel like strangers in their own land.[13] The White supremacists at the "Unite the Right" rally in Charlottesville, Virginia, in 2017 chanted, "You! Will Not! Replace Us!" In 2019, White supremacists interrupted a book reading by the author of the aptly-titled *Dying of Whiteness* with the chant, "This land is our land!"[14] When you are used to being the norm, any act of tilting toward equality can feel like a mammoth loss. This point is conveyed by Jason Stanley, author of *How Fascism Works*, in the quotation that begins this chapter.[15]

Entitled Resentment and the Trump Voter

We see the effectiveness of the racial bribe offered to White people today. Shortly after the 2016 US presidential election, in trying to understand the surprising results of Trump's win, many pundits reported that White, working-class, rural voters won it for Trump. Donald Trump spoke to their economic anxieties more effectively than Hillary Clinton, and so they voted for him. In fact, Trump and Clinton voters did not differ on income. Trump voters were hardly the poorest of the poor. The median annual income of Trump supporters was $82k, slightly *above* that of Clinton supporters ($77k).[16] Trump followers were less likely than others to be looking for work, less likely to be unemployed or part-time employed.[17] And those who had recently lost a job were no more likely to vote for Trump.[18] Whereas Trump and Clinton voters did not differ significantly on income, they did differ on education. Those without a college education—especially if they were White—were more likely to vote for Trump.[19]

The attitudes and beliefs of Trump voters are representative of an entitled person feeling wronged. In Chapter 2, we examined ideologies that contribute to prejudice, discrimination, and entitlement. Two of those, authoritarianism and social dominance orientation are common to Trump voters, relative to Clinton voters.[20] Recall that these are individuals who see the world as a dangerous and threatening place, consisting of a dog-eat-dog world of competition. Intolerance to variety, an adherence to law and order, and rigid retrograde values are common. Authoritarians are typically triggered by threat and fear so they fit into Trump's fear-of-the-Other rhetoric like a hand in a glove. Those voters who believed that the "American way of life is threatened" voted for Trump.[21] Those who felt the established hierarchy was being upended voted for Trump. For working-class White voters without college degrees, fears about immigrants and cultural displacement were more powerful factors than economic concerns in predicting support for Trump.[22] Trump voters more than Clinton voters tended to fear the Other. Consistent with what we know about the entitled, Trump voters did not need to know a lot about minorities in order to be opposed to them. In fact, Trump's White supporters had less contact with people of color than other Americans. Racial isolation of Whites at the zip code level was one of the strongest predictors of Trump support.[23] In other words, the less contact White people had with people of color, the more likely they were to vote for Trump. And as the distance from the Mexican border increased so did Trump support.[24] Those who think that dominant groups (Whites, Christians, and men) are discriminated against were more likely to support Trump.[25] They were also more likely to believe that discrimination against White people was at least as bad as discrimination against people of color.[26] Trump voters were also more likely than Clinton voters to believe that the United States has become too soft, and that men are being punished for being men.[27]

The concept of losing out to minorities as a result of perceived wrongs is highly salient to Trump voters. They have been told to expect a lot, so while they continue to do significantly better economically than people of color,[28] they misperceive their advantages and think they should be *much* better off. Some Trump voters certainly felt like they were being ripped off, but they were not any more disadvantaged than Clinton voters. Instead, what seems to be salient to Trump supporters is the *feeling* of deprivation. Trump adherents felt deprived relative to what they perceived other less-deserving groups have gotten. The subjective feeling of loss matters because it is a precursor to aggression. For instance, one study found that those who *felt* a loss of socioeconomic status tended to demonstrate trait aggression (proneness to anger and violence).[29] They agree with statements such as, "I have threatened people I know."[30] Similarly, when asked questions such as, "To what extent do you feel like a winner compared to other Americans," those who do not feel like winners are more likely to possess trait aggression.[31] Again this is about the perception of disadvantage, not actual disadvantage.

It probably doesn't help matters that Trump supporters identify with some of the wealthiest people in the United States—people like Donald Trump. Their support for the ultra-wealthy exacerbates this unrealistic assessment of their own place in the world. White men who supported Trump tend to feel they should be doing much better than they are, and they think women and minorities are unjustly elevated. Trump voters have been convinced to blame marginalized groups rather than the super rich who actually engineer, benefit from, and perpetuate growing income inequality that hurts most everyone in the United States.

Trump's victory might be viewed admirably when it is attributed to a groundswell of support from previously ignored workers, compared to if it were attributed to those whose status is irrationally threatened by minorities, Muslims, and immigrants.[32] Group threat and intolerance (e.g., racism) of others is a harder thing to make palatable to the media and the electorate than claiming Trump supporters' concerns were about economics. Ta-Nehisi Coates writes that the media focus on one subcategory of Trump voters—the

White working class—is puzzling, given the breadth of his White coalition.[33] But if you can reduce Trump's election to the working class and evangelicals, then the role of racism is diminished or it's laundered through White economic anxiety. Coates says, "the point of white supremacy—to ensure that that which all others achieve with maximal effort, white people (particularly white men) achieve with minimal qualification." "Black workers suffer because it was and is our lot. But when white workers suffer, something in nature has gone awry." It's time to take complaints seriously when they come from White workers. So, while at first blush, addressing the complaints of the economically disadvantaged seems like progress, this is not true when it is actually a ruse to hide a racist agenda.

Dying of Whiteness

For his book *Dying of Whiteness*, physician Jonathan M. Metzl interviewed White people in Missouri, Tennessee, and Kansas, where many are in desperate economic conditions.[34] When you consider Trump support at the community level by zip code, you find that Trump supporters—compared to Clinton supporters—came from areas where education rates are low, health outcomes are bad, disability rates are high, and there's greater reliance on Social Security income and the Earned Income Tax Credit.[35] Harkening back to DuBois's psychological wage of Whiteness, the struggling Whites that Metzl interviewed have foregone government assistance they desperately need because they believe government aid would also help people of color who do not deserve it. Immigrants, "welfare queens," and other moochers are taking advantage of the system, according to this distorted (and self-destructive) way of thinking. Metzl found that chronically ill and even dying White people he interviewed refused to sign up for the Affordable Care Act— known as *Obamacare*—which would have provided them much needed medicine, tests, and doctor visits, because of their belief that Obamacare is part of the government spending to help undeserving minorities.

In 2016, the state of Missouri passed Senate Bill 656, making guns available nearly everywhere and for almost anyone. SB 656 eliminated requirements for firearm training, background checks, and permits needed for conceal carry. It expanded the Castle Doctrine—the notion that you can shoot someone in your house or property without being prosecuted. It expanded "stand-your-ground" protections for people who kill someone because the victim was perceived to be dangerous. The idea is that more guns lead to more safety and less crime. Metzl found that the loosening of gun laws has not resulted in White people protecting themselves from marauding gangs and thieves. Rather, the loosening of gun laws resulted in increased suicides, partner violence, and accidental deaths. Open access to firearms has disproportionately affected White people, White rural men in particular. White men account for nearly 80% of all gun suicides, even though they represent less than 35% of the population.[36] Missouri's state motto, the *Show Me State*, might more accurately be called the *Shoot Me State*.[37]

There's also the tax cuts that benefit the rich but are supported by the poor and working-class Whites who Metzl interviewed. Tax cuts for the wealthy have resulted in gutting public school funding, initially with the result of starving low-income minority districts. However, because the school funding cuts were not severe enough to make up for tax cuts for the wealthy, the funding cuts soon bled into White suburban, middle-class districts. As one Kansas legislator admitted, "the fire that we set in the fields burned all the way up to the home."[38] Politicians capitalize on White anxiety and the "mortal trade-offs White Americans make in order to defend an imagined sense of whiteness."[39] Metzl describes the policy and legislation that capitalizes on White racial resentment as "backlash governance."[40] White politicians push deregulation, lax gun laws, and state funding cuts for health care, schools, and food assistance to help the poor and working-class—policies that hurt the voters who keep electing them.

The psychological wage of Whiteness is powerful. Rather than seeing equity and diversity as helping everyone, Metzl's subjects expressed a willingness to die for their place in the hierarchy rather than participate in a system that puts them on the same level as immigrants and people of color. Their investment in Whiteness blinds them to how politicians use racial resentment as a tool for class exploitation.

Anti-Affirmative Action

Today the white male is the enemy. I've seen too many qualified white males passed over for promotions or advancement in favor of a woman and/or minority. Qualifications don't matter these days, rather your gender and race matter.

—White man, engineer, age 47[41]

Affirmative action in the United States is an obvious target for dominant group members who perceive they have been wronged by "diversity."
Affirmative action makes for easy criticism because it is commonly misun-
derstood as a quota system that results in the hiring of women and people
of color over more qualified White men. Quotas are illegal and are not part
of affirmative action programs. Instead, affirmative action refers to a set of
strategies to bring workers into the pool who are available and qualified but
are underrepresented in organizations and companies.[42] Those who are
against affirmative action tend to argue that it violates meritocracy, a topic
we explored in Chapter 2. The anti-affirmative action argument that turns on
the myth of meritocracy says that those who were previously shut out of the
workplace and university—people of color and women—are getting "special
advantages" under affirmative action. This premise is based on the notion
that the playing field is otherwise level *except* for affirmative action, which
puts its thumb on the scale for women and people of color.[43] The widespread
college admissions cheating scandal in 2019 shows that the constituency
really putting their thumbs on the scale is rich people who buy and cheat
their way into elite schools. Nonelite White men should direct their ire upward, but their racial and gender attitudes have them directing their anger
downward.

Opponents of affirmative action and defenders of the beleaguered White
man seem utterly confident in their belief that less-qualified people of color
and women are getting jobs that more qualified White men are not. It's curious that they know so much about other people's resumes. In reality, it would
be rare for a job candidate to know another person's qualifications for a job
to which they are both applying—even if they work in the same department
of a competing candidate. They don't know the details of competitors' experience, they haven't seen how they answer interview questions, and so on.

People have a variety of reasons for rejecting affirmative action programs.
Some people assert that affirmative action violates meritocracy and fairness,
or even harms the recipients of it. These claims tend to fall apart when you
take a closer look. Do White people object to affirmative action because they
believe it harms White people or because they believe it harms people of
color? One study presented White college students with different versions
of an article about affirmative action policy.[44] One version argued that affirmative action harms White people; another version claimed it helps White
people. For those who read the article claiming that affirmative action harms
Whites, they were more likely to endorse the harm-to-beneficiary objection

than when they read information that promoted the idea that affirmative action does not harm Whites. Thus, the White respondents in this study professed concern about the damage affirmative action supposedly does to people of color, but only when they were presented with the idea that it harms White people. In other words, they appear to care about the effect affirmative action has on the outgroup, but in fact they are more concerned with the impact on their group.

These findings complement an early study that examined explanations for people's resistance to affirmative action. Stephen Johnson engaged White participants in a problem-solving task.[45] They were told they would be competing with someone in a different room for the best solution to a problem. Participants were led to believe their competitor was either African American or White. After the task, each participant was told they had lost the competition, but the reasons for losing varied. Half were told they lost because of their competitor's superior problem-solving abilities. The other half, however, were told that although both the participants and the competitors performed similarly, the competitor was deemed the winner because they were from a poor background, were economically disadvantaged, and had probably faced injustices in their life. Obviously, this second condition was set up to induce the belief of preferential treatment in favor of the competitor, akin to what people think affirmative action does. After the participants were informed they had lost, the experimenter presented an opportunity for retaliation by telling each participant that their judgment of the other person was an important factor in the final decision to award points and that if the participant had anything negative to say about the other person, the experimenter would take that into account when awarding points to the competitor. The participant would not receive extra points, but they could prevent the other person from receiving the extra points. Using this analogy of affirmative action, if the participants were against affirmative action solely on the basis of merit—that people should not gain what they haven't earned—the participants would penalize the competitors who won due to previous disadvantage, regardless of the competitor's race. If racial prejudice was a factor in the participants' decisions, they would penalize the African American competitor more than the White competitor.

Did it matter whether the competitor in this study was White or Black when it came to the participant retaliating? It did not matter when the participants thought they lost due to the others' superior performance. In fact, when the participant's loss was believed to be because of the other person's better performance, the participants were less retaliatory toward the Black competitor than toward the White competitor. However, when the participant's loss in the competition resulted from the other person having been given the advantage due to their deprived background, the participants retaliated against the African American competitors more than they did against the White competitors. Discrimination against Black participants occurred even though those discriminating gained nothing for themselves by retaliating. It appears that the White participants in Johnson's study disliked preferential treatment, but they didn't mind it so much when White participants received it.[46] Both studies undermine the fallacy of the claim that opposition to affirmative action programs is about fairness, not racism.

Rattled and Fragile

The thing is, when we have the feeling that we are forced to change, then it's gonna be, that's in my opinion, the wrong way, you know? So if you want to change the trick is not to force it, and do it in a very clever way. That you change without noticing. That would be the perfect way.
—White man, firefighter, Amsterdam, NL[47]

Another feature of entitlement is how challenging it is to feel decentered. There are many examples in recent years of the rattling of dominant group members—the confusion and panic that comes from the prospect of not being number one. Members of preferred groups are easily triggered because they are used to being both centered and also left alone. In recent decades there have been modest gains in women's rights, some progress for people of color, and recognition and acceptance of queer people. The world feels upside down to the entitled.

Backlash always accompanies social progress. The celebrations of marriage equality were promptly followed by legislators introducing "religious freedom" bills that would allow businesses to refuse service to queer patrons. The shift toward recognizing transgender people as fully human resulted in dozens of so-called bathroom bills around the United States that would make it a violation of the law for a transgender person to use the bathroom of their gender. As plantation tours in the US South begin to address the brutality of slavery more accurately, some White visitors aren't having it. The very mention of slavery is resisted by some tourists who seem to believe that tours are inserting politics into something they believe is apolitical.[48] It is difficult to fathom what tourists expect to hear about at a former slave plantation, if not slavery. At the same time, White people are fighting the removal of confederate statues that litter the country—monuments that should have never been erected in the first place any more than monuments to Adolf Hitler and Joseph Goebbels should proliferate in Germany.

Who Counts as American?

Perhaps the most difficult and delicate question that confronts our powers that be is the handling—the safe and proper treatment—of our American-born Japanese, our Japanese-American citizens by the accident of birth. But who are Japanese nevertheless. A viper is nonetheless a viper wherever the egg is hatched.
                    —W. H. Anderson, *Los Angeles Times*, 1942[49]

And I think about the probational nature of my Chinese-American existence, in a sense that, in better times, in normal times, there are certain stereotypes that are cast upon me when I walk down the street. But in a moment of crisis, when it seems plausible that the country where I was born could be responsible for an unprecedented pandemic, that I become a person of suspicion, and I become someone who is quite easy perhaps to target all your ire and anxieties, and that maybe it gave him temporary relief to be able to identify someone or something as the cause for his hurt and for his anxieties.
                    —Chinese American journalist, Jiayang Fan, 2020[50]

One of the pillars of entitled resentment is the idea that White people are the real Americans and that Brown and Black people are not fully and legitimately American. As we saw in the last section, the demographic shift of the United States has White people rattled. This is the notion that Whites are losing their status as the norm, as the ones in charge, as those that epitomize the ideal. The election of Barack Obama challenged the racial hierarchy that has advantaged White people for so long.[51] Donald Trump got his political start by accusing President Obama in 2011 of not being an American-born citizen, a requirement for the presidency, and, therefore, of being an illegitimate presence in the Oval Office. Perhaps at a different moment in US history,

Trump's half-baked allegation would have been easily dismissed. However, in 2011, many people were ready to listen. White people were primed to believe that people of color are not real Americans. Only Whites are legitimate Americans. Experience and experiments tell us so.

Donald Trump described a Latinx judge born in Indiana as biased against Trump's racist policies because the judge is "Mexican," "Hispanic," and "Spanish." Trump insisted that the judge should recuse himself because of his heritage.[52] America has a long history of considering the only legitimate Americans to be White Americans. People of color, even those who have lived in America for centuries, including, ironically, Native Americans, are seen as interlopers, and not real Americans. The incarceration of Japanese Americans—predominantly American citizens of Japanese heritage born in the United States, as well as Japanese immigrants—is but one example of the belief that those with white skin are the only true Americans. During World War II, the US government arrested and incarcerated 120,000 Japanese Americans, for no other reason except they were of Japanese descent.[53] Their land and personal property were seized, and they were put into militarized camps and horse stalls that were repurposed to house humans.

If you ask White people directly if they think that Asian Americans or African Americans are less American than White Americans, they report seeing Asians and Blacks as *somewhat* less American than Whites. However, if you ask them to answer this question with implicit measures, when respondents don't have time to control their attitudes and modulate their responses, results are stark. Thierry Devos and Mahzarin Banaji paired ethnic faces with American symbols (e.g., American flag, Mt. Rushmore) and European symbols (e.g., Flemish Lion, 20-cent Swiss coin). White people are much more likely to associate Americanness with White faces than with African American or Asian faces. A follow-up study found that even famous Asian American actors are viewed as less American than famous foreign White (British and French) actors.[54] Consistently, White Americans see White people as more American than Latinx Americans, Asian Americans, African Americans, and even Native Americans.[55]

When the racial demographic shift from a White majority to a non-White majority is made salient to White people, they hunker down and constrict. For example, one study presented White Americans with two different narratives about the United States: one emphasized the demographic shift of the United States to what has been called *majority-to-minority*—the trend that finds that White people will soon become the numeric minority relative to people of color. Other participants were told about general geographic movement—not tied to race/ethnicity. When Whites were made to think about the majority-minority racial shift, their attitudes shifted as well. Whites endorsed more conservative ideology. They expressed more support for conservative positions on both race-related issues (affirmative action and immigration) and race-neutral issues (funding defense). However, when the researchers added information indicating that the racial shift would not result in the loss of White people's status, their attitudes did not increase their conservatism.[56] This study reveals how the framing of an issue can manipulate voters. Race-baiting politicians can and do cynically couch the demographic change in the language of loss for White people in order to gain support for conservative policies.

Whites who want to maintain White power and status do so in quite convoluted ways. The interpretation of hate crimes is a telling indicator of this. Prejudiced Whites are more likely to use free speech as an excuse if the victim of a hate crime is African American. In a study where White participants were set up with a scenario of a bias crime directed at a Black or White person, prejudiced White people believed the hate speech should be protected by the First Amendment if the victim is Black, but not when the victim is White.[57] In other words, prejudiced Whites are hesitant to call hate speech a problem if the victim is Black rather than White. In contrast, low-prejudice participants appropriately rated the act as less protected by freedom of speech rights and more strongly as a hate crime when the target was Black versus White. The use of free-speech principles is applied unevenly and strategically depending on how prejudiced one is.

Entitled to Fragile Feelings

White Fragility

The rattling of dominant group members by the perceived progress of those on the margins manifests at the macro level (e.g., antagonism to government aid to poor people) and the micro level (e.g., defensiveness about the topic of racism). White fragility and fragile masculinity reflect examples of micro responses. Robin DiAngelo coined the term *White fragility* to capture how some White people get rattled when they have to account, in any way for, or acknowledge the existence of, racism.[58] We have already explored some conceptions and phenomena that trigger White fragility, such as exposing meritocracy as a myth. Dominant group members come to believe that their privileges feel like equality and that they deserve things they have not necessarily earned. As a result, attempts at equality can feel like oppression against White people. This is based on the false belief that racism is an individual pathology reflected only in hate groups, White supremacists, or perhaps, elderly relatives who use racial slurs. If someone doesn't hold membership in these categories, they cannot be racist and the problem of racism has nothing to do with them.

White people tend to see racism as about an individual's bad intentions, rather than bias that is inherent in our institutions. If the topic of racism is raised, a White person can easily feel defensive and personally confronted. The conversation quickly becomes about how that individual White person is not racist, rather than about the issue of racism. White people experience the privilege of individuality—viewing themselves as individuals with unique characteristics, experiences, desires, and preferences. In contrast, people of color are seen as belonging to a group with members that are similar to each other.[59] Therefore, many White individuals view racism through an individualized lens, and if the topic of racism comes up, they feel personally targeted. Robin DiAngelo cites example after example of how White fragility manifests interpersonally.[60] For example, White people tend to control conversations about race or conversations with people of color by speaking first, last, and most often. They engage in the disingenuous invalidation of racial equality by "just playing devil's advocate." They might play the outraged victim of "reverse racism" or accuse people of color of "playing the race card" when they bring up prejudice.

DiAngelo has a particular frustration with White women who cry in cross-race interactions.[61] While crying in response to racism might seem like an admirable gesture of solidarity, DiAngelo exposes the White privilege embedded in this gesture. When a White woman cries over some aspect of racism, the attention immediately goes to her, demanding time, energy, and attention from everyone in the room when they should be focused on ameliorating racism. Racism becomes about White distress, White suffering, and White victimization. DiAngelo argues that because we so seldom have authentic and sustained cross-racial relationships, White women's tears do not feel like solidarity to people of color. Tears driven by White guilt are self-indulgent and are not helpful to people of color. Those mired in guilt tend to be self-focused and ineffective; guilt functions as an excuse for inaction. In addition, White tears are a reminder to people of color that White people do not notice racism on a daily basis. Since many White individuals have not learned how racism works and their role in it, their tears may come from shock and distress about what they didn't know or recognize. For people of color, White tears are an enactment of racial insulation and privilege. And because Whites see their tears as specific to them as individuals, they may take offense when people of color find them frustrating and annoying.

Robin DiAngelo also situates White women's tears in the long historical backdrop of Black men being tortured and murdered based on a White woman's distress. Many Black men and children have been lynched for allegedly whistling at a White woman, or simply talking to them. Many Black women have been lynched for allegedly failing to show White women sufficient respect. White women's tears have been the trigger (or excuse) for the terrorism by Whites against African Americans. Not knowing or being sensitive to this brutal history is another example of White centrality, individualism, and lack of racial humility.[62]

Fragile Masculinity

> Someone once said, "Men are afraid that women will laugh at them. Women are afraid that men will kill them."
> —June in *The Handmaid's Tale*[63]

Another dominant group examined in these pages also experiences fragility, and this dynamic has been popularly called *fragile masculinity*. Its underlying mechanisms have some similarities with White fragility. Recall our discussion in Chapter 4 on *precarious manhood*. Unlike womanhood, manhood is hard won and easily lost, and, therefore, some men go to great effort to perform it—for the most part for other boys and men—sometimes to their own and others' detriment.[64] Men will go out of their way to not appear unmanly or feminine—they adhere to an *antifemininity mandate*. For example, men are reluctant to take jobs that women do. Men hold out for diminishing coal-mining jobs when they should be applying for home health aid jobs. In contrast, women have been more flexible and have pushed themselves into men's jobs; men have not pushed themselves into women's jobs.[65]

There are consequences of the investment in maintaining manhood for individual men, as well as the rest of us. Men learn to be fixated on performing masculinity, which often entails aggression. Men tend to believe aggression is more typical than it actually is—as we learned earlier. They falsely believe that women are attracted to aggressive men, when, in fact, women tend to view aggression as weak and impulsive, a loss of self-control, and not sexy or charming.[66]

Entitlement tells White men they shouldn't have to bow down to those they perceive to be below them. In 2018, Markeis McGlockton, an African American man, pushed a White man to the ground because the man was yelling at his partner outside a convenience store. The man pulled out a gun and shot and killed McGlockton and was not prosecuted because of Florida's stand-your-ground law.[67] Stand-your-ground laws and gun ownership are manifestations of feeling entitled to never back down. Gun owners often justify owning or carrying a gun with fears of violent crime; however, over the same period in which gun purchases have risen, violent crime has dropped. In truth, support for gun rights for White men is linked to perceived threats to their racial privilege.[68] Gun popularity among men is linked to threats to their gender status as well. How do we know? First, men with higher sexism scores believe it should be easier to buy guns; men with lower sexism scores say it should be more difficult to buy guns.[69] Second, firearm background checks increase in communities where married men, but not married women, have lost their jobs.[70] Presumably, recently unemployed men become interested in guns at a time they feel vulnerable. In addition, when wives out earn their husbands, gun sales increase.[71] These men seem to see guns as one way to shore up masculinity. As we saw earlier, Jonathan Metzl's work finds that guns are used by White men as a means of preserving racial privilege, even as Whites wind up being disproportionately harmed by the presence of guns.[72]

It turns out in laboratory studies it's pretty easy to threaten men's masculinity into panic that then motivates them toward compensation. Consider the following study. Julia Dahland her colleagues asked young and mostly White men to complete a "gender knowledge test."[73] During this test participants were asked questions such as, "What is a dime in football?" and "Do you wear Manolo Blahniks on your head or feet?" The respondents were then randomly put into either a threat condition—being told they scored similar to the average women—or a no-threat condition—being told they scored like the typical man. Their grouping had nothing to do with their actual answers on the test. Men threatened by being associated with women were more likely to feel embarrassed by their responses and angry, and they wanted to display dominant behaviors. Anger predicted greater endorsement of ideologies that implicitly promote men's power over women. Specifically, men's social dominance orientations and benevolent sexism (and both are correlated with entitlement) increased if they were exposed to the masculine threat. How did the threatened men in this study appease that threat to their masculinity? By endorsing the legitimacy of men's societal power over other groups, particularly women.

Sexualizing Women Who Outperform Men

Another strategy for masculinity recovery is for some men to demean and sexualize women who have hurt their feelings. Dahl and her colleagues also looked at men's reactions to being outperformed by women.[74] In this study, men were led to believe they were playing a computer game with another participant. Men were told the study was about people who succeed in "action-oriented and competitive environments." They were given some SAT questions. After, they were told that their teammate was a woman. In the threat condition, they were told the woman outperformed them. In the no-threat condition, they outperformed her. The men were then instructed to pick avatars (characters that represented each player) for themselves and their partners. The women's avatars varied on how much clothing they were wearing. How did the men respond when they believed they were outperformed by a woman? They reported greater public embarrassment and anger relative to the men who believed they outperformed the woman. The reactions of these embarrassed men in turn predicted the avatars they chose for the women. The men who were angered at being outperformed chose more sexually revealing avatars for the women than did the men who were not angered by being outperformed by a woman. That is, increases in anger predicted men's increased sexualization of the woman who outperformed them. Sexualizing women who outperform you is a relatively subtle form of dominance, making it difficult to detect and resist. At the same time, sexualizing women is so common in popular culture that this strategy to repair harmed masculinity provides a socially appropriate, non–physically violent means of asserting power and repairing masculinity.

Donald Trump routinely used this strategy against women who stood up to him, disagreed with him, or demonstrated too much competence and confidence. For example, he tweeted the following about Senator Kirsten Gillibrand: "Lightweight Senator Kirsten Gillibrand, a total flunky for Chuck Schumer and someone who would come to my office 'begging' for campaign contributions not so long ago (and would do anything for them), is now in the ring fighting against Trump."[75] Implied in his tweet is that Gillibrand would trade sexual favors for campaign contributions.

Entitlement and Rage

When Southern whites made the choice to go to war with America they did so because however much racism had been embedded in the nation from the start, they didn't find our commitment sufficient. And that's saying a lot. They chose a side. It was a side of even more *oppression, even* more *mistreatment than that which the North had been helping dish out upon black bodies and upon indigenous peoples for many a generation. It is the same choice the white nationalists are making now. In a nation where they as whites already have half the unemployment rate of people of color, one-third the poverty rate, and 12 times the median net worth of black and brown folks, they are choosing to go all in for even greater dominance, even greater hegemony.*

—Tim Wise[76]

Thus far in this chapter we have considered the role of entitlement in feeling deprived, aggrieved, and ripped off. We have considered the confusion, irritation, and fragility produced by the feeling of being sidelined by minorities. This section considers the aggrieved, entitled person's emotional reactions to feeling decentered: out of control, irrational, prone to reckless projection, and punishing rage over perceived demotion.

Bigotry as Bonding

Even before Trump took office, experts on authoritarianism had sounded the alarm on his tendency toward a tyrannical style of governing.[77] Trump's anti-immigration position, the America First rhetoric, demands for loyalty above experience and expertise, referring to journalists as enemies of the people, and his authoritarian personality and social dominance orientation are consistent with fascist politics.[78] In her article, "Trump's not Hitler, he's Mussolini," Fedja Buric contextualizes the Trump campaign rally in a fascist context.[79] Buric describes the carnivalesque atmosphere of his rallies. Attendees came together to rough up protestors as an exercise in fascist community building. Trump egged on his followers by saying things like, "I'd like to punch him in the face!" Trump's inability to condemn Nazis after the "Unite the Right" rally in Charlottesville, Virginia, in 2017, also fits into the context of White bonding—or perhaps more specifically *White supremacist* bonding. When asked to comment on the horror of hundreds of White supremacists and Nazis marching in the streets of Charlottesville and fighting counter protestors, Trump's summation of the event included, "I think there's blame on both sides," "you had people that were very fine people, on both sides."[80] To be clear, Trump is criticizing and then complimenting both White supremacists and counter protestors against White supremacists—the two groups were equivalent in Trump's eyes.

In Chapter 2 we considered the powerful role that individualism plays in the United States. Americans tend to over rely on individualism as an explanation of one's successes or failures. Those who have succeeded have done it by their own grit and guts, and those who have failed have only themselves to blame. Individualism says it's not institutional structures (laws, policies, and practices) that make it more likely certain people will succeed or struggle. The bootstrap mentality is highly appealing—even iconic—to many Americans. The individualist perspective benefits the already wealthy and powerful. However, it is a myth that many who are not wealthy and powerful have absorbed and embraced, albeit to their own detriment.

As enamored with going it alone as many Americans are, some Americans come together to commit acts of terror. We saw White bonding when lynchings of African Americans were common in the US South and elsewhere. The murders of African Americans were community events for White spectators. Lynchings were advertised in newspapers, and crowds gathered to ogle and celebrate these crimes. Postcards were made of the murders; spectators took "souvenirs" that included victims' clothing and body parts. The purpose of lynchings was to terrorize Black communities. However, they also served to bond White communities together. Terror against African Americans solidified Whites' sense of superiority and legal impunity, as the perpetrators were almost never prosecuted for their crimes. Whites felt entitled to do this out in the open with no penalty and no discouragement from law enforcement.

Similar White bonding occurred during the 1943 Zoot Suit Riots in Los Angeles when White military servicemembers terrorized the Mexican American community, beating and stripping the men of their clothing.[81] In the first days of the riot the violence was confined to White servicemembers who clashed with Mexican American youth in streets and other public areas. However, within a few days, other White people saw the opportunity to put "uppity" Latinx youth in their place and joined in the violence. The White community of Los Angeles imagined itself as joining together against a threat of out-of-control brown-skinned ruffians. In August 2020, a police officer in Kenosha, Wisconsin, shot an unarmed Black man seven times. People of color in the community and White allies responded with daily protests. A group of White armed vigilantes (self-described as a "militia") came to the protests, apparently believing they were entitled to keep order. One of the vigilantes, a 17-year-old unlawfully armed with an AR-15 rifle, shot three protestors, and killed two.[82] History is replete with White citizens feeling entitled and emboldened to keep the racial order.

Men's street harassment and sexual assault of women can be viewed through the lens of male bonding—or at least as a patriarchal performance of women's mistreatment in the service of maintaining standing among other men. Recall the discussion from Chapter 4 of Jackson Katz's observation that the mistreatment of girls and women, rather than being condemned, actually lifts boys' and men's status in some peer groups. Objectifying and dehumanizing women is a form of homosocial bonding for some men. Brett Kavanaugh's performance during his nomination hearing for the US Supreme Court in 2018 contained many lows—Kavanaugh's fits of anger that the seat he felt entitled to may be lost because of allegations of sexual assault in his youth; the Republicans' embrace of bluster and petulance as a rhetorical tool of entitled resentment.[83] Lili Loofbourow writes about the sexual assault allegations against Kavanaugh as a performance for other young men and the pursuit of male approval.[84] Loofbourow argues the alleged sexual assault and sexual misconduct committed by Kavanaugh in high school and college was done in front of other young men for their benefit and with the goal of elevating Kavanaugh's status among men. And just as Kavanaugh's entitlement would predict, the Republican men on the Senate Judiciary Committee circled the gender wagons, ensuring that Kavanaugh's behavior was not subject to any true investigation or scrutiny. Even Kavanaugh's yearbook remarks are a good example of homosocial bonding at the expense of girls. In their "senior memories," Kavanaugh and his friends imply they all had sex with a girl from a local high school. Donald Trump performed for TV host Billy Bush in a recording in which Trump brags about kissing women without their consent and grabbing their genitals. Bush encourages Trump by laughing. When the recording surfaced during Trump's 2016 presidential campaign, he dismissed the conversation as "locker room talk"—another form of bonding between men. Sexual assault is sometimes something men do for other men.[85]

These incidents of White bonding and men's bonding demonstrate a profound privilege of the entitled. Dominant group members feel entitled to mistreat others without the threat of consequences. They are rarely punished socially or criminally for their conduct. In fact, they are sometimes elevated due to such conduct. Members of socially-preferred groups not only learn that they can get away with the mistreatment of the marginalized, but also the mistreatment bonds preferred groups together in their shared sense of dominion.

The Rage Against Uppity Minorities

White bonding and, to some extent, men's bonding, often occurs in the context of backlash against marginalized people's progress, or a lack of proper deference shown to the dominant group. For example, when groups of men harass women on the street, they are conveying to the woman that if she dares appear in public alone, then she's up for grabs.

It's worth taking a look at how this sort of backlash punishment can be measured experimentally. These experiments allow one to expose the double standards people use to judge people based on whether they are members of dominant or subordinated groups. One experiment asked White college students to rate the performance of an employee based on a summary of information about the person.[86] The person was either African American or White and was either in a supervisory or subordinate job. So, there were four different versions of the employee to be evaluated, but each student evaluated only one version. The participants gave higher ratings to the White supervisor than the Black supervisor even though the information provided about each was identical. The opposite judgment occurred in the evaluation of the subordinate employees. The students rated the Black subordinate higher than the White subordinate even though the information provided about each employee was identical. Another experiment found that when White respondents evaluated a low- and high-ability White or African American person, they rated the high-ability White person as somewhat more intelligent than themselves but rated the high-ability Black person as significantly less intelligent than themselves.[87]

Both studies reveal a racial bias. The White respondents in these studies felt comfortable with an African American in a subordinate role—they evaluated this person more favorably than a White person in the same role. In contrast, the respondents in these studies were uncomfortable when an African American employee was in a high-status position that reflected competence. For some White people, it is inconceivable that a person of color could be more competent than a White person. Therefore, rather than acknowledging the success of a person of color, they reject it.

We find similar patterns attributable to high-achieving professional women. A study by Madeline E. Heilman and her colleagues illustrates how women pay a social penalty for competence.[88] Heilman gave American college students packets that contained a profile of either a clearly successful or ambiguously successful woman or man in a male-dominated job (assistant vice president in mechanics and aeronautics). All information about the employee was identical except for the employee's gender. Students were asked to rate the candidate on competence, likeability, and interpersonal hostility. When students rated the employee's competence, successful women and men were evaluated equally—they were both given credit for their successes. When information about the candidate's performance was ambiguous, the woman was rated as less competent than the man. Consistent with our discussions from previous chapters, men are assumed to be competent even with mixed evidence. Conversely, women do not receive the presumption of competence and are therefore judged negatively when the evidence is mixed.

Patterns regarding the likability of candidates were also predictable demonstrating antipathy toward boundary-busting women. When there was ambiguity about the candidate's performance, there was no difference between the likeability ratings of women and men targets. But when there was clear evidence of success, the woman was liked less than the man. In fact, the clearly successful woman was liked less than the candidates in all other conditions (i.e., the clearly successful man, the ambiguously successful man, and the ambiguously successful woman). A similar pattern emerged in terms of judgments of hostility. The woman candidate was rated as less hostile than the man in the ambiguous performance outcome condition but was rated as more hostile than the man in the clearly successful condition. However, when success is explicit, women are viewed as less likable than men. Women, although rated less competent than men when information about them was ambiguous, are at least rated as less hostile interpersonally. These patterns hold for both women and men raters; so, these gender stereotypic norms, and the tendency to penalize women who violate them, are meaningful for both women and men respondents. Heilman further found that dislike was associated with not being recommended for promotions and salary increases.[89]

Men can feel comfortably entitled to recognition and credit even when it's not quite deserved. Women are credited with competence, but they are disliked for their competence, whereas men are not. Two important caveats to Heilman's studies: First, these punitive judgments about women occurred only when women were occupying male-dominated jobs, not when they oc-cupied female-dominated jobs. Therefore, what is salient to evaluators of these women is the fact that they are out of place—they are violating gender stereotypes about what work women should and should not do. Second, men who violate gender stereotypes also face a penalty. Heilman has found that men who were successful in female-stereotyped jobs were judged as ineffec-tual and afforded less respect than women occupying the same position.[90]

Salient here is the discussion in Chapter 2 regarding the *dominance* or *hubris penalty*. Subordinated groups pay a hubris penalty or a dominance penalty when they appear too confident, or too competent, as was the case in Heilman's study. This hubris/dominance penalty was tested in an experi-ment where research participants, all of whom were familiar with American football, read a passage about an African American or White professional football player who spiked the ball and danced immediately after scoring a touchdown versus the same player not engaging in such a celebration. Respondents then rated how arrogant they perceived the player to be and recommended a salary for the player for the following year. The participants viewed the two celebrating players as equally arrogant; however, they recommended that the celebrating African American player receive a salary that was 17% lower than the celebrating White player. There was no differ-ence in salary recommendations for the noncelebrating players.[91]

The Heilman study on women and the study of professional football players demonstrate something more than dominant group members being resistant to competence or confidence of women and men of color. In both studies there are salary implications for the judgments of competent women and confident men of color. Those making these judgments punished each group by preventing promotions or negatively affecting future salary. Minorities can pay a literal price for acting out of their designated position and making dominant group members feel uncomfortable. It's worth noting that men in professional settings who do not conform to the masculine stereotypes of assertiveness and competitiveness experience a modesty penalty.[92] Modest men are disliked because they are perceived as weak and uncertain. However, unlike perceptions of African American men and women from the studies above, modest men do not face employment or salary discrimination.

Women of color and White women face the dominance penalty, but the penalty may be harsher for women of color. For example, Latinx women college instructors with strict teaching styles pay a dominance penalty relative to White (Anglo) women professors with the same teaching style.[93] Another study found that compared to White women who do pay a professional penalty for dominance, Asian women do not. However, Asian American women are perceived to be lower in leadership ability than similarly situated White women.[94]

There's a history of White people responding with violence to what they perceive as a Black person acting out of their subordinated position, and men responding violently to women who don't stay in their place. It is a common motivation for rapes and lynchings. White people and men believe that African Americans and women should behave in a way that matches their status. If they are seen as too proud, or arrogant, or confident, they pay a hubris penalty. They are punished for not embracing their lower status. The Zoot Suit Riots, described earlier, is an example of Mexican American youth paying a hubris penalty for being too confident and not deferential to Anglos on public streets. The zoot suit was seen by Anglos as a symbol of Mexican American arrogance. The flamboyant style was seen as audacious and arrogant by the Anglo community. In fact, when the young men were beaten by Anglo servicemembers, they were also stripped of their symbol of arrogance—their suits were torn off them, leaving them in shreds of clothing. Some servicemembers took as souvenirs pieces of the zoot suit, harkening back to "souvenirs" taken from lynching victims.[95]

The Rage of the Dissed Man

In Chapter 2 we looked at attitudes that are correlated with feelings of entitlement. One set of attitudes, benevolent and hostile sexism, provides a framework for understanding the punishment of women who are too competent or confident, or men punishing women for rejecting them. Benevolent sexism is a set of attitudes that women should be nurturing, quiet, ladylike, and accommodating. Benevolent sexism rewards women for behaving according to these traditional gender roles. The rewards are empty, with gestures such as women having doors opened for them or being released first in a theoretical hostage situation. But what about women who don't behave according to traditional gender roles? What about ambitious, competitive, nonnurturing, or sexually active women? They are punished by the same attitudes. In this way, benevolent sexism is a protection racket. It sets up a situation of a hostile environment for women, but if they behave themselves and are subservient to men, those potentially threatening men will actually protect them. For the women who do not comply with the rigid gender constraints of benevolent sexism, they are punished in a variety of ways. Jessica Valenti uses the term *misogynist terrorism* to describe the ways men attack women—online or in person.[96] There is simply no equivalent with reversed genders. Women do not (and because it is systemic, cannot) punish in similar ways. Men's punishment of women in many cases results from men's maladaptive strategies for dealing with strong emotions, including anger and embarrassment.

Revenge porn is one phenomenon by which men punish women, and this revenge is usually the aftermath of a woman rejecting a man. A man, usually the ex-partner of the victim, posts online sexually explicit photos of the victim that she either did not know were taken or were taken in the context of a relationship. Revenge porn is the purposeful attempt to ruin the life of the woman, as it often identifies the victim by name and may include her e-mail or physical address. The result can be not only embarrassment and humiliation, but also other men contacting the victim, going to her home and harassing and stalking her. The fact that there are groups and forums on the Internet where men can find support for this behavior justifies and normalizes it to some men.[97] There is no equivalent pattern of women ex-partners engaging in online revenge in a way that threatens the life and livelihood of the victim. Revenge porn is gendered behavior of men lashing out against the women they can no longer control. Trolling comes down to the same root—the entitled man who thinks his right to free speech is equivalent to his right to be noticed and heard, and whose reaction to being ignored is to escalate until he cannot be ignored anymore.[98]

Men's Violence Against Transgender Women

The violence against transgender women in recent years epitomizes entitled resentment and backlash against progress. In the last couple of decades, transgender individuals have begun to be recognized for the gender they are rather than the gender assigned to them at birth. Transgender people, as well as gender nonbinary people, have demanded respect and recognition of their humanity even in the face of rejection from family members and strangers. Consistent with most movements toward progressive equality, the recognition of transgender people as fully human and worthy of dignity is matched with violent backlash. Violence against trans individuals tends to be especially gruesome and "personal," meaning the violence is close up, sometimes involving torture and mutilation. Violence against transgender women, especially transgender women of color, has become so frequent that the American Medical Association has declared it an "epidemic."[99]

Transgender activist and actor, Laverne Cox captures the entitled resentment of antitrans violence when she says, ". . . when we are living our lives, so many times just walking down the street as a Black trans woman, people saw it as some sort of affront to them, when men would find themselves attracted to me because I was walking down the street, and they would get upset about that."[100] A consistent thread that runs through men's violence against transgender women is the man feeling "fooled" or "tricked" by the victim. In fact, one defense strategy used by men who have murdered transgender women is a trans "panic" defense.[101] The revelation that the woman a man is attracted to is transgender and not a "real" woman in the man's mind is such a profound deception that the man lashes out in violence. Notice the shift in responsibility and victimhood here. The perpetrator of murder frames himself as the victim of a profound deception.

A related thread that runs through transgender violence is the misgendering of transgender victims of violence by law enforcement, news media, or lay people. Misgendering occurs when one intentionally or unintentionally refers to a person or uses language to describe a person that doesn't align with their affirmed gender. Referring to a trans woman as "he" or "really a guy" is an act of misgendering. It is the epitome of entitlement that strangers, or anyone other than the transgender person themselves, believe they have a right to decide what to call the person. If someone tells you their name and their gender, why would you feel comfortable calling them something else? If your name is *Luís*, I don't just decide to call you *Frank*. Cisgender people feel entitled to determine how a transgender person should be treated and what identity they should have. This practice epitomizes the entitlement of socially-preferred groups.

Entitlement and Men's Intimate Partner Violence

The rage of the rejected man plays out not just on the Internet but interpersonally. For instance, when a man feels disempowered relative to his partner, he may respond with aggression. The reverse tends not to be true. A study of White heterosexual couples in New Zealand is revealing.[102] In romantic relationships, the person who is more dependent on the relationship—the person who identifies more strongly with the relationship and is more emotionally or cognitively involved than their partner—possesses less power in the relationship. This study looked at couples' communication styles based on how much power each partner has in the relationship. Men who possessed low relationship power because they were more dependent on their partner exhibited greater aggressive communication (criticism, domineering) during the couple's conflict discussions. Specifically, they were more aggressive when they were unable to influence their partner and thus had low situational power (getting their partner to agree with them). In contrast, women's relationship to power was not associated with aggression. In other words, the women partners who had low relationship power did not behave aggressively with their mates. Interestingly, in these conflict interactions, the women were more verbally aggressive than their partners overall, but their verbal aggression was independent of their power status.

What accounts for men's aggression as a result of low power? Follow-up analyses found that the men in the study responded aggressively to lower power because low power threatens masculinity; men low in relationship power reported a reduction in masculinity on the days they had low situational power, and such drops in masculinity predicted a greater probability of men behaving aggressively toward their partner. In other words, aggression for these men was an attempt to repair their masculinity. It was when situational power—the ability to influence a partner—was undermined that aggression occured in men. The implication of this study is that we can predict men's aggression from whether or not they feel disempowered. Some men are highly sensitive to feeling disrespected. Traditional gender roles tell men they should be.

In her book on men's domestic violence, *No Visible Bruises*, Rachel Louise Snyder writes that violence is rooted in men's entitlement.[103] Violence is a result of a shared belief system wherein perpetrators have been told they are the authority in their lives and they should be respected and obeyed. Men are at the top of the human hierarchy. Men learn to have a sense of ownership over the world, themselves, and their partners. For these men, violence is the strategy for bringing things back to status quo when their expectations are frustrated. Snyder, who observed men in antiviolence programs, found that the decision to not engage in violence was not the most difficult part of their journey. Rather, it was learning that they have been fed a line about what they are supposed to be like, what masculinity means, and what being a man means. Many participants feel relieved when they learn they have been coerced into their violence and are not born with it. Boys' and men's socialization sadly distances them from the people around them. It limits their range of thinking, feeling, and behaving and keeps them boxed in by their own narrow ideas of what men could be and how men could behave.

This chapter has included a heavy dose of discussion about anger and aggression. Certainly, anger and aggression play significant roles in men's lives because they are so closely tied to traditional gender roles. However, when we consider the role of gender and entitlement in domestic violence, we must consider anger in a deeper way. Anger is not necessarily at the root of domestic abuse even if it may be used as a tool—a way for a man to bring back stasis and status. Men who are perpetrators of domestic abuse target their partners and children for abuse, but usually not others. In other words, perpetrators may not be walking around seething in anger, even though they do use violence to control others. Most often it is not directed at outsiders—only those they feel entitled to brutalize, that is, their woman partners. One study of men in domestic violence programs found that participants did not have substantial levels of anger, and that only a small percentage were in the unusually high range. Only about 25% are so-called rageaholics.[104] The domestic abuser's anger is targeted at their partner or her family. As a result, friends and acquaintances of abusers are often surprised to hear they committed an assault. These men treat many people in a respectful manner. They know how to treat people well but feel entitled to treat their victims differently.

Domestic violence generally refers to intimate partner or family abuse. But a significant amount of violence in home spaces includes violence against domestic workers—usually women of color—in someone else's home. Entitlement plays a role in this dynamic in several ways, from employers who are men who feel entitled to both the labor and the bodies of the women they hire, to women employers who rely upon domestic workers without considering the exploitation in which they are complicit. Some White women, including women who consider themselves feminists, feel entitled to pursue their economic and professional endeavors while someone else does the care work that makes their professional work possible. Domestic workers—often immigrant women of color—face economic exploitation and everyday violence. Women in these jobs face widespread sexual abuse, yet their workplaces are generally excluded from laws such as Title VII that are supposed to protect workers from sexual harassment.

The most important contributor to boys' and men's violence is gender socialization. Men learn that violence—particularly directed at people they think belong to them or those they believe should be subservient to them—is a reasonable reaction to bring back everyone to their rightful place. Men's violence is not inevitable but it is entitled and can be unlearned. Jessica Valenti argues that society is failing boys. Society has failed to raise them to believe they can be men without inflicting pain on others, failing to teach them that they are not entitled to women's sexual attention, and failing to allow them an outlet for understandable human fear and foibles that will not label them "weak" or unworthy.[105]

Conclusion

The entitled person's sense of being wronged is not merely psychological in nature. It occurs at macro and micro levels. At the macro level, while subordinated groups struggle, cynical politicians and dominant group members themselves invoke dominant group victimization. These groups' desire to "make America great again" are harkening back to a previous time in the country's history when classist, racist, sexist, hierarchical, and patriarchal power was even more entrenched. To the beneficiaries thereof, the world was properly aligned and change was and is threatening. Entitled resentment manifests in interpersonal interactions as well, where individual dominant group members punish subordinated groups who are perceived to act out of their assigned roles. At this micro level, individuals suffer psychological wounds because their sense of what they imagine they deserve is not sufficiently better than what those in the lower rungs have or are perceived to have.

White people have accepted a racial bribe in the form of a psychological wage of Whiteness, that tells them they cannot be as bad off as people of color, no matter what—because they are White. The myth of meritocracy tells White people that if they work hard, they can be rich and powerful, and this belief keeps them invested in this hierarchy. Therefore, many poor and working-class Whites do not build coalitions with poor and working-class people of color to fight against the unprecedented growth of income inequality in the last 40 years. They choose to resist and disidentify with those who would be natural allies, if not for racism. One tragic result of this dynamic is that government programs meant to help those who are struggling financially are unpopular with the White Americans most in need because these programs also help people of color. It is intolerable for some White people to be put in the same class as people of color. To use Jonathan Metzl's words, they are willing to die of Whiteness in the form of a lack of health insurance, increasing gun suicides, and foregoing food assistance. The 2016 presidential election demonstrated that White people appear to vote in their racial self-interest, not their economic self-interest.

Entitlement is a set of expectations that are not necessarily deserved but is nonetheless deeply rooted. When things don't go their way, preferred groups respond with confusion, fragility, and anger. When attention is turned to marginalized groups, there is a similar response. As a matter of course, White people do not want to hear about racism. They tend to think that people of color are not equal Americans so they are not worthy of legitimate recognition. Men don't want to deal with successful women. They want jobs and college entry free from competing with illegitimate competitors—women.

Cisgender people and heterosexuals are annoyed by gender-neutral restrooms and Pride parades. Marginalized people should not be center stage, however briefly. A month of Black History means they get attention for a whole month? Or in response to Pride parades, a few dozen men and White supremacists organized the "Straight Pride" march in 2019 in Boston.[106]

Entitled resentment can result in more than annoyance at being sidelined: it can resemble hotter emotions such as rage directed at uppity (i.e., confident) minorities. Punishment of minorities who are perceived to step out of line has historic and present-day manifestations ranging from denigrating their competence in a job search, to sexualization of women, to rape and other forms of violence. The antifemininity mandate reinforced in boys' and men's peer groups, and the instrumental use of women as methods of raising a man's status, make women alien to some men. Some men spend so much time trying to distinguish themselves from women and anything feminine that it is nearly impossible for those men to view women as human beings, as individuals requiring regard and having subjectivity. Society has done a woeful job of teaching men how to deal with their emotions, especially the emotions of hurt, sadness, anger, and disappointment. Therefore, some men's response to being rejected by women is to respond wildly disproportionately in the form of doxing, publishing revenge porn, committing acts of domestic abuse, or carrying out a mass shooting.

Finally, the entitled resentment that results from feeling wronged can be weaponized on a grand scale. In his book, *How Fascism Works: The Politics of Us and Them*, Jason Stanley writes that fascism offers a tried-and-true explanation for perceived loss by dominant group members who are accustomed to being centered but are easily led to view gestures toward equality as a source of victimization. Stanley notes, "The exploitation of the feeling of victimization by dominant groups at the prospect of sharing citizenship and power with minorities is a universal element of contemporary international fascist politics."[107] "This sense of loss, which is genuine, is manipulated in fascist politics into aggrieved victimhood and exploited to justify past, continuing, or new forms of oppression."[108] Stanley further argues that empires in decline are particularly susceptible to fascist politics because of this sense of loss. Donald Trump's politics were effective for his core group of supporters and that unsurprisingly parallels the United States' decline on the global stage.

Notes

1. Page 98: Stanley, J. (2018). *How fascism works: The politics of us and them.* Random House.
2. United States Environmental Protection Agency. (2017, June 19). Toxicological threats of plastic. https://www.epa.gov/trash-free-waters/toxicological-threats-plastic#what-type.
3. Trump Make America Great Again Committee. (n.d.). Trump straws-pack of 10. https://shop.donaldjtrump.com/products/trump-straws?_pos=1&_sid=c0a54f22c&_ss=r.
4. Swim, J. K., Gillis, A. J., & Hamaty, K. J. (2019). Gender bending and gender conformity: The social consequences of engaging in feminine and masculine proenvironmental behaviors. *Sex Roles.* https://doi.org/10.1007/s11199-019-01061-9.
5. Rosenberg, E. (2018, March 28). The vegans came to protest his restaurant. So this chef carved a deer leg in the window. *The Washington Post.* https://www.washingtonpost.com/news/food/wp/2018/03/28/the-vegans-came-to-protest-his-restaurant-so-this-chef-carved-a-deer-leg-in-the-window/.
6. Van Kessel, P., & Quinn, D (2020, October 29). Both Republicans and Democrats cite masks as a negative effect of COVID-19, but for very different reasons. *Pew Research Center.* https://www.pewresearch.org/fact-tank/2020/10/29/both-republicans-and-democrats-cite-masks-as-a-negative-effect-of-covid-19-but-for-very-different-reasons/.
7. Blumer, H. (1958). Race prejudice as a sense of group position. *Pacific Sociological Review, 1*(1), 3–7. https://doi.org/10.2307/1388607.

8. The Intrusion of Caste in Everyday Life section in: Wilkerson, I. (2020, July 1). America's enduring caste system. *New York Times Magazine*. https://www.nytimes.com/2020/07/01/magazine/isabel-wilkerson-caste.html?smid=em-share&login=email&auth=login-email.

9. Blumer, H. (1958). Race prejudice as a sense of group position. *Pacific Sociological Review, 1*(1), 3–7. https://doi.org/10.2307/1388607.

10. The Inevitable Narcissism of Caste section in: Wilkerson, I. (2020, July 1). America's enduring caste system. *New York Times Magazine*. https://www.nytimes.com/2020/07/01/magazine/isabel-wilkerson-caste.html?smid=em-share&login=email&auth=login-email.

11. Du Bois, W. E. B. (1935). *Black reconstruction in America*. Harcourt, Brace and Co.

12. Goldstein, N. J., & Hays, N. A. (2011). Illusory power transference: The vicarious experience of power. *Administrative Science Quarterly, 56*(4), 593–621. https://doi.org/10.1177/0001839212440972.

13. Hochschild, A. R. (2018). *Strangers in their own land: Anger and mourning on the American Right*. The New Press.

14. Rodrigo, C. M. (2019, April 28). White nationalists interrupt author, chant "This land is our land" in DC bookstore. *The Hill*. https://thehill.com/blogs/blog-briefing-room/news/441045-white-nationalists-interrupt-author-chant-this-land-is-our-land.

15. Stanley, J. (2018). *How fascism works: The politics of us and them*. Random House.

16. Rothwell & Diego-Rosell (2016), cited in: Pettigrew, T. F. (2017). Social psychological perspectives on Trump supporters. *Journal of Social and Political Psychology, 5*(1), 107–116. https://doi.org/10.5964/jspp.v5i1.750.

17. Rothwell & Diego-Rosell (2016), cited in: Pettigrew, T. F. (2017). Social psychological perspectives on Trump supporters. *Journal of Social and Political Psychology, 5*(1), 107–116. https://doi.org/10.5964/jspp.v5i1.750.

18. Mutz, D. C. (2018). Status threat, not economic hardship, explains the 2016 presidential vote. *Proceedings of the National Academy of Sciences, 115*(19). https://doi.org/10.1073/pnas.1718155115.

19. Pew Research Center. (2018, August 9). An examination of the 2016 electorate, based on validated voters. https://www.people-press.org/2018/08/09/an-examination-of-the-2016-electorate-based-on-validated-voters/.

20. Pettigrew, T. F. (2017). Social psychological perspectives on Trump supporters. *Journal of Social and Political Psychology, 5*(1), 107–116. https://doi.org/10.5964/jspp.v5i1.750.

21. Mutz, D. C. (2018). Status threat, not economic hardship, explains the 2016 presidential vote. *Proceedings of the National Academy of Sciences,115*(19). https://doi.org/10.1073/pnas.1718155115.

22. Cox, D., Lienesch, R., & Jones, R. P. (2017, May 9). Beyond economics: Fears of cultural displacement pushed the white working class to Trump: PRRI/The Atlantic report. *PRRI*. https://www.prri.org/research/white-working-class-attitudes-economy-trade-immigration-election-donald-trump/.

23. Rothwell, J., & Diego-Rosell, P. (2016). Explaining nationalist political views: The case of Donald Trump. *SSRN Electronic Journal*. https://doi.org/10.2139/ssrn.2822059.

24. Cited in Pettrigrew, T. F. (2017). Social psychological perspectives on Trump supporters. *Journal of Social and Political Psychology*, *5*(1), 107–116. https://doi.org/10.5964/jspp.v5i1.750.

25. Mutz, D. C. (2018). Status threat, not economic hardship, explains the 2016 presidential vote. *Proceedings of the National Academy of Sciences*, *115*(19). https://doi.org/10.1073/pnas.1718155115.

26. Cox, D., Lienesch, R., & Jones, R. P. (2017, May 9). Beyond economics: Fears of cultural displacement pushed the white working class to Trump: PRRI/The Atlantic report. *PRRI*. https://www.prri.org/research/white-working-class-attitudes-economy-trade-immigration-election-donald-trump/.

27. Cox, D., Lienesch, R., & Jones, R. P. (2017, May 9). Beyond economics: Fears of cultural displacement pushed the white working class to Trump: PRRI/The Atlantic report. *PRRI*. https://www.prri.org/research/white-working-class-attitudes-economy-trade-immigration-election-donald-trump/.

28. Gould, E., & Schieder, J. (2018, May 17). Poverty persists 50 years after the Poor People's Campaign: Black poverty rates are more than twice as high as white poverty rates. *Economic Policy Institute*. https://www.epi.org/publication/poverty-persists-50-years-after-the-poor-peoples-campaign-black-poverty-rates-are-more-than-twice-as-high-as-white-poverty-rates/.

    Jones, J. (2017, February 13). The racial wealth gap. How African-Americans have been shortchanged out of the materials to build wealth. *Economic Policy Institute*. https://www.epi.org/blog/the-racial-wealth-gap-how-african-americans-have-been-shortchanged-out-of-the-materials-to-build-wealth/.

29. Greitemeyer, T., & Sagioglou, C. (2016). Subjective socioeconomic status causes aggression: A test of the theory of social deprivation. *Journal of Personality and Social Psychology*, *111*(2), 178–194. https://doi.org/10.1037/pspi0000058.

30. Greitemeyer, T., & Sagioglou, C. (2016). Subjective socioeconomic status causes aggression: A test of the theory of social deprivation. *Journal of Personality and Social Psychology*, *111*(2), 178–194. https://doi.org/10.1037/pspi0000058.

31. Greitemeyer, T., & Sagioglou, C. (2016). Subjective socioeconomic status causes aggression: A test of the theory of social deprivation. *Journal of Personality and Social Psychology*, *111*(2), 178–194. https://doi.org/10.1037/pspi0000058.

32. Mutz, D. C. (2018). Status threat, not economic hardship, explains the 2016 presidential vote. *Proceedings of the National Academy of Sciences*, *115*(19). https://doi.org/10.1073/pnas.1718155115.

33. Coates, T. (2017 October). The first White president. *The Atlantic*. https://www.theatlantic.com/magazine/archive/2017/10/the-first-white-president-ta-nehisi-coates/537909/.

34. Metzl, J. M. (2019). *Dying of whiteness: How the politics of racial resentment is killing America's heartland*. Basic Books.

35. Rothwell, J., & Diego-Rosell, P. (2016). Explaining nationalist political views: The case of Donald Trump. *SSRN Electronic Journal*. https://doi.org/10.2139/ssrn.2822059.

36. Metzl, J. M. (2019). *Dying of whiteness: How the politics of racial resentment is killing America's heartland*. Basic Books.

37. Metzl, J. M. (2019). *Dying of whiteness: How the politics of racial resentment is killing America's heartland.* Basic Books.

38. Page 13: Metzl, J. M. (2019). *Dying of whiteness: How the politics of racial resentment is killing America's heartland.* Basic Books.

39. .Vanderbilt.edu.   https://news.vanderbilt.edu/vanderbiltmagazine/dying-of-whiteness-how-the-politics-of-racial-resentment-is-killing-americas-heartland/.

40. Page 7: *Dying of whiteness: How the politics of racial resentment is killing America's heartland.* Basic Books.

41. Berman, J. (2019, April 2). White men who can't get jobs say they're being discriminated against. *MarketWatch.* https://www.marketwatch.com/story/that-google-engineer-isnt-alone-other-white-men-say-theyre-discriminated-against-2018-01-09.

42. For a review of what affirmative action is and is not, please see Chapter 6 in: Anderson, K. J. (2010). *Benign bigotry: The psychology of subtle prejudice.* Cambridge University Press.

43. Berman, J. (2019, April 2). White men who can't get jobs say they're being discriminated against. *MarketWatch.* https://www.marketwatch.com/story/that-google-engineer-isnt-alone-other-white-men-say-theyre-discriminated-against-2018-01-09.

44. O'Brien, L. T., Garcia, D., Crandall, C. S., & Kordys, J. (2010). White Americans' opposition to affirmative action: Group interest and the harm to beneficiaries objection. *British Journal of Social Psychology, 49*(4), 895–903. https://doi.org/10.1348/014466610X518062.

45. Johnson, S. D. (1980). Reverse discrimination and aggressive behavior. *The Journal of Psychology: Interdisciplinary and Applied, 104*(1), 11–19.

46. Johnson, S. D. (1980). Reverse discrimination and aggressive behavior. *The Journal of Psychology: Interdisciplinary and Applied, 104*(1), 11–19.

47. Glass, I. (Host). (2019, September 29). Burn it Down. (No. 684) [Audio podcast episode]. In *This American Life.* https://www.thisamericanlife.org/684/burn-it-down.

48. Knowles, H. (2019, September 8). As plantations talk more honestly about slavery, some visitors are pushing back. *The Washington Post.* https://www.washingtonpost.com/history/2019/09/08/plantations-are-talking-more-about-slavery-grappling-with-visitors-who-talk-back/.

49. Addison, B. (2012, June 13). Apologizing for mistakes of the past. *Long Beach Post.* https://lbpost.com/news/apologizing-for-mistakes-of-the-past

50. The New York Times. "I Become a Person of Suspicion." The Daily. https://www.nytimes.com/2020/04/10/podcasts/the-daily/racism-chinese-coronavirus-asian-americans.html?showTranscript=1.

51. Tatum, B. D. (2017). *Why are all the Black kids sitting together in the cafeteria?* Basic Books.

52. Rosenberg, E. (2018, February 5). The judge Trump disparaged as "Mexican" will preside over an important border wall case. *The Washington Post.* https://www.washingtonpost.com/news/politics/wp/2018/02/05/the-judge-trump-disparaged-as-mexican-will-preside-over-an-important-border-wall-case/.

53. History.com Editors. (2020, February 21). Japanese internment camps. *History.* https://www.history.com/topics/world-war-ii/japanese-american-relocation.

54. Devos, T., & Banaji, M. R. (2005). American = White? *Journal of Personality and Social Psychology, 88*(3), 447–466. https://doi.org/10.1037/0022-3514.88.3.447.

55. Devos, T., & Mohamed, H. (2014). Shades of American identity: Implicit relations between ethnic and national identities. *Social and Personality Psychology Compass, 8*(12), 739–754. https://doi.org/10.1111/spc3.12149.

56. Craig, M. A., & Richeson, J. A. (2014). On the precipice of a "majority-minority" America: Perceived status threat from the racial demographic shift affects White Americans' political ideology. *Psychological Science, 25*(6), 1189–1197. https://doi.org/10.1177/0956797614527113.

57. Roussos, G., & Dovidio, J. F. (2018). Hate speech is in the eye of the beholder: The influence of racial attitudes and freedom of speech beliefs on perceptions of racially motivated threats of violence. *Social Psychological and Personality Science, 9*(2), 176–185. https://doi.org/10.1177/1948550617748728.

58. Kegler, A. (2016, July 22). The sugarcoated language of white fragility. *HuffPost.* https://www.huffpost.com/entry/the-sugarcoated-language-of-white-fragility_b_10909350.

59. See Chapter 1 in: Anderson, K. J. (2010). *Benign bigotry: The psychology of subtle prejudice.* Cambridge University Press.

60. DiAngelo, R. (2015, April 9). White fragility: Why it's so hard to talk to White people about racism. *The Good Men Project.* https://goodmenproject.com/featured-content/white-fragility-why-its-so-hard-to-talk-to-white-people-about-racism-twlm/.

61. DiAngelo, R. (2015, April 9). White fragility: Why it's so hard to talk to White people about racism. *The Good Men Project.* https://goodmenproject.com/featured-content/white-fragility-why-its-so-hard-to-talk-to-white-people-about-racism-twlm/.

62. DiAngelo, R. (2015, April 9). White fragility: Why it's so hard to talk to White people about racism. *The Good Men Project.* https://goodmenproject.com/featured-content/white-fragility-why-its-so-hard-to-talk-to-white-people-about-racism-twlm/.

63. Fiore, N. (Writer), Herrera, J. (Writer), & Skogland, K. (Director). (2018, June 6). Women's Work. (Season 2, Episode 12) [Hulu series episode]. In S. Kockin, B. Miller, E. Moss, E. Tuchman, M. Barker, W. Littlefield, I. Chaiken, F., et al. (Executive producers), *The Handmaid's Tale.* Daniel Wilson Productions, Inc.; The Littlefield Company; White Oak Pictures; MGM Television.

64. Vandello, J. A., & Bosson, J. K. (2013). Hard won and easily lost: A review and synthesis of theory and research on precarious manhood. *Psychology of Men & Masculinity, 14*(2), 101–113. https://doi.org/10.1037/a0029826.

65. Vedantam, S., Shah, P., Boyle, T., & Cohen, R. (Hosts). (2018, October 1). "Man up": How a fear of appearing feminine restricts men, and affects us all. [Audio podcast episode]. In *Hidden Brain.* NPR. https://www.npr.org/2018/10/01/653339162/-man-up-how-a-fear-of-appearing-feminine-restricts-men-and-affects-us-all.

66. Vandello, J. A., & Bosson, J. K. (2013). Hard won and easily lost: A review and synthesis of theory and research on precarious manhood. *Psychology of Men & Masculinity, 14*(2), 101–113. https://doi.org/10.1037/a0029826.

67. Wootson, C. (2018, July 23). He is accused of killing someone in a parking spot dispute. Authorities say he was standing his ground. *The Washington Post.* https://www.

washingtonpost.com/news/post-nation/wp/2018/07/21/hes-accused-of-killing-someone-in-a-parking-spot-dispute-authorities-say-he-was-standing-his-ground/?utm_term=.6cd681eb0bf2.

68. Carlson, J. (2015). Mourning Mayberry: Guns, masculinity, and socioeconomic decline. *Gender & Society, 29*(3), 386–409. https://doi.org/10.1177/0891243214554799.

69. Cassino, D., & Besen-Cassino, Y. (2019). Sometimes (but not this time), a gun is just a gun: Masculinity threat and guns in the United States, 1999-2018. *Sociological Forum, 35*(1), 5–23. https://doi.org/10.1111/socf.12565.

70. Cassino, D., & Besen-Cassino, Y. (2019). Sometimes (but not this time), a gun is just a gun: Masculinity threat and guns in the United States, 1999-2018. *Sociological Forum, 35*(1), 5–23. https://doi.org/10.1111/socf.12565.

71. Cassino, D., & Besen-Cassino, Y. (2019). Sometimes (but not this time), gun is just a gun: Masculinity threat and guns in the United States, 1999-2018. *Sociological Forum, 35*(1), 5–23. https://doi.org/10.1111/socf.12565.

72. Metzl, J. (2019). *Dying of whiteness.* Basic Books.

73. Dahl, J., Vescio, T., & Weaver, K. (2015). How threats to masculinity sequentially cause public discomfort, anger, and ideological dominance over women. *Social Psychology, 46*(4), 242–254. https://doi.org/10.1027/1864-9335/a000248.

74. Dahl, J., Vescio, T., & Weaver, K. (2015). How threats to masculinity sequentially cause public discomfort, anger, and ideological dominance over women. *Social Psychology, 46*(4), 242–254. https://doi.org/10.1027/1864-9335/a000248.

75. Trump, D. J. [@realDonaldTrump]. (2017, December 12). *Lightweight Senator Kirsten Gillibrand, a total flunky for Chuck Schumer and someone who would come to my office "begging" for* [Tweet]. Twitter. https://twitter.com/realDonaldTrump/status/940567812053053441.

76. Wise, T. (2017, August 16). If it's a civil war, pick a side: Donald Trump, White nationalism and the future of America. *Tim Wise.* http://www.timwise.org/2017/08/if-its-a-civil-war-pick-a-side-donald-trump-white-nationalism-and-the-future-of-america/. Also, the statistics offered in this quotation can be found from:

Jones, J. (2018, October 30). Black unemployment is at least twice as high as white unemployment at the national level and in 12 states and D.C. *Economic Policy Institute.* https://www.epi.org/publication/2018q3_unemployment_state_race_ethnicity/.

Jones, J. (2017, February 13). The racial wealth gap. How African-Americans have been shortchanged out of the materials to build wealth. *Economic Policy Institute.* https://www.epi.org/blog/the-racial-wealth-gap-how-african-americans-have-been-shortchanged-out-of-the-materials-to-build-wealth/, and Gould, E., & Schieder, J. (2018, May 17). Poverty persists 50 years after the Poor People's Campaign: Black poverty rates are more than twice as high as white poverty rates. *Economic Policy Institute.* https://www.epi.org/publication/poverty-persists-50-years-after-the-poor-peoples-campaign-black-poverty-rates-are-more-than-twice-as-high-as-white-poverty-rates/.

77. Gessen, M. (2016, November 10). Autocracy: Rules for survival https://www.nybooks.com/daily/2016/11/10/trump-election-autocracy-rules-for-survival/.

Snyder, T. (2017). *On tyranny: Twenty lessons from the twentieth century.* Tim Duggan Books.

78. Stanley, J. (2018). *How fascism works: The politics of us and them.* Random House.

79. Buric, F. (2016, March 12). Trump's not Hitler, he's Mussolini: How GOP anti-intellectualism created a modern fascist movement in America. *Salon.* https://www.salon.com/2016/03/11/trumps_not_hitler_hes_mussolini_how_gop_anti_intellectualism_created_a_modern_fascist_movement_in_america/.

80. Holan, A. (2019, April 26). In context: Donald Trump's "very fine people on both sides" remarks (transcript). *Politifact.* https://www.politifact.com/article/2019/apr/26/context-trumps-very-fine-people-both-sides-remarks/.

81. Gerber, M. (2018. June 4). Zoot Suit Riots: After 75 years, L.A. looks back on a violent summer. *Los Angeles Times.* https://www.latimes.com/local/lanow/la-me-ln-zoot-suit-riots-anniversary-20180604-story.html.

82. Thebault, R., & Armus, T. (2020, August 30). Dueling narratives fuel opposing views of Kenosha protest shooting. *The Washington Post.* https://www.washingtonpost.com/nation/2020/08/30/kenosha-shooting-victims-defense/.

83. St. Felix, D. (2018, September 28). The Ford-Kavanaugh hearings will be remembered for their grotesque display of patriarchal resentment. *The New Yorker.* https://www.newyorker.com/culture/cultural-comment/the-ford-kavanaugh-hearings-will-be-remembered-for-their-grotesque-display-of-patriarchal-resentment.

84. Loofbourow, L. (2018, September 25). Brett Kavanaugh and the cruelty of male bonding. *Slate.* https://slate.com/news-and-politics/2018/09/brett-kavanaugh-allegations-yearbook-male-bonding.html.

85. Tolentino, J. (2018, September 26). Brett Kavanaugh, Donald Trump, and the things men do for other men. *The New Yorker.* https://www.newyorker.com/news/our-columnists/brett-kavanaugh-donald-trump-and-the-things-men-do-for-other-men.

86. Knight, J. L., Hebl, M. R., Foster, J. B., & Mannix, L. M. (2003). Out of role? Out of luck: The influence of race and leadership status on performance appraisals. *Journal of Leadership & Organizational Studies, 9*(3), 85–93. https://doi.org/10.1177/107179190300900308.

87. Dovidio, J. F., & Gaertner, S. L. (1991). Changes in the expression and assessment of racial prejudice. In H. J. Knopke, R. J. Norrell, & R. W. Rogers (Eds.), *Opening doors: Perspectives on race relations in contemporary America* (pp. 119–148). University of Alabama Press.

88. Heilman, M. E., Wallen, A. S., Fuchs, D., & Tamkins, M. M. (2004). Penalties for success: Reactions to women who succeed at male gender-typed tasks. *Journal of Applied Psychology, 89*(3), 416–427. https://doi.org/10.1037/0021-9010.89.3.416.

89. Heilman, M. E., Wallen, A. S., Fuchs, D., & Tamkins, M. M. (2004). Penalties for success: Reactions to women who succeed at male gender-typed tasks. *Journal of Applied Psychology, 89*(3), 416–427. https://doi.org/10.1037/0021-9010.89.3.416.

90. Heilman, M. E., & Wallen, A. S. (2010). Wimpy and undeserving of respect: Penalties for men's gender-inconsistent success. *Journal of Experimental Social Psychology, 46*(4), 664–667. https://doi.org/10.1016/j.jesp.2010.01.008.

91. Hall, E. V., & Livingston, R. W. (2012). The hubris penalty: Biased responses to "Celebration" displays of Black football players. *Journal of Experimental Social Psychology, 48*(4), 899–904. https://doi.org/10.1016/j.jesp.2012.02.004.

92. Moss-Racusin C. A., Phelan J. E., & Rudman L. A. (2010). When men break the gender rules: status incongruity and backlash against modest men. *Psychology of Men & Masculinities, 11*(2), 140–151. https://doi.org/10.1037/a0018093.

93. Anderson, K. J., & Smith, G. (2005). Students' preconceptions of professors: Benefits and barriers according to ethnicity and gender. *Hispanic Journal of Behavioral Sciences, 27*(2), 184–201. https://doi.org/10.1177/0739986304273707.

94. Tinkler, J., Zhao, J., Li, Y., & Ridgeway, C. L. (2019). Honorary Whites? Asian American women and the dominance penalty. *Socius: Sociological Research for a Dynamic World, 5*. https://doi.org/10.1177/2378023119836000.

95. Tovares, J. (Writer & Director). (2002, February 10). Zoot Suit Riots. (Season 14, Episode 8) [TV series episode]. In J. Crichton, M. Drain, M. Samels, & S. Bellows (Executive Producers), *American Experience*. WGBH-TV.

96. Valenti, J. (2018, April 26). When misogynists become terrorists. *The New York Times*. https://www.nytimes.com/2018/04/26/opinion/when-misogynists-become-terrorists.html.

97. DeKeseredy, W. S., & Schwartz, M. D. (2016). Thinking sociologically about image-based sexual abuse: The contribution of male peer support theory. *Sexualization, Media, & Society, 2*(4), 1–8. https://search-ebscohost-com.ezproxy.uhd.edu/login.aspx?direct=true&db=edb&AN=122380599&site=eds-live&scope=site.

98. Chu, A. (2015, August 29). Celebrity killer culture: When grandiosity, privilege and entitlement turn attention-seeking into violence. *Salon*. http://www.salon.com/2015/08/28/celebrity_killer_culture_the_history_of_how_grandiosity_privilege_and_entitlement_turn_attention_seeking_into_violence/.

99. AMA adopts new policies on first day of voting at 2019 Annual Meeting. https://www.ama-assn.org/press-center/press-releases/ama-adopts-new-policies-first-day-voting-2019-annual-meeting.

100. "A backlash against our existence": Laverne Cox speaks out on violence against trans women of color. *Democracy Now*. https://www.democracynow.org/2019/10/7/laverne_cox_violence_trans_women_of.

101. Trans woman's killer used the "gay panic defense." It's still legal in 42 states. *Vice.com*. https://www.vice.com/en_us/article/a3xby5/trans-womans-killer-used-the-gay-panic-defense-its-still-legal-in-42-states.

102. Overall, N. C., Hammond, M. D., McNulty, J. K., & Finkel, E. J. (2016). When power shapes interpersonal behavior: Low relationship power predicts men's aggressive responses to low situational power. *Journal of Personality and Social Psychology, 111*(2), 195–217. https://doi.org/10.1037/pspi0000059.

103. Snyder, R. L. (2019). *No visible bruises: What we don't know about domestic violence can kill us*. Bloomsbury.

104. Cited on page 153 in: Snyder, R. L. (2019). *No visible bruises: What we don't know about domestic violence can kill us*. Bloomsbury.

105. Valenti, J. (2018, April 26). When misogynists become terrorists. *The New York Times.* https://www.nytimes.com/2018/04/26/opinion/when-misogynists-become-terrorists.html.

106. Betancourt, S. (2019, August 31). Boston "straight pride" parade dwarfed by large counter-protest. *The Guardian.* https://www.theguardian.com/world/2019/sep/01/boston-straight-pride-parade-arrests.

107. Page 95: Stanley, J. (2018). *How fascism works: The politics of us and them.* Random House.

108. Page 99: Stanley, J. (2018). *How fascism works: The politics of us and them.* Random House.

Conclusion

Not everything that is faced can be changed. But nothing can be changed until it is faced.

—James Baldwin[1]

The goal of this book was to analyze the crucial role of entitlement in understanding the persistence of inequality and, specifically, the backlash against efforts toward equality. This book situates entitlement among other drivers of inequality—power and privilege. Examining power and privilege helps to explain why inequality exists and persists. An analysis of entitlement allows us to understand the perpetuation of inequality in a more nuanced and precise way. Entitlement showcases the hyper-emotional reaction of backlash by the entitled in response to their perception of being sidelined or having their relative status decreased in the social hierarchy.[2] Entitlement is key to this reaction and it often results in rage, stemming from the dominant groups' perception of minority progress. While most of the examples in this book have been contemporary, entitlement is central to understanding both the vicious backlash of the last few years and most, if not all, of the history of the United States. Understanding entitlement's role in persistent inequality should help activists and organizers, policy makers, journalists, researchers, and nonacademics understand the entrenchment rooted in one's sense of deservingness. Entitlement is not genetic. It is learned, so it can be unlearned. But we have to see it, understand its workings, and care about its consequences.

Entitled Resentment's Consequences for People

Inequality pummels marginalized groups while illegitimately elevating socially-preferred groups. Both interpersonal and institutional inequality persists in healthcare, the legal system, housing, employment, and education. Income inequality between the richest and poorest in the United States is more extreme than any comparable country.[3]

Enraged, Rattled, and Wronged. Kristin J. Anderson, Oxford University Press. © Oxford University Press 2021. DOI: 10.1093/oso/9780197578438.003.0008

Inequality devastates the marginalized and benefits the preferred. However, there are also negative consequences for the entitled. Entitled people tend to be overconfident in the assessments of their own skills and performance. This tendency makes them ignorant to their own limitations and their ability to recognize when they need to improve. Power constrains and streamlines one's thinking. Power holders tend to rely on stereotypes to quickly make sense of their surroundings. They are less likely than those with diminished power to bother with careful, deliberate thinking. Laboratory studies reveal that power holders tend to be self-serving in their decision-making and evaluations of things and people. In this way, entitled people are, to some degree, disconnected from reality and thus are not interacting with the world in an authentic way.

Entitlement makes people cognitively inflexible but also behaviorally, professionally, and politically unable to adapt to change. In contrast to dominant groups—the groups with a surplus of entitlement—members of marginalized groups cannot take much for granted. They have to be flexible whether it be during interactions with those in power (e.g., law enforcement, employers) or retooling their skills to adapt to changes in the job market. Dominant group members do not believe they should have to change and adapt, and they react emotionally when they are asked to do so. Christianity is unquestionably the dominant religion in the United States, yet some Christians react to the inclusive greeting "Happy Holidays" with the overwrought and irrational response that there is a war on Christmas.[4] Entitled people fashion themselves as victims when they are not.

There are practical consequences of entitlement for those with excess amounts of it. As we saw from Jonathan M. Metzl's interviews, economically struggling White people support policies that are self-destructive to themselves and their communities. Too many White people vote according to their racial status, against their economic status. They support politicians who offer policies that objectively advantage the wealthy and harm working-class and poor White people. Working-class and less-educated Whites vote for politicians who keep gun laws loose, and easy access to firearms disproportionately affects White men in suicides (and mass shootings, which affect the rest of us). They vote for politicians who give massive tax breaks to the wealthiest Americans—the very people who do not need tax cuts—while cutting much needed aid, such as health care, early childhood education programs, and school lunch programs, to poor and working-class people. White voters who are challenged economically seem to accept the racial bribe offered to them by elites. Rather than *actual* wages, they accept the psychological wage of Whiteness in exchange for their higher position in the racial hierarchy. Isabel Wilkerson argues that, "Everyone in the caste system is trained to covet proximity to the dominant caste."[5] The rage struggling White people feel is not directed upward toward the wealthy, but downward or horizontally toward poor people, and people of color in their own economic group who also face racism. Entitlement compels those who have it to co-sign inhumane policies in order to keep the power they believe they deserve. Among those many Americans who are simultaneously in dominant (e.g., White, male) and subordinate (e.g., working-class) groups, entitlement tricks them into disowning those in similar circumstances where coalitions could be created. The pact that working-class Whites have made with politicians who enrich themselves and their friends only serves to perpetuate income inequality that directly impacts these very same working-class White people.

Entitled Resentment's Consequences to the Planet

There are broader consequences of entitled resentment beyond individuals' health, safety, and resources, as if those consequences are not breathtaking enough to provoke radical change. The refusal of dominant group members to adapt to needed change is exemplified in the denial of environmental catastrophe from climate change. The United States has been out of step with comparable nations on climate action, and the Trump administration actually reversed the modest regulations in place to stem climate change.[6] The United States also has a greater concentration of "climate deniers" than comparable nations.[7] There are myriad reasons for this dangerous dynamic that are beyond the scope of this book. However, the issue of climate change denial does speak to some of the issues in this book. Entitlement can help us understand climate change denial. Consider our discussions of anti-intellectualism, individualism, and fragile masculinity. US leaders such as Donald Trump, and many in the Republican Party, dismiss accepted scientific principles when it furthers their political goals.[8] Look no further than the Trump administration's delayed and inept response to the outbreak of COVID-19 in 2020.[9] The Republican Party has long supported empirically bankrupt initiatives such as abstinence-only education, attempts at solving drug abuse by just saying "No," and the extreme wing of the party opposes the teaching of evolution. Antiscience attitudes, which were linked to entitlement in Chapter 5, contribute to climate change denial.

Recall the discussion of individualism in Chapter 2. The ideology that attributes success and failure solely to the individual is baked into American identity. In order to slow the negative effects of climate change, both individual and collective behavior change is required. As a global community, we must consume less, reuse more, and cut our reliance on fossil fuels. Such changes, however, are incompatible with the "American way of life," which is defined by high consumption and ever-expanding material prosperity.[10] Some Americans feel entitled to not be inconvenienced in the slightest, and they are unwilling to forego any comforts or modify their behavior in the least bit, all of which are required to deal with the catastrophic crisis of climate change.

One of the correlates of entitlement—social dominance orientation—predicts climate change denial. Those who support group-based hierarchies and dominance over others also believe in human domination over nature.[11] In other words, those who orient toward social dominance seem to believe they are going to tell nature what to do, not vice versa. People with social dominance orientations also support the status quo[12] and would likely reject any initiatives that would require people to change their behavior—for instance, consuming less, reusing more, and lowering reliance on fossil fuels.

Women are more likely than men to support legislation to combat climate change.[13] Perhaps because women are more concerned about climate change than men, environmental concerns seem too feminine for some men. Recall the study finding that people questioned the sexual orientation of men who recycle.[14] Several writers have linked attitudes of climate change denial to fragile masculinity. "Petro-masculinity" is a term that captures the link between the desire for fossil fuel extraction and masculinity.[15] Researchers coined the term "cool dude effect" to capture how White, politically conservative men are particularly susceptible to climate change denial compared to other Americans.[16] These researchers conclude, "climate change denial seems to have become almost an essential component of conservative white male identity."[17] And consistent with discussions in earlier chapters, the researchers found that the more these men *think* they know about global warming, the more they deny it.[18] Eating animals is the second largest contributor to human-caused greenhouse gas emissions, and thus plant-based diets are a crucial strategy for combating climate change. And yet, eating meat has long been viewed and defended as manly,[19] and thus veganism is associated with femininity, and vegan men are dismissed as "soyboys" and "beta males."[20] In this regard, fragile masculinity is endangering the planet.

Entitled Resentment's Consequences for Democracy

Donald Trump is a fascist. And when it comes to democracy versus fascism, I'm sorry there are not fine people on both sides. So you need to choose, Donald Trump or the American people. This is the time to get off the Trump train. Cuz he just told you where the train is going and it's not a passenger train. And he'll load you on it some day too.
                            —Stephen Colbert, November 5, 2020[21]

Entitlement could end democracy. The grievance politics of the entitled has knocked down some crucial pillars that have historically upheld democracy in the United States. Consider the election of Donald Trump, who, in terms of worldview and ideology, is an authoritarian (in addition to having a cruel social dominance orientation). But his authoritarian tendencies are not confined to inside his head. His authoritarian governance was reflected in his immigration policies, his attacks on refugees and religious minorities, and his emphasis on so-called law and order. Trump sucked up to other authoritarians around the world including Jair Bolsonaro in Brazil, Rodrigo Duterte in the Philippines, Recep Tayyip Erdoğan in Turkey, and even North Korea leader Kim Jong-un, about whom Trump has said, "And then we fell in love. No really. He wrote me beautiful letters. They were great letters. And then we feel in love."[22]

Trump interacted with his political enemies, and the media as an authoritarian as well. He felt entitled to face no opposition, and he used the power of the state to try to stifle opposing views or any honest accounting of his policies and behavior. According to Steven Levitsky and Daniel Ziblatt in their book, *How Democracies Die*, Trump checks off the main four boxes of authoritarianism: (1) He described the news media as an enemy of the people, (2) he said he may not accept the outcome of an election if he lost, (3) he accused his political rivals of being corrupt, and (4) he stoked violence at his campaign rallies.[23] These steps are crucial to intimidate and silence real and imagined opponents.

According to Levitsky and Ziblatt, Trump is part of a long line of authoritarian demagogues that have gained popularity throughout US history.[24]

There was Henry Ford in the 1920s, Huey Long in the 1930s, Joseph McCarthy in the 1950s, and George Wallace in the 1960s. What is different about these demagogues of earlier decades is that they were never able to get close to the White House. Politicians in their own parties eventually stopped them. Not so for Trump. Why was 2016 different? And why, after knowing him so well, did he come close to being re-elected in 2020? There are no doubt multiple reasons we got Trump but there are a couple of factors that directly relate to the topic of this book: the radicalization of the Republican Party, the lack of popularity of Republican policies, and Republicans' resorting to unethical and unconstitutional tactics to win.[25] These factors center on and exploit entitled resentment of those who think they should be on top but feel left behind. A significant Republican voting bloc is those who believe that women and minorities—those who reliably vote as Democrats—are taking over the country. White men vote Republican even though many will suffer economically. Republican politicians can win by taking advantage of the entitled resentment and stoking it.

Republicans also win by cheating.

Republican initiatives are unpopular among Americans in general. Their tax cuts that benefit the rich are unpopular.[26] Their position on gun control, which is to have no control over guns, is unpopular.[27] Their position against the Affordable Care Act is unpopular.[28] Their position against Medicare-for-All is unpopular.[29] Their position on immigration is unpopular.[30] Their position against the right to abortion is unpopular.[31] Their position denying climate change is unpopular.[32] Their position on prematurely "reopening the economy" during the 2020 Coronavirus pandemic was unpopular.[33] When your policies are not supported by the people, you have to find ways to stop the people from weighing in. And thus, in an ostensible democracy, the only way for Republicans to win is by cheating.

This characterization is not hyperbolic as comprehensive analyses of voter disfranchisement by Carol Anderson[34] and Ari Berman carefully document.[35] If everyone eligible to vote, votes, Republicans lose. "I don't want everybody to vote," conservative strategist Paul Weyrich declared in 1980.[36] In 2020, Donald Trump admitted, "you'd never have a Republican elected in this country again" if Congress made it easier to vote by mail.[37] And sure enough, only a few hours after the polls closed in the 2020 presidential election, Trump falsely declared victory and stated, "We want all voting to stop."[38]

So what have Republicans done? Gerrymandering congressional districts to maintain power is one strategy that both Republicans and Democrats are guilty of, creating noncompetitive districts for their own candidates. Republicans only win by engaging in undemocratic voter disfranchisement, which hurts not only Democrats but democracy itself. Republican legislators have made it nearly impossible for specific groups of people to vote including poor people, students, and communities of color. These communities reliably vote for Democrats, not Republicans, and so the Republican strategy is to close polling locations in these communities, restrict early voting, disallow voting on the weekend when fewer people work, limit voting by mail (even during a global pandemic), require specific kinds of identification (e.g., a hunting license but not a university ID), launch modern-day poll taxes (see Florida, 2020),[39] and illegitimately and illegally remove Latinx and African American registered voters from the voting rolls.[40]

When voting ends, democracy ends.

Notes

1. Page 103: Baldwin, J. (2017). *I am not your Negro: A major motion picture directed by Raoul Peck*. Vintage International.
2. Major, B. (1994). From social inequality to personal entitlement: The role of social comparisons, legitimacy appraisals, and group membership. In M. P. Zanna (Ed.). *Advances in experimental social psychology* (Vol. 26) (pp. 293–355). Academic Press.
3. Schaeffer, K. (2020, February 7). 6 facts about economic inequality in the U.S. *Pew Research Center*. https://www.pewresearch.org/fact-tank/2020/02/07/6-facts-about-economic-inequality-in-the-u-s/.
4. Stack, L. (2016, December 19). How the "war on Christmas" controversy was created. *The New York Times*. https://www.nytimes.com/2016/12/19/us/war-on-christmas-contro7 0versy.html.
5. The inevitable narcissism of caste section in: Wilkerson, I. (2020, July 1). America's enduring caste system. *New York Times Magazine*. https://www.nytimes.com/2020/07/01/magazine/isabel-wilkerson-caste.html?smid=em-share&login=email&auth=login-email.
6. Schwartz, J. (2019, August 29). Major climate change rules the Trump administration is reversing. *The New York Times*. https://www.nytimes.com/2019/08/29/climate/climate-rule-trump-reversing.html.
7. Milman, O., & Harvey, F. (2019, May 8). US is hotbed of climate change denial, major global survey finds. *The Guardian*. https://www.theguardian.com/environment/2019/may/07/us-hotbed-climate-change-denial-international-poll.
8. Otto, S. L. (2012, November 1). Antiscience beliefs jeopardize U.S. democracy. *Scientific American*. https://www.scientificamerican.com/article/antiscience-beliefs-jeopardize-us-democracy/.

9. Friedman, L., & Plumber, B. (2020, October 7). Trump's response to virus reflects a long disregard for science. *The New York Times.* https://www.nytimes.com/2020/04/28/climate/trump-coronavirus-climate-science.html.

10. Collomb, J-D. (2014). The ideology of climate change denial in the United States. *European Journal of American Studies.* https://doi.org/10.4000/ejas.10305.

11. Häkkinen, K., & Akrami, N. (2014). Ideology and climate change denial. *Personality & Individual Differences, 70,* 62–65. https://doi.org/10.1016/j.paid.2014.06.030.

12. Häkkinen, K., & Akrami, N. (2014). Ideology and climate change denial. *Personality & Individual Differences, 70,* 62–65. https://doi.org/10.1016/j.paid.2014.06.030.

13. Arbuckle, M., & Mercer, M. (2020). Economic outlook and the gender gap in attitudes about climate change. *Population & Environment,* Preprints, 1–30.

14. Swim, J. K., Gillis, A. J., & Hamaty, K. J. (2019). Gender bending and gender conformity: The social consequences of engaging in feminine and masculine pro-environmental behaviors. *Sex Roles.* https://doi.org/10.1007/s11199-019-01061-9.

15. Cited in: MacKenzie, M. Opinion. Is fragile masculinity the biggest obstacle to climate action? *ABC News.* https://www.abc.net.au/news/2019-12-15/is-fragile-masculinity-the-biggest-obstacle-to-climate-action/11797210.

16. McCright, A. M., & Dunlap, R. E. (2011). Cool dudes: The denial of climate change among conservative white males in the United States [electronic resource]. *Global Environmental Change, 21*(4), 1163–1172. https://doi.org/10.1016/j.gloenvcha.2011.06.003.

17. McCright, A. M., & Dunlap, R. E. (2011). Cool dudes: The denial of climate change among conservative white males in the United States [electronic resource]. *Global Environmental Change, 21*(4), 1163–1172. https://doi.org/10.1016/j.gloenvcha.2011.06.003.

18. McCright, A. M., & Dunlap, R. E. (2011). Cool dudes: The denial of climate change among conservative white males in the United States [electronic resource]. *Global Environmental Change, 21*(4), 1163–1172. https://doi.org/10.1016/j.gloenvcha.2011.06.003.

19. Adams, C. J. (2002). *The sexual politics of meat: A feminist-vegetarian critical theory.* Continuum.

20. Cited in: MacKenzie, M. Opinion. Is fragile masculinity the biggest obstacle to climate action? *ABC News.* https://www.abc.net.au/news/2019-12-15/is-fragile-masculinity-the-biggest-obstacle-to-climate-action/11797210.

21. Colbert, S., Licht, C., Purcell, T., & Stewart, J. (2020, November 5). Keep calm and count on! (Season 6, Episode 31) [TV series episode]. *The Late Show with Stephen Colbert.* https://www.youtube.com/watch?v=TeSiJmLoJd0&t=1s.

22. Manchester, J. (2018, October 1). Trump's comments on falling in love with Kim Jong Un "shocking and appalling," says conservative writer. *The Hill.* https://thehill.com/hilltv/rising/409245-trumps-comments-on-falling-in-love-with-kim-jong-un-are-shocking-and-appalling.

23. Levitsky, S., & Ziblatt, D. (2018). *How democracies die.* Crown.

24. Levitsky, S., & Ziblatt, D. (2018). *How democracies die.* Crown.

25. Timm, J. C. (2019, September 3). North Carolina judges slam GOP gerrymandering in stinging ruling, reject district maps. *NBC News*. https://www.nbcnews.com/politics/politics-news/north-carolina-judges-toss-maps-slam-gerrymandering-stinging-ruling-n1049411.

26. Sides, J. (2017, November 18). Here's the incredibly unpopular GOP tax reform plan—in one graph. *The Washington Post*. https://www.washingtonpost.com/news/monkey-cage/wp/2017/11/18/heres-the-incredibly-unpopular-gop-tax-reform-plan-in-one-graph/.

27. Montanaro, D. (2019, August 10). Americans largely support gun restrictions to "do something" about gun violence. *NPR*. https://www.npr.org/2019/08/10/749792493/americans-largely-support-gun-restrictions-to-do-something-about-gun-violence.

28. Younis, M. (2020, March 9). Americans' approval of ACA holds steady. *Gallup*. https://news.gallup.com/poll/287297/americans-approval-aca-holds-steady.aspx.

29. Weixel, N. (2020, January 30). Poll: Narrow majority favors "Medicare for All." *The Hill*. https://thehill.com/policy/healthcare/480719-poll-narrow-majority-favors-medicare-for-all.

30. Newport, F. (2018, June 20). Americans oppose border walls, favor dealing with DACA. *Gallup*. https://news.gallup.com/poll/235775/americans-oppose-border-walls-favor-dealing-daca.aspx.

31. Pew Research Center (2019, August 29). Public opinion on abortion. *Pew Research Center*. https://www.pewforum.org/fact-sheet/public-opinion-on-abortion/.

32. Funk, C., & Hefferon, M. (2019, November 25). U.S. public views on climate and energy. *Pew Research Center*. https://www.pewresearch.org/science/2019/11/25/u-s-public-views-on-climate-and-energy/.

33. Epstein, K. (2020, April 22). Just 14% of Americans support ending social distancing in order to reopen the economy, according to a new poll. *Business Insider*. https://www.businessinsider.com/poll-most-americans-support-coronavirus-social-distancing-measures-2020-4.

34. Anderson, C. (2018). *One person, no vote: How voter suppression is destroying our democracy*. Bloomsbury.

35. Berman, A. (2015). *Give us the ballot: The modern struggle for voting rights in America*. Farrar, Straus, and Giroux.

36. Blue, M. (2015, September 24). Seven times conservatives have admitted they don't want people to vote. *Right Wing Watch*. https://www.rightwingwatch.org/post/seven-times-conservatives-have-admitted-they-dont-want-people-to-vote/.

37. Levine, S. (2020, April 8). Trump urges Republicans to "fight very hard" against voting by mail. *The Guardian*. https://www.theguardian.com/us news/2020/apr/08/trump-mail-in-voting-2020-election.

38. Burns, A., & Martin, J. (2020, November 4). As America awaits a winner, Trump falsely claims he prevailed. *New York Times*. https://www.nytimes.com/2020/11/04/us/politics/election-trump-biden-recap.html.

39. Villareal, d. (2020, August 18). Modern-day "poll tax" amendment in Florida faces court battle before election. *Newsweek*. https://www.newsweek.com/modern-day-poll-tax-amendment-florida-faces-court-battle-before-election-1526013.

40. Anderson, C. (2018). *One person, no vote: How voter suppression is destroying our democracy*. Bloomsbury.

  Berman, A. (2015). *Give us the ballot: The modern struggle for voting rights in America*. Farrar, Straus, and Giroux.

Index

women (*cont.*)
  divorce filings, 148–49
  domestic violence, 12, 115–16, 122, 169, 206–7
  dominance penalty, 201–2
  gender entitlement learned from parents, 88–89
  gender policing, 110–12
  honor culture in Southern US, 164
  illusory power transference, 23
  inmates, discipline of, 95
  internalization of media messages, 130
  intimate partner violence, 115–16, 204–7
  mansplaining, 158
  marriage rituals, 22
  masculine honor beliefs about, 165–66
  online abuse of, 117–18
  peer groups, effect on, 108–10
  reproductive rights of, 10
  self-citation by, 44–45, 156
  self-report measures of entitlement, 30–32
  sexualization of outperforming, 195
  smiling by, 86–87, 153
  social penalty for competence, 200–1
  in television and film, 123–26
  violence against transgender women, 203–4
  White fragility, 192–93
worldviews, 6, 7. *See also* authoritarianism; social dominance orientation
  individualism and meritocracy, 48–52
  parents, role of, 77–80
  political conservatism and rigidity, 52–54
wronged, sense of being
  anti-affirmative action, 185–88
  dying of Whiteness, 184–85
  in Trump voters, 182–84

zero-tolerance policies, 94–95
Ziblatt, Daniel, 222–23
Zoot Suit Riots in Los Angeles, 197, 202